J. K. LASSER'S

Business Tax Techniques

A GUIDE TO EXECUTIVE

TAX-SAVING DECISIONS

by the J. K. Lasser Tax Institute

EDITOR:
BERNARD GREISMAN, *Member of the New York Bar*

DIRECTORS:
BERNARD GREISMAN, LEE GRAY, T. R. LASSER

SIMON AND SCHUSTER · NEW YORK

LIBRARY OF CONGRESS CATALOG CARD NUMBER: 66-28652
DESIGNED BY EVE METZ
MANUFACTURED IN THE UNITED STATES OF AMERICA
BY H. WOLFF BOOK MFG. CO., NEW YORK

Preface

BUSINESS TAX TECHNIQUES is a practical guide to reducing the tax cost on business investments. It can be used profitably by both businessmen and professionals. It guides the executive to the available alternatives in making business decisions, at the time of organizing, buying, selling, reorganizing or liquidating a business. Special attention has been drawn to techniques of realizing capital gains from business activity and other methods of withdrawing profits at the lowest possible tax cost. The scope of BUSINESS TAX TECHNIQUES can be quickly found by scanning the topical table of contents following this preface.

We have, wherever possible, tried to simplify the discussions by keeping technical terminology at a minimum. The use of examples and illustrations help to make difficult material clear to the reader.

We take this opportunity to acknowledge with thanks the invaluable professional assistance of Samuel H. Okoshken of the New York Bar.

Bernard Greisman, Director
J. K. Lasser Tax Institute

Table of Contents

CHAPTER I

Choosing a Form of Doing Business

Tax planning can reduce taxes throughout the life of your business. Your first planning step is to choose a proper form of doing business. You can operate as a sole proprietor, in a partnership with others, or through a corporation. The nature of your business often determines which form you select. Thus, if you have a business where there is danger of personal injury to your customers or clients, a corporation may be the best form to shield against your being personally liable in a lawsuit.

Tax considerations will probably determine your choice where you are not forced by business or legal reasons to select a particular form of business. If you are in a high tax bracket and you expect substantial profits from the start, a corporation is probably the best form to shield your business income from your personal tax bracket. On the other hand, if you anticipate losses until the business matures, a sole proprietorship or partnership will allow you to report losses on your personal return, or else you may form a corporation and make a stockholder (Subchapter S) election to report corporate income or losses.

In this chapter, there is: (1) A brief general outline of the tax consequences of operating as a sole proprietorship, partnership, and corporation accompanied by checklists of the advantages of each form, and (2) methods of estimating the tax cost of each form.

The Sole Proprietorship

How the sole proprietor is taxed. In a sole proprietorship, business operations are treated as an integrated part of the owner's activities. Thus, the tax law does not treat a proprietorship as a separate taxpayer or even as a separate tax-reporting unit. The sole proprietor keeps separate business records detailing business income, deductions, inventories and capital acquisitions and dispositions. He reports his business profit or loss on Schedule C, Form 1040. The net profit or loss is then combined with his other income.

Advantages and disadvantages of a sole proprietorship. The advantages of a sole proprietorship are: (1) Facility of formation. The sole proprietorship is the easiest form of ownership to get underway. (2) Freedom of action. You are not bound by restrictive laws, corporate charters or partnership agreements. In certain cases, however, you must conform to licensing laws and other state regulatory laws. (3) Individual control and maximum centralization of authority. Since you are the sole owner, you may act promptly on your decisions or "hunches," without going through red tape encountered in more complicated organizations. (4) Secrecy of operation. There are no stockholders or "silent partners" to take into the owner's confidence. You must, however, file a certificate of doing business in most states, which requires you to disclose the nature of your business. (5) Ease of termination. It is terminable at any time without burdensome legal formalities. Thus, you may continue your business only so long as it remains profitable.

The disadvantages of a sole proprietorship are: (1) Unlimited liability. You are personally liable for all debts of the business, not merely for your investment. Your creditors can reach your personal assets, such as stock investments and your home, to cover business debts. (2) Difficulty of raising capital. You are generally limited to your personal funds or personal credit. The sole proprietorship is therefore unsuited for large enterprises and is often unable to compete with larger concerns. (3) Personnel difficulties. Competent and valuable employees with managerial ability generally are discontented serving as mere employees; they prefer an interest in the business. Thus, capable employees are likely to start a competing business. (4) Inability to get the benefits from qualified pension and profit-sharing plans, and other fringe benefits available to employees of a business.

The Partnership

How the partnership is taxed. For some purposes, the partnership activities are attributed to the individual owners as if they were sole proprietors. For other purposes, the partnership itself is treated as a unit divorced from the individual partners. For example, the tax law requires the partnership entity to compute and report income and losses but does not require the partnership itself to pay taxes. On the other hand, it requires the partners in their personal returns to report their share of partnership income or loss. Thus, the individual partner for tax reporting purposes is in generally the same position as a sole proprietor.

Advantages and disadvantages of the partnership. The advantages of a partnership are:

1. *Division of profits*. Profits may be divided in accordance with both the capital and services contributed. Moreover, each class of contribution may be rewarded separately, a certain return for capital investment and a different return for services or abilities contributed.

2. *Freedom of action*. There are usually no limitations on what a partnership may do, other than those self-imposed by the partnership agreement.

3. *Division of responsibilities*. The partnership permits specialization in management. Each partner can handle that aspect of the business for which he is best suited by experience and knowledge.

4. *Flexibility of operation*. Since the partnership is a contractual relationship, its objectives, capital, and membership may be changed to meet changing needs.

5. *Increased sources of capital*. The resources of several individuals are naturally greater than those of one individual. As larger capital becomes necessary, partners may be added. Even if this procedure is not practical, the combined credit resources of existing partners afford greater possibility of expansion. The borrowing capacity of the partnership is greater than that of the individual. It may even be said to be greater in proportion to capital than that of corporations, because of the liability for debts which the partners must assume.

6. *Retention of individual control*. Even though risk and responsibility are divided among partners, the individual partner retains some control. If he is dissatisfied, he can withdraw and thus dissolve the firm, or he can force his partners to buy him out.

7. *Personnel advantages*. The partnership can offer more incentive to the key employees than can the individual proprietorship. Reward

for efficiency or excellence of service may be admission to the partnership, either as a general partner, or as a special partner, according to the partnership agreement.

The disadvantages of a partnership are:

1. *Unlimited liability.* Partners are usually jointly and severally liable for all debts of the firm. Generally speaking, the more numerous the partners, the greater the risk of each individual partner. The larger the scale of the partnership operation, the greater his liability.

2. *Impermanency of existence.* Partnerships may usually be terminated voluntarily, by agreement of the parties, or they are terminated involuntarily by the acts of the partners, by certain events (such as death, insanity, or insolvency of a partner), or by court action.

3. *Lack of entity.* Each partner generally has authority to act as agent for the partnership. Each might render it liable for damages by his acts. A partner usually can make contracts which, within the scope of the partnership business, are binding on the partnership and the other partners. Generally, a partnership cannot sue, or be sued by, one of its partners.

4. *Capital limitations.* When an enterprise needs large amounts of capital, the partnership form is usually impracticable. A partnership with too many partners becomes clumsy.

5. *Ease of disruption.* A serious problem in a partnership is the ease with which the whole organization may be disrupted or disorganized. Personality or policy clashes among partners, the death of a partner, dishonesty, or unfair practice may cause difficulties which can be solved only by dissolution of the partnership.

6. *Limited marketability of interest.* A partnership interest is usually not readily marketable. Generally, the partnership agreement provides that the partner must sell to a copartner or to an outsider, only with the consent of the partners.

7. *Difficulty of centralizing authority.* It is difficult to centralize or circumscribe authority in the partnership. So far as third persons are concerned, one partner has as much authority as another on each question.

The Corporation

How the corporation is taxed. A corporation differs radically from a partnership or sole proprietorship because it is generally treated as a separate and distinct unit from its owners. Legally, it is treated as an artificial person having rights and duties all its own. The tax law adopts this legal principle and treats it as a separate taxpayer, thus creating the problem of double taxation: (1) The tax paid by the corporation on its earnings and (2) the tax paid by the owners when they receive these earnings in the form of dividends. Despite this expense, the corporation, because it is treated as a separate taxpayer, may provide many tax advantages not available to either a proprietorship or partnership. The stockholders working for the corporation as employees are eligible for fringe benefits they could not acquire as proprietors or partners. Some of these benefits have an immediate tax saving effect, such as medical expense reimbursement and the sick pay exclusion. Others provide long-term benefits, such as taxfree build-up of funds in a pension or profit-sharing plan. In addition, the corporation may be used to accumulate after-tax income for ultimate distribution to the stockholders at preferred capital gain rates or at no income tax cost at all where stock is held until death.

Advantages and disadvantages of the corporation. The advantages of a corporation are:

1. *Limited liability.* Liability is usually limited to the amount of stock issued.

2. *Continuity of existence.* Change of ownership through transfer of stock has no effect on the existence of the corporate form.

3. *Continuity of management.* Change of ownership through transfer of stock need not affect management.

4. *Acquisition of new capital.* A successful corporation may seek as much capital as it needs. Investors have greater confidence in the securities of a corporation than in those of other forms of doing business.

5. *Personnel advantages.* The corporation can offer more opportunity to the efficient and ambitious employee and thus secure topflight personnel. Opportunity to secure stock in the corporation is an incentive to effort.

6. *Limitation of power to bind.* Power to bind the corporation is limited to designated directors, officers, and agents. Any one partner can bind all partners, perhaps disastrously.

7. *Control of minorities.* While minorities have adequate representation, dissident minorities are usually not as difficult to manage as they are in partnerships.

8. *Transfer of interests.* Corporate shares provide a means of investment that can be transferred to heirs with comparative ease. A partner's heir cannot succeed to his status as a partner without the consent of the other partners.

The disadvantages of a corporation are:

1. *Difficulty of formation.* Forming a corporation involves formality and expense.

2. *Control and regulation.* The corporation is subject to governmental control and regulation. It has to file reports and tax returns.

3. *Interstate limitations.* If a corporation wants to do business in states other than the one in which it is organized, it must usually qualify in the other states and pay their fees and taxes.

4. *Charter limitations.* The scope of activity of the corporation is limited by the purposes set out in the corporate charter. This difficulty may be eliminated by making the original charter broad or by amending it. The corporation's outstanding stock may not be more than the amount authorized by its charter.

5. *Inflexibility of operation.* Some types of transactions must be authorized by the directors or stockholders. It may be difficult to get quick action on many important transactions.

6. *Possible liability of stockholders.* The corporate form has sometimes been disregarded. Stockholders have been held individually liable where the corporation is used for fraud, evasion of the law, monopoly, or personal gain of a dominant stockholder.

7. *Division of profits.* In a partnership, profits can be divided arbitrarily, as desired, in ratio to capital or services contributed. If the corporation divides profits it must do so in proportion to stockholdings. Profits can be distributed only after a declaration of dividends by the directors. Limitations are often placed upon the amount of distributions. These vary with states. Generally, the laws try to prohibit impairment of capital by the payment of dividends.

8. *Minority stockholders.* Minority stockholders sometimes have no means of protection against some acts of majority stockholders.

9. *Separate ownership and management.* The divorcing of management from ownership may lead to abuse. Constant change of management is dangerous when continuity of effort is needed.

10. *Dissolution.* Dissolution of the corporation may be an involved process.

The Subchapter S Corporation

The Subchapter S corporation is an ordinary corporation that elects to receive special tax treatment. It may not have more than 10 stockholders and one class of stock. Where these and other requirements are met, the corporation pays no tax; its income or losses are passed through to the stockholders.

Although the Subchapter S corporation's profits and losses pass directly to its stockholders, the corporation is still a separate entity for all other purposes. Thus, the Subchapter S corporation is available as a means for providing fringe benefits for its stockholder-employees in the same manner as a regular corporation.

Advantages of a Subchapter S corporation. They are: (1) Increased charitable contribution deduction. By combining the corporate limitation on charitable deductions with your own, you can increase your allowable maximum. (2) Tax sheltered fringe benefits. As a corporate employee you are entitled to fringe benefits such as qualified pension and profit-sharing plans, sick pay exclusion, and accident and health insurance. (3) Better timing of income distributions. If the Subchapter S corporation operates on a taxable year differing from that of its stockholders, it can time its distributions to cover two tax years. (4) Passthrough of business losses. Losses in the first years of the corporation's life (or even in later years) are passed through to the stockholders and are deductible against ordinary income from other sources. (5) Capital gains on sales of assets can be passed through to stockholders. (6) Starting a new corporation with a fiscal year to postpone payment of taxes for a year. For example, if you start your company with a fiscal year beginning February 1, 1968, you do not have to report undistributed corporate income earned in 1968 until the due date of your individual 1969 return on April 15, 1970. (7) Avoiding the accumulated earnings penalty tax. When a company is in danger of the penalty tax, the Subchapter S election can be made so that the penalty cannot be imposed on corporate income during the years the election is in force.

The disadvantages are: (1) Prior net operating losses may be wasted by a company making the election. (2) A new stockholder may be subject to ordinary income earned before he was a stockholder. Although he is a stockholder for only part of the year, he must report his share of the income for the entire year. (3) Income taxed to stockholders but not withdrawn can be taxed again if the election is terminated. (4) If the electing corporation receives dividends, it is not entitled to the usual 85% dividends received deduction.

Comparing the Tax Cost of Each Business Form

For purposes of comparing tax costs, you can put a partnership, sole proprietorship, and Subchapter S corporation into one category, since only one tax is paid by the proprietor, partner or stockholder. In the other category is the regular, non-Subchapter S corporation. This business form generally involves double taxation, first to the corporation and then to the stockholder when the after-tax profits are distributed. However, the effect of the double taxation can be minimized or sometimes eliminated by various income-splitting methods. As a general rule, in splitting income between yourself and a corporation, you must try to place into two low tax brackets income that would normally be taxed in one high bracket. You split business income between yourself and a corporation by drawing from the corporation amounts which it then deducts from its gross income. Drawing salary as a stockholder-employee is the usual method of splitting income. Sometimes you can also get income-splitting by drawing interest on loans you have made to the company; but this method is far more susceptible to Treasury disallowance than salary withdrawals (*see* page 45). Another means is payment by the company of expenses you incur in entertaining customers and traveling on business trips. This, too, is subject to Treasury review and possible disallowance. However, in all cases, to the extent a corporation can deduct payments to you, there is only one tax.

Individual Tax Rates

Below, for your convenience, are tax rates that are used in the comparison of tax costs on page 20.

TAX RATES FOR THE HEAD OF A HOUSEHOLD

IF YOUR TAXABLE INCOME IS		YOUR TAX IS		
Over	But not over	This	Plus following percentage	Over this
$0	$1,000	$0	14%	$0
1,000	2,000	140	16%	1,000
2,000	4,000	300	18%	2,000
4,000	6,000	660	20%	4,000
6,000	8,000	1,060	22%	6,000
8,000	10,000	1,500	25%	8,000
10,000	12,000	2,000	27%	10,000
12,000	14,000	2,540	31%	12,000
14,000	16,000	3,160	32%	14,000
16,000	18,000	3,800	35%	16,000
18,000	20,000	4,500	36%	18,000
20,000	22,000	5,220	40%	20,000
22,000	24,000	6,020	41%	22,000
24,000	26,000	6,840	43%	24,000
26,000	28,000	7,700	45%	26,000
28,000	32,000	8,600	46%	28,000
32,000	36,000	10,440	48%	32,000
36,000	38,000	12,360	50%	36,000
38,000	40,000	13,360	52%	38,000
40,000	44,000	14,400	53%	40,000
44,000	50,000	16,520	55%	44,000
50,000	52,000	19,820	56%	50,000
52,000	64,000	20,940	58%	52,000
64,000	70,000	27,900	59%	64,000
70,000	76,000	31,440	61%	70,000
76,000	80,000	35,100	62%	76,000
80,000	88,000	37,580	63%	80,000
88,000	100,000	42,620	64%	88,000
100,000	120,000	50,300	66%	100,000
120,000	140,000	63,500	67%	120,000
140,000	160,000	76,900	68%	140,000
160,000	180,000	90,500	69%	160,000
180,000		104,300	70%	180,000

TAX RATES—IF YOU FILE A JOINT RETURN

IF YOUR TAXABLE INCOME IS		YOUR TAX IS		
Over	But not over	This	Plus following percentage	Over this
$0	$1,000	$0	14%	$0
1,000	2,000	140	15%	1,000
2,000	3,000	290	16%	2,000
3,000	4,000	450	17%	3,000
4,000	8,000	620	19%	4,000
8,000	12,000	1,380	22%	8,000
12,000	16,000	2,260	25%	12,000
16,000	20,000	3,260	28%	16,000
20,000	24,000	4,380	32%	20,000
24,000	28,000	5,660	36%	24,000
28,000	32,000	7,100	39%	28,000
32,000	36,000	8,660	42%	32,000
36,000	40,000	10,340	45%	36,000
40,000	44,000	12,140	48%	40,000
44,000	52,000	14,060	50%	44,000
52,000	64,000	18,060	53%	52,000
64,000	76,000	24,420	55%	64,000
76,000	88,000	31,020	58%	76,000
88,000	100,000	37,980	60%	88,000
100,000	120,000	45,180	62%	100,000
120,000	140,000	57,580	64%	120,000
140,000	160,000	70,380	66%	140,000
160,000	180,000	83,580	68%	160,000
180,000	200,000	97,180	69%	180,000
200,000		110,980	70%	200,000

TAX RATES—IF YOU ARE SINGLE

IF YOUR TAXABLE INCOME IS		YOUR TAX IS		
Over	But not over	This	Plus following percentage	Over this
$0	$500	$0	14%	$0
500	1,000	70	15%	500
1,000	1,500	145	16%	1,000
1,500	2,000	225	17%	1,500
2,000	4,000	310	19%	2,000
4,000	6,000	690	22%	4,000
6,000	8,000	1,130	25%	6,000
8,000	10,000	1,630	28%	8,000
10,000	12,000	2,190	32%	10,000

TAX RATES—IF YOU ARE SINGLE (*continued*)

IF YOUR TAXABLE INCOME IS		YOUR TAX IS		
Over	But not over	This	Plus following percentage	Over this
12,000	14,000	2,830	36%	12,000
14,000	16,000	3,550	39%	14,000
16,000	18,000	4,330	42%	16,000
18,000	20,000	5,170	45%	18,000
20,000	22,000	6,070	48%	20,000
22,000	26,000	7,030	50%	22,000
26,000	32,000	9,030	53%	26,000
32,000	38,000	12,210	55%	32,000
38,000	44,000	15,510	58%	38,000
44,000	50,000	18,990	60%	44,000
50,000	60,000	22,590	62%	50,000
60,000	70,000	28,790	64%	60,000
70,000	80,000	35,190	66%	70,000
80,000	90,000	41,790	68%	80,000
90,000	100,000	48,590	69%	90,000
100,000		55,490	70%	100,000

Corporate Tax Rates

The corporate tax rate structure is simpler than that applied to individuals. There is a *normal* tax of 22% and a *surtax* of 26%. The first $25,000 of corporate income is subject to a surtax exemption. In other words, the first $25,000 of corporate income is subject to the normal rate of 22%. All income in excess of $25,000 is subject to the 48% combined rate.

Corporate capital gains. Net long-term capital gains are included in the corporate income unless the corporation elects to have them taxed at the alternative tax rate of 25%. If the corporate ordinary income is below $25,000, net long-term capital gains are generally included in ordinary income because the tax rate is only 22%. Where, however, the corporate ordinary income exceeds $25,000, the alternative tax for capital gains is usually elected.

You cannot include some long-term capital gains as ordinary income and have the remainder of the net long-term capital gains taxed at the 25% alternative rate. Where ordinary income is below (but close to) the $25,000 level, it may be advisable to have the entire long-term capital gain taxed at the alternative tax rate even though part of the gain might have been subject to the 22% tax rate.

EXAMPLES:

1. Corporation's ordinary income is $23,000; net long-term capital gains amount to $10,000. If the $10,000 capital gain is added to the $23,000 ordinary income, for a total of $33,000, the total tax would come to $9,340 ($5,500 on first $25,000 at 22%, plus $3,840 on next $8,000 at 48%). If, however, the alternative tax is applied to the $10,000 capital gain, the total tax would come to only $7,560 ($5,060 on the $23,000 ordinary income at 22%, plus $2,500 on the capital gain of $10,000 at 25%). So, using the alternative tax saves $1,780.

2. Corporation's ordinary income is $10,000; net long-term capital gains are $16,000. If the $16,000 capital gain is combined with the ordinary income for a total of $26,000, the tax will come to $5,980 ($5,500 on the first $25,000 at 22% plus $480 on the next $1,000 at 48%). If the alternative tax is used, the total tax comes to $6,200 ($2,200 on the ordinary income of $10,000 at 22%, plus $4,000 on the $16,000 capital gain at 25%). So, here, by not using the alternative tax, even though the total income then rises above the $25,000 surtax exemption, $220 less is paid.

Corporate penalty tax. The corporation may be subject to additional penalty taxes. There is a tax of 27½% on the first $100,000 of unreasonably accumulated income plus 38½% on the excess over $100,000. There is also a penalty tax of 70% imposed on the undistributed income of personal holding companies. What you can do to avoid these tax penalties is discussed at page 147.

Figuring Tax on Business Income

Here are some general observations on the relationship between personal and corporate tax rates. If the business will produce taxable income of $25,000 or less, the corporate tax will be higher than the tax you would pay if on your personal return your taxable income (including the business income) is less than—

$12,000 on a joint return
6,000 on a single return
8,000 on a head-of-household return.

Over $25,000, corporate tax will be higher than the tax on your personal return if you report income (including the business income) of less than—

$44,000 on a joint return

22,000 on a single return

36,000 on head-of-household return

If your personal income exceeds these figures then the corporation will pay a lower tax on income over $25,000.

Below are three examples outlining the type of computations you make in comparing the tax costs of a corporation and individual ownership. Your determination should include these steps:

1. You compute how much you would personally pay if you reported all of the business income either in an unincorporated organization or in a corporation subject to a Subchapter S election.

2. You compute how much the corporation would pay if it reported the income.

3. You compute how much you would pay on income withdrawn annually (as a salary or dividend) from the corporation and how much the corporation would pay after the withdrawal.

4. If any income is accumulated in the corporation for future distribution, you compute how much tax you would pay at that time.

In the examples below, it is assumed that the withdrawals are at capital gain rates. Capital gain is possible when you sell or redeem your stock in the corporation or the corporation is liquidated. But be aware that this anticipated capital gain may not be realized if the sale, redemption, or liquidation falls within the collapsible corporation rules or some other disguised dividend transaction. Note, Social Security taxes and the possibility of surplus accumulation penalties are not considered in these examples.

EXAMPLES:

1. You have a joint taxable income of $20,000 from sources other than the projected business. You estimate the business will return a taxable income of $10,000. If you were to report the income on your joint return, you pay a tax of $7,880 on $30,000. If you incorporate and make no deductible withdrawals such as a salary, the corporation pays a tax of $2,200 ($10,000 × 22%). At the same time, you pay a tax of $4,380 on your $20,000 income. Thus, the total tax incurred by you and the corporation is $6,580. ($4,380 + $2,200.) This is $1,300 ($7,880 − $6,580) less than if you had reported all the income on your return. However, there remains a potential tax to be paid on the income of $7,800 ($10,000 − $2,200) remaining in the company.

If you withdraw the amount as a dividend, the ordinary tax attributed to the dividend would be $2,648 assuming that your income from other sources remains at $20,000. Thus, the tax attributed to $10,000 of corporate income would be $4,848 ($2,200 + $2,648). If you had originally reported the income on your return, the tax attributed to $10,000 would be $3,500, or $1,348 less. Obviously, if you personally need the $10,000, you might not incorporate; or if you do incorporate, you would try to withdraw the $10,000 in the form of deductible salary and interest or elect to report the income under a Subchapter S election. In that way, the corporation would not incur tax on the income.

But assume you do not currently need the income earned by the corporation; that it can be left in the corporation. It could be reinvested or used as working capital for an additional return of income. You would then anticipate its withdrawal at a later time when you could receive it at capital gain rates. Assuming that you were able to receive the $7,800 at capital gain rates and your income from other sources remained at $20,000, the capital gains tax on the $7,800 would be $1,248. Thus, the total tax attributed to the $10,000 would be only $3,448 ($2,200 + $1,248), $52 less than reporting all the income on your return at the time it was earned ($3,500 − $3,448).

Retention of earnings in a corporation becomes more advantageous as your personal tax bracket increases, provided of course, income can later be withdrawn at capital gain rates. There is also a possibility that the potential tax on the earnings may be eliminated, at least for your family, if you should die while owning the stock. At your death, the cost basis of the stock is increased to its fair market value. This boost or step-up will reflect the value of earnings retained.

2. You have a joint taxable income from other sources of $10,000. You estimate your business will produce a taxable income of $30,000. If you were to report this income on your personal return, you would pay a tax of $12,140. The tax attributed to the reporting of $30,000 on your return is $10,320. If you were to incorporate, the corporate tax would be $7,900. If you were to receive the remaining $22,100 at capital gain rates (and your other income remained at $10,000), the tax attributed to the distribution would be $2,896, so that the tax attributed to the business income of $30,-000 would be $10,796 ($7,900 + $2,896). This comparison ($10,796 as compared with $10,320) shows that the corporation should not be used to accumulate all the income in expectation of capital gain return.

But now determine the tax if you took a deductible salary of $10,000. Your personal tax on taxable income of $20,000 would be $4,380 ($2,560 attributed to the $10,000 salary). The corporate tax on its remaining $20,000 would be $4,400. Assuming that the remaining $15,600 ($20,000 − $4,400) could be received by you at capital gain rates when you had other income of $10,000, the tax attributed to $15,600 would be $1,944. Thus, the total tax attributed to $30,000 would be $8,904 ($1,944 + $4,400 + $2,560). Therefore, income splitting between your personal tax and the corporation with deductible salary would be preferable both to reporting all the business income on your return or to accumulating all the corporate income in the corporation.

3. You have a joint taxable income of $44,000 on which $14,060 in taxes is due. You intend to invest in a business that produces taxable income of $25,000. If you incorporate, the corporate tax on $25,000 would be $5,500. If you did not withdraw the remaining $19,500 from the corporation until it could be recovered at capital gain rates, the capital gain tax on the withdrawal would be $4,875, making a total tax attributed to the $25,000 of $10,375. If you did not incorporate (or incorporated and made a Subchapter S election) and reported all of the $25,000 personally, the tax attributed to the $25,000 would be $13,110. This is $2,735 more than incurred by the corporation and yourself on a later distribution at capital gain rates ($13,100 — $10,375). At this level, it would be preferable to use the corporation as a tax shelter. If you had to withdraw funds currently, any withdrawals taxable on your return would be at higher rates than incurred by the corporation plus the potential capital gain tax due on a later distribution. For example, assume that you withdrew $10,000 as a salary. The tax attributed to the withdrawal would be $5,060, so that the effective tax of about 50.6% on the $10,000 is considerably higher than the corporate rate of 22% plus a potential tax of 25% or 47%.

Fixing Reasonable Compensation

Payment of salaries to employee-stockholders (as explained in the previous pages) provides a means of reducing the overall tax burden of the corporation and its owners. The corporation deducts the payment to the extent it is reasonable in amount, resulting in one tax paid by the employee. The problem is how to fix compensation and avoid possible disallowance of the deduction for the salary.

The challenge of reasonableness comes up frequently on Treasury audit of corporate tax returns. Unless the full amount can be substantiated, the corporation faces partial disallowance of the deduction or the issue may be used as a bargaining point by the auditor for the reducing or disallowing of other deductions.

The Treasury considers these points in determining whether a salary is reasonable: (1) Duties performed by the employee, (2) volume of business handled, (3) the character and amount of his responsibility, (4) the complexities of the business, (5) the amount of time required, (6) the cost of living in the community where he lives, (7) his ability and achievements, and (8) the amount of his pay in comparison with the corporation's gross and net income.

The Treasury reviews each individual salary, not the aggregate salaries paid to all employees. Thus, total salaries may be reasonable in amount, but a salary paid to one employee may be found unreasonable. In addition, the eight facts listed above are viewed at the time the contract for services was made, not when the compensation was actually paid or accrued.

Often a crucial fact is whether the salary is comparable to salaries received by other executives in similar companies in the industry. Sometimes a record of substantial dividend payments over past years may negate the Treasury challenge.

In publicly-held corporations, large salaries paid to key men are rarely questioned because it is assumed the amount was set in arm's length bargaining. Similarly, salaries paid to non-stockholder-employees are rarely questioned because it is assumed they were also arrived at at arm's length. But salary arrangements in closely-held corporations with employee-stockholders usually lack the element of objective bargaining. However, an attempt should be made to give a compensation arrangement the coloring of an impersonal transaction. The following discussion reviews what you should or should not do in fixing compensation.

Pro-rated salaries according to stockholdings. Equal stockholders want equal returns on their investment in salaries as well as dividends. But pro-rated salaries bear close resemblance to dividend distributions. If stockholder Jones does more work than stockholder Smith, Jones should be paid more because of the extra work. This will tend, also, to avoid the claim that part of the salaries paid to both were dividends.

Do not write the salary authorization in the corporate minutes in terms of stockholdings. Even if the salary is reasonable, you create an unnecessary danger to a full deduction. Pro-rated salaries, however, are not conclusive proof of disguised dividends. You may still prove the reasonableness of the amounts.

Fixing salaries too low when corporation is set up. When a Treasury agent considers a salary payment too high, he may review past returns to compare former salaries. If your corporation has a history of fluctuating salaries, high salaries in high earnings years, and low salaries in lean years, he has additional evidence for his disallowance of part of the salary deduction. If it is possible, without draining necessary working capital from the business, set salaries at a reasonably high point from the very beginning. This provides a base for the future, and the net operating losses that may result from the initial high salaries may be used as carryovers for up to five years. You may also consider having the corporation credit the salary on the books without actually paying it. But there is a potential tax danger in this plan: If you own more than 50% of the corporate stock and do not receive payment of the credited salary after two and a half months after the close of the tax year, the corporate deduction is disallowed.

Establishing salaries at the beginning of the year. If you fix or increase your salary at the end of the year when profits are known, you create a strong impression that the salary includes a disguised dividend. Some tax men suggest writing an agreement covering a number of years. If it turns out that working capital is depleted in a given year, actual payment can be withheld, or you can contribute part of your salary to the capital of the corporation (which increases your stock basis) or become a creditor of your corporation. If you become a creditor, you must be careful of a "thin capitalization" situation, which occurs when there is too much debt outstanding and not enough stock.

Payment for past services. Large salary payments for several years can sometimes be justified by showing lack of available funds in prior years to fully compensate the employee. You must also show that prior salaries were reasonable. Corporate minutes from prior years recording the fact that the salary paid was necessarily low is the type of proof the Treasury wants to see. You should earmark the part of the compensation payment covering past services.

Use of contingent salary arrangements. Your corporation may have widely fluctuating earnings from year to year, and you may not want to fix a salary that would prove too large in a lean year. At the same time, you do not want to wait until the year's profits become ascertainable before fixing the salary, since this arrangement may lend support to a Treasury claim of unreasonableness. The use of the contingent salary agreement may be a compromise.

Treasury regulations generally allow deductions for "contingent compensation paid pursuant to a free bargain between the employer and the individual made before services are rendered," even if "it may prove to be greater than the amount that would ordinarily be paid."

When the Treasury questions a salary based on a contingent agreement, it will look at the circumstances existing at the inception of the agreement, not at the year in which the questioned salary is paid. However, a legitimate contingency arrangement may not always escape question. Thus, where a president-stockholder begins gradually to withdraw from active management and participation in the firm, the situation as it exists at the time of payment must be examined. In this case, a large salary payment would likely be disallowed as a deduction.

Reasonableness of bonuses. In determining whether a bonus is excessive, the Treasury will view it as part of total compensation. If total compensation is reasonable, the bonus is deductible by the corporation, regardless of the fact that the bonus may be larger even than the regular compensation.

Agreements to repay part of salary that Treasury finds excessive. If the Treasury holds that part of a stockholder-employee's salary was unreasonable and the employee voluntarily returns that part to the corporation, he cannot escape tax on that salary. The corporation, of course, gets no deduction and treats the returned portion as a contribution to capital, or it may even result in income to the corporation. You can hedge against this undesirable result by providing in an agreement between the corporation and stockholder-employees, or in the corporate minutes that, if the Treasury finds part of a salary unreasonable, it *must* be returned. It is important to create a definite obligation on the part of the employee, or else the Treasury will claim it was a voluntary repayment. Under this arrangement, the employee originally pays a tax on the full amount, but he gets a tax deduction in the year it is refunded to the corporation. The corporation has no income because it is merely collecting a debt which was created in the original agreement.

The validity of this agreement may be challenged by the Treasury. If the agreement is to work, it, or a notation in the minutes, must be in existence at the time the salary is paid to the employee. Creating the obligation when the Treasury finally determines the salary is unreasonable is too late. However, consider the possible effect of the existence of the agreement. It may suggest to the Treasury agent that the corporation is paying excessive salaries.

CHAPTER II

Organizing a Corporation

THE CORPORATION you will organize will be a separate taxpayer. It follows that if you give the corporation property and in return receive its stock, an exchange has occurred.

You must decide before incorporation whether it is to your advantage to incur a tax on this exchange or to qualify it as a nontaxable exchange. Generally, nontaxable exchange is easier to arrange than a taxable exchange because the tax law is designed to facilitate nontaxable exchanges.

You will generally *want* to incur tax in the following types of situations:

To give the corporation a stepped-up basis for property, the basis of which in your hands is less than its present market value. For example, you own a building with an adjusted basis of $50,000 and a present market value of $100,000. If you were to transfer the building to a corporation (which you control) in return for stock under the nontaxable exchange rules explained below, no tax would be incurred. However, the corporation would list and take depreciation on the building at a basis of $50,000. If you were to negotiate a taxable exchange, you might realize capital gain on your $50,000 profit and the corporation would take depreciation basis on a basis of $100,000. It is necessary to point out that in planning a taxable transaction, you have to avoid not only the nontaxable exchange rules on page 32, but also another rule that treats as ordinary income gain on a sale of depreciable property to a controlled corporation.

To avoid dealer status if you are in the real estate business. You own a large undeveloped tract that has appreciated in value. You can sell the tract at a capital gain profit. You estimate that if you subdivided the property, you would be able to realize a greater profit. But, you fear that if you engage in the subdivision and sale, you might be taxed as a dealer, and your entire gain subjected to ordinary income rates. To realize capital gain on your present appreciation and still engage in the subdivision, you may want to transfer the property in a taxable exchange to a corporation that would engage in the subdivision and sale. You estimate that your net return from the capital gain on the exchange with the corporation and on the profits earned by the corporation, even though taxable at ordinary income rates would exceed what you would net on the bulk sale of the undeveloped tract.

To realize a deductible loss. You individually own property the basis of which in your hands exceeds its present market value. In transferring the property you prefer to realize an immediate loss, which is barred if the nontaxable exchange rules apply. In arranging a loss sale with a corporation, you must also try to avoid the rule that disallows losses on sales between a 50% controlling stockholder and his corporation.

Before discussing how to avoid the nontaxable exchange rules, it is, of course, necessary to know the nontaxable exchange rules.

Requirements for Taxfree Incorporation

Cash or other property must be transferred to the corporation in exchange solely for stock or securities of that corporation. Immediately after the transfer, the transferors (such as partners, where a partnership is being incorporated or a sole proprietor, if his business is being incorporated) must own at least 80% of the combined voting power of the corporation and 80% of all other classes of stock.

EXAMPLE:
> Green owns assets that have a basis in his hands of $10,000 and are now worth $100,000. If he transfers them to a corporation in exchange for all of its stock, he has no taxable gain. The basis for the stock he receives is $10,000; the basis to the corporation for the assets received from Green is also $10,000.

The stock or securities received do not have to be in proportion to each transferor's proportionate interest in the total property transferred to the corporation. A disproportionate receipt of stock or secu-

rities will not upset the taxfree status of the exchange. But a disproportionate distribution of stock or securities among the transferors may
result in gifts subject to gift tax or taxable compensation.

EXAMPLES:

Father and son organize a corporation with 100 shares of common
stock. The father transfers property worth $8,000 to the corporation for 20
shares. The son transfers property worth $2,000 for 80 shares. There is no
gain or loss on these transfers. The incorporation is taxfree. But the facts
indicate that the father apparently made a gift to his son of the disproportionate number of shares. If so, they may be subject to gift tax. However,
the son might have rendered his father services not related to the assets
transferred or to the corporate business. In such a case, the disproportionate stock ownership could be viewed as pay for these services. If so, the son
would have taxable income on the fair market value of the extra 60 shares,
and the father would have gain or loss for the difference between his basis
for the 60 shares and their fair market value. Of course, if the compensation were deductible for tax purposes (for example, for services in connection with the father's business), the father would also be entitled to a tax
deduction for the market value of the 60 shares.

Services to the corporation are not "property." So, if a party, who
has rendered services only, receives stock from the corporation in return for past services or services to be rendered in the future, the value
of the stock is taxed as compensation. In counting for the necessary
80% control, stock received for services is included.

EXAMPLE:

Jones owns property worth $18,000 which cost him $10,000. He also
performs some services for the F Corporation. The services are worth
$2,000. F Corporation has 100 shares outstanding, all owned by Green. F
issues 400 shares of stock (worth $20,000) to Jones in exchange for his
property ($18,000) and his services ($2,000). Immediately after the exchange, he owns 80% of the F stock. He has no taxable gain on the transfer of the property to F. But he has taxable compensation of $2,000 on the
stock issued for his services.

What is a security? For a taxfree incorporation, the transfer of
property to the corporation has to be in exchange solely for stock or
securities. A 30-day note is not a security, but an obligation running
more than five years will usually qualify as a security. Other examples
of corporate obligations that have been held to be securities: 20-year

debenture bonds, 10-year debenture bonds, interest-bearing notes payable annually in five to nine years, six and one-half year secured notes, unsecured 10-year notes, and five-year secured coupon notes. These were held *not* to be securities: Interest-bearing, secured notes payable in 45 to 105 days, demand notes, 12-month notes, and notes payable monthly from three to 15 months.

Partially-Taxed Incorporations

If assets in addition to the stock or securities are received by the stockholders, the market value of the additional assets (often referred to as "boot") is taxable. The amount taxable cannot exceed the gain on the exchange.

EXAMPLE:

Adams and Brown, equal partners, transfer partnership assets worth $50,000 to a corporation. They have 100% control after the exchange. Their combined basis for the property transferred is $10,000. Adams receives stock worth $25,000; he recognizes no gain. Brown receives stock worth $15,000 and $10,000 cash. Brown has an actual profit of $20,000 ($25,000 minus $5,000). But he is taxed only on the cash of $10,000.

Transfers of Properties to Corporation Need Not be Simultaneous

Transfers of properties made at different times by two or more persons may be taxfree provided the several transfers are part of a single plan and are made promptly under an agreement. If one of the transferors, soon after the exchange, sells or gives his stock to an outside party, the original exchange remains taxfree if the sale or gift was not part of the original plan.

The 80% test is not met if you agree in advance to transfer part of the stock to others, leaving you with less than 80%, or if you acquired the 80% merely as one step in a series of transactions intended to give the other parties part of the stock. Even if there is no commitment that stock subsequently be sold, there is danger that the transfer will not satisfy the 80% test. It may be advisable to wait some time between the transfer to the corporation and the sale of the stocks received. Of course, if the sale involves 20% or less of the voting power of voting stock or 20% or less of any other class of stock, the "control" requirement would not be violated by an immediate sale.

Transfers of Property to an Existing Corporation

Taxfree incorporation rules apply equally to transfers to an existing corporation, providing that after the transfer the transferor meets the 80% test. This can present a problem on a transfer to an existing corporation by one stockholder.

EXAMPLES:

1. John Swift owns all the stock of Rapid Delivery Corporation. Several years after the corporation was formed, John transfers additional property to the corporation having a basis to him of $1,000 and a market value of $10,000. The corporation issues to John additional stock valued at $10,-000. The transaction is tax-free because John meets the 80% test after the transfer.

2. Smith and Jones form Smith-Jones, Inc. At the time of incorporation, Smith transferred property worth $50,000 to the corporation (having a basis to him of $10,000) and Jones paid in $50,000 in cash. Smith and Jones each received 5,000 shares of stock, the entire amount of stock issued by the corporation. Although Smith received only 50% of the stock, the 80% test was met on the incorporation because Smith and Jones together met the 80% test. Five years later, Smith transfers additional property to the corporation worth $10,000 for which he has a basis of $5,000. The corporation issues Smith 1,000 additional shares of stock (assume for this illustration that the book value of the stock has remained $10 per share). After this transfer, Smith owns 6,000 of 11,000 shares outstanding, 54½% of the outstanding stock. He does not meet the 80% test. He cannot count Jones' stock because Jones has not made a transfer to the corporation at this time. So, Smith has a taxable gain of $5,000 on this exchange.

Assume, when Smith transferred the property to the corporation for 1,000 shares, Jones also transferred a piece of property worth $100 to the corporation for 10 shares of stock. Can Smith and Jones be considered transferors together because they each transferred property to the corporation at the same time? Treasury regulations say no. A relatively small amount of stock issued to someone who already owns considerable stock in the corporation will not be considered the issuance of stock in exchange for property where the primary purpose of the transfer is to make tax free another stockholder's transfer to the corporation.

Transfers of Liabilities May Result in Tax

Often assets transferred to a corporation in exchange for stock are subject to liabilities, as for example, a building subject to a mortgage. Whether the corporation takes subject to or assumes the liability, the taxfree nature of the transaction is not usually upset.

Generally, the liability taken over by the corporation is not treated as a distribution of "boot" to the stockholder transferring the property, but his basis for his stock is reduced by the amount of liability taken over by the corporation.

You may realize taxable income on transferring property subject to liabilities to a corporation when (1) the transfer is part of a tax-avoidance plan, or (2) the liability exceeds your basis for the property transferred to the corporation.

EXAMPLES:

1. *The general rule.* Smith transfers to his corporation property with a basis to him of $10,000 in exchange for stock with a fair market value of $8,000 and cash of $3,000. The corporation also assumes Smith's debts of $4,000. Smith has 80% control of the corporation after the exchange. The gain on the transaction is as follows:

Stock	$8,000
Cash	3,000
Liability assumed	4,000
Total received by Smith	$15,000
Less: Basis for property transferred	10,000
Gain on the exchange	$5,000

Only $3,000 of the gain is taxable. This is the amount of cash which is treated as "boot." The assumed liabilities are not treated as boot.

2. *Tax avoidance transfers.* Same facts as above except there was no bona fide business purpose for the transaction; the purpose of the transfer was to avoid taxes. The $4,000 of assumed liabilities is treated as "money received on the exchange" and the full $5,000 of the gain is taxed. An example of a tax avoidance scheme is mortgaging property shortly before transferring it to the corporation.

3. *Liabilities exceed basis.* Brown owns several pieces of property having a total basis to him of $20,000. One piece with a basis of $10,000 is subject to a $30,000 mortgage. He transfers all these properties to a corporation in return for all of its stock. Whether the corporation assumes the mortgage or merely takes the property subject to it, he has $10,000 capital gain. Gain is the difference between the $30,000 mortgage and his basis for all the property he transferred to the corporation ($20,000). Whether he has long-term or short-term gain depends on how long he held the properties transferred.

If some were held six months or less and the rest for more than six months, the relative fair market values of each type determine how much of the gain is long-term and how much is short-term. Thus, if half the property (based on value) was held more than six months and the balance for a lesser period, half the gain is long-term and the balance short-term. If the assets transferred were not capital assets in Brown's hands, he has ordinary income.

What if the assumption of a mortgage, or taking subject to it, may be taxable because of two reasons: (1) tax avoidance, or (2) the liabilities exceed basis? The transaction is considered as falling within the tax avoidance area. This means that *all liabilities* taken over by the corporation are treated as money received. This may result in a much larger taxed gain than if the transaction fell into the basis rule under which only the excess of the liabilities over basis is taxable.

Tax on the transfer of property with a mortgage in excess of basis may be avoided by transferring enough other property with a sufficient basis to offset the amount of the excess mortgage. The total liability is compared to the total basis of all the property transferred to the corporation.

EXAMPLE:

Cronin owns property with a basis of $25,000; the mortgage on the building is for $50,000. He also owns vacant land with a basis of $25,000. If he transfers only the building to the corporation in exchange for its stock, $25,000 attributed to the excess mortgage is taxable. He can avoid tax by transferring the land. The $50,000 received when he mortgaged the property is his without tax; the corporation repays the mortgage. There is, of course, the danger that this type of transaction may be viewed as a tax avoidance scheme.

Incorporating a Partnership

When a partnership is incorporated, one of two steps may be followed: (1) The partnership transfers all the partnership assets and liabilities to the corporation in exchange for stock, securities, and any "other property" and then distributes to each partner his pro rata share of what the partnership got from the corporation. (2) The partnership first distributes to each partner his pro rata share of partnership assets and liabilities and then each partner individually transfers what he received from the partnership to the corporation in exchange for stock, securities, and perhaps "other property." In either case, the entire transaction can be taxfree or partially taxable in the same manner as a transfer of a sole proprietorship to a corporation.

If the transaction is partially taxable, such as where "boot" is received or the corporation takes over liabilities in circumstances that cause the transferor to be taxed, the nature of the gain depends on the type of property transferred. On the transfer of capital assets, the gain is capital gain; on the transfer of assets that give ordinary income, such as assets subject to depreciation recapture, the gain is ordinary income. Where there are a number of assets, the total gain is divided between capital gain and ordinary income in proportion to the relative values of all the assets transferred.

Transfer of Depreciable Property

Where depreciable assets are transferred to a corporation, a special rule converts what would otherwise be capital gain to ordinary income. If the transferor, together with his spouse, minor children and minor grandchildren, owns the required 80% control, any taxed gain on the depreciable property would be taxable as ordinary income and not capital gain.

Note that the test is whether or not the property is depreciable by the corporation, not by the transferor. So, if you transfer a personal residence to the corporation, the gain is taxable as ordinary income if the residence is depreciable by the corporation.

How Depreciation Recapture Applies to Incorporation

A taxfree transfer of depreciable property solely in exchange for stock of your controlled corporation will not give rise to tax under the depreciation recapture rules. The corporation's basis for the property is the same as transferor's, but it may, if it later sells the asset, realize ordinary income.

In a partially taxfree transfer in which gain is taxed to the extent of the receipt of cash or short-term notes, ordinary income due to additional depreciation is realized but it cannot exceed taxable gain realized on the transfer to the corporation.

EXAMPLE:

You transfer depreciable property to a corporation in exchange for $1,000 cash and stock in the corporation worth $9,000. Your property has a fair market value of $10,000, adjusted basis of $4,000. You have realized a $6,000 gain on the transaction ($10,000 − $4,000). If you had received only stock, no part of the gain would be taxed on the exchange. But as you received cash, $1,000 of the gain is taxed. Now let us assume $1,000 of the depreciation taken on the property is subject to ordinary income tax. All of the $1,000 gain realized on the transfer is taxable as ordinary income.

Transfer of Accounts Receivable May Create Taxable Income

When an unincorporated business transfers accounts receivable to a corporation, the Treasury holds that the corporation takes the accounts receivable at face value, but a bad debt reserve cannot be transferred. Since the unincorporated business is left with a reserve it no longer needs, the reserve becomes ordinary income. Several cases dealing with the sale of the assets of the business to a third party have sustained the Treasury's position. But a court refused to side with the Treasury in a case dealing with a taxfree incorporation. The court said the transfer consisted of the *net* receivables, that is, the face value of the accounts receivable less the reserve for bad debts. Since the value of the stock which the sole proprietor received was equal to that net value, he realized no gain on the transfer. As it is not clear if the Treasury is willing to follow this court decision, here are ways of dealing with accounts receivable and a bad debt reserve in an unincorporated business preparing to incorporate:

1. Do not transfer the accounts receivable to the corporation. Thus there is no immediate income arising from the bad debt reserve. If you collect more than the net value of the receivables, the unused bad debt reserve becomes ordinary income at that time.

EXAMPLE:

You have $10,000 of accounts receivable and a bad debt reserve of $3,000. If eventually, you collect $8,000 on those accounts, $2,000 of worthless accounts will be charged to the bad debt reserve. The balance of $1,000 will be taxable as ordinary income.

2. Sell the accounts receivable to a third party for their net value. If they are sold at an amount in excess of the net value at which you carry them, that excess will be taxable at the time of sale.

EXAMPLE:

Assume the same figures in the example above, $10,000 receivables, $3,000 reserve. You sell all the receivables to a third party for $7,500. That gives you a $2,500 loss on the sale, but you now have a $3,000 reserve you do not need. Net result, $500 income ($3,000 unneeded reserve less $2,500 loss). In effect, you sold the accounts at $500 over your net value.

3. Before transferring the accounts to the corporation, examine them carefully and determine partial or full worthlessness of each account. Write these worthless amounts off against the reserve before transferring the accounts.

EXAMPLE:

Assuming $10,000 of receivables and a $3,000 reserve, an examination of the accounts establishes that $2,500 is definitely worthless (a combination of partial and full worthlessness of the individual accounts). Write off the $2,500 against the reserve, reducing the reserve to $500. The accounts receivable are now reduced to $7,500 and transferred to the corporation. Then, if the Treasury position is upheld against you, the amount taxable to you as the unneeded reserve is only $500.

Basis of Property on Incorporation

If you	*Find your basis this way*
Transfer property for only stock or securities.	Your basis for the stock or securities is the basis of property transferred to the corporation.
Transfer property for stock or securities and also get cash and "other property."	Your basis for the stock or securities is the basis of the property transferred to the corporation less the amount of cash you received and the value of the other property. If you have a taxable gain on the transaction, the amount of the gain increases your basis for the stock or securities. The basis of "other property" you received on the exchange is its fair market value.
Transfer property for stock or securities. The corporation assumes your liability, but you	Your basis for the stock or securities is the basis for the property you transferred less the

have no taxable gain under the rules covering assumption of liabilities.

Same as the previous case but you have a taxable gain on the transaction.

Receive stock and securities or several classes of stock on the exchange.

amount of the liabilities assumed.

After reducing your basis for the amount of the liabilities assumed (as in the previous case), add to your basis the taxable gain on the transaction.

You figure your basis for all the stocks and securities you receive under the four rules above. You allocate the basis among the various classes of stock or stock and securities in proportion to their fair market values.

How to Avoid a Taxfree Incorporation

As previously explained, a disadvantage of taxfree incorporations is that the corporation takes as its basis for depreciation, depletion, and resale of the properties you transfer to it the same basis you had for those properties. So, assets worth considerably more than their bases must still be carried by the corporation at their bases to you. If you are willing to pay the tax, often at capital gain rates, you can step up the corporation's basis of the property transferred to it to market or near-market value.

Several approaches can be used to avoid the taxfree rules and give the corporation a fair market value for the transferred property:

1. Transfer the property to an already existing corporation in which outsiders own stock and you receive less than 80% of the voting stock. Do not set up the corporation right before the transfer. Otherwise, both the transfers to the corporation (of cash or other property) by the outsiders and by you may be considered as part of one plan. Then, the 80% control test is met and the entire transfer is taxfree.

2. The corporation is first organized by transfers of cash for stock, a taxfree transaction. The stockholders may or may not include those who will later transfer property to the corporation by way of sale. Later, the appreciated properties are sold to the corporation in a separate sale at a value that can be defended as market value. The terms of

the sale are similar to terms that would be set on a sale to complete strangers. In that case, where a separate sale is established, the transaction is treated as a sale, rather than a taxfree transfer. This is so even though securities (long-term indebtedness by way of mortgage notes, for example) are received. Of course, if those who "sell" the property to the corporation and receive securities do not own 80% of the stock, there could not in any case be a taxfree transaction. A direct sale requires careful timing. There must be an interval of time between the date of incorporation and the date of sale. But even with this precaution, there is always the possibility that the Treasury might argue that the direct sale made after the incorporation was part of the original incorporation.

You will probably not want to use the sale approach (even though it is recognized as a separate sale) where the sale is being made by an individual who himself (or together with his spouse, minor children and minor grandchildren) owns 80% or more of the corporation's stock. If the property being transferred is depreciable in the corporation's hands (and it is likely to be), any realized gain will be ordinary income to the stockholder. You may be willing to pay capital gain rates in order to step up basis, but it may not make tax sense in your tax bracket to trade corporate depreciation deductions for a tax at ordinary income rates.

3. Before the transfer, put a mortgage on the property in excess of basis. Then, when the property is transferred to the corporation, the liability in excess of basis is taxable (see page 36). The taxable amount is added to the corporation's basis for the property it has received. The danger here is that the transaction might be viewed as a tax avoidance scheme. In that case, the amount of the entire mortgage, not only the excess over basis, will be taxed.

4. Instead of receiving only securities (stocks and bonds) on the exchange, you take back short-term or demand notes. Short-term or demand notes are not treated as securities and are taxable when received in an exchange with a corporation. As a result, the basis of the property transferred to the corporation is increased by the amount of taxable gain realized by you.

Be careful in drawing the terms of short-term notes. They should not resemble secured debentures. Their term should be no longer than five years. Also be aware that if a substantial amount of short-term or demand notes are given, the corporation may be considered to have a "thin capitalization." In that event, the notes will be treated as securities and the transfer of property will be treated as a taxfree exchange with the result that there will be no increase in the adjusted basis of the assets received by the corporation. The corporation will not receive any interest deduction on its notes, and any principal or interest payments will be taxed to you as dividends.

EXAMPLE:

Property has a basis of $50,000 and fair market value of $125,000. You transfer it to a corporation for stock of $100,000 and a short-term note of $25,000. Gain of $25,000 (measured by the note) is taxable. The basis of the property to the corporation is $75,000 (your original basis of $50,000 plus the amount of taxable gain of $25,000).

CHAPTER III

Capitalizing the Corporation

An IMPORTANT STEP in setting up a corporation is proper capitalization. You can base your corporation's capital structure on common stock, preferred stock, and debt, such as bonds and notes. Not only legal and financial considerations but also tax consequences will influence your choice. For example, the Subchapter S corporation rules limit an electing corporation to only one class of stock. This might be sufficient reason for a decision not to issue preferred stock despite other reasons in favor of such issue. If a Subchapter S election is not desired, you may want to use preferred stock as an income-splitting or estate planning device.

To reduce the double tax on corporate income payable to stockholders, you may want to capitalize partially with long or short-term debt. The corporation deducts interest paid on loans, avoiding the double tax on income paid to the stockholders on the debt. When the debt is finally repaid, no income is realized as usually occurs when stock is redeemed. However, as will be explained in this chapter, debt financing runs risks.

After the discussion on debt financing, you will find when and how to use "Section 1244" stock which allows you to convert a long-term capital loss into an ordinary loss if the corporation fails.

Finally, the use of preferred stock and tax penalties involved in certain preferred stock issues are discussed.

Debt Financing: Thin Incorporation

The question that must be answered is to what extent debt financing is needed, and if the debt structure can withstand a challenge by a Treasury agent. In general, debt financing as a tax device is not required if the property held by the corporation will provide large depreciation deductions to offset the taxable income. Neither is it necessary if substantial current earnings are to be accumulated in the corporation.

By disallowing interest deductions and taxing retirements of the debt as stock redemptions, the Treasury is quick to strike at debt financing as a subterfuge for equity capital. This is the risk of thin incorporation capitalization. Investors have been willing to run the risk as the Treasury has not been altogether successful in barring thin incorporation. There is no tax law provision covering the subject. Congress has not been able to agree on legislation barring the use of debt financing in close corporations. However, as the Treasury has forced taxpayers to court to support their debt financing, court decisions—some of which have been favorable—suggest some guides or tests in measuring the bona fides of a debt situation. They can be summarized as follows:

Is the capital and credit structure of the new corporation realistic? What is the business purpose, if any, of organizing the new corporation? Are the stockholders the actual promoters of the new venture? Do the noteholders bear the principal risks of loss from the business? Would other investors make such advances? Is there a lack of reasonable expectation of repayment and do the noteholders attempt to enforce the obligations? Other pointers looked for are:

1. Are the instruments of debt an actual evidence of a valid debt? The character of these instruments—the relationship they set up between the holder and the issuer—determines the debt's tax status. What name is given to the instruments is unimportant. If the actual nature of the instruments is held to disclose a stockholder relationship, they will not be considered as evidences of debt.

2. Do the stockholder loans proportionately relate to the number of shares held? An affirmative answer is held to indicate an intent to preserve the original relationship of the stockholders in the assets of the corporation. The debt may be held to be a contribution to capital.

3. Would the corporation be able to obtain this kind of loan (amount, term or rate) from outsiders on the basis of its business standing? The best substantiation for this is the conclusion of experts. An expert's thorough analysis showing that the amount of the loan, the

interest payment, the amortization provisions, and the maturity dates are realistically in line with an actual debt will carry considerable weight with the court.

4. Is the debt the only working capital of the corporation? If so, the debt is considered to be stock. It is, generally, the proceeds of the original stock issue which supply the beginning working capital.

5. Are the loans to be repaid from corporate earnings? An investment based on prospective earnings is usually the mark of risk capital, that is, a stock investment. An actual loan is generally safeguarded by tangible assets of the borrower. A loan to be paid from future earnings takes on the character of a stock investment.

6. What is the status of the stockholder-lender as compared with that of other creditors in the event of bankruptcy? Does the stockholder-lender follow other lenders in priority of claim? This indicates that the relationship is not considered a complete debtor-creditor one, even by the parties themselves. It would be difficult to make the court find otherwise.

7. Does the corporation itself treat the obligations as a debt? It may not be decisive for the court that the corporation has set up the obligation as a debt and regularly provides for interest payments. The absence of such provision, however, is almost conclusive evidence that the parties did not consider the obligation as a valid debt.

A court may look at the ratio between debt and the equity capital. A high ratio of debt to equity would be evidence of undercapitalization. But even a more favorable and balanced ratio might not be sufficient to sustain the character of the loans as debt. A 20- or 30-to-1 ratio of debt to stock will be difficult to sustain. Interest deductions have been disallowed where the ratio of debt to capital was as low as 6.5 to 1 and 4.4 to 1. Thus it is difficult in any one case to point out one single circumstance as the determining factor that influenced the court's decision on the subject. The following suggestions, although no guarantee of success against a Treasury disallowance, are minimum precautions to follow where debt financing is used:

1. A reasonable ratio between the debt and capital is essential. The equity investment should be appropriate to the operational needs of the business. If possible, loans to the corporation should be made in installments, not at one time.

2. There must be evidences of indebtedness such as notes and bonds with a fixed interest and a reasonable maturity date. Debt tied to collateral or to a mortgage is helpful.

3. The stockholders, if possible, should not make the loans in proportion to their stockholders.

4. It might be possible to have a third party lend the money to the corporation, with the stockholders guaranteeing the loan (even putting up their own property as collateral). At least one court has found that this type of arrangement avoids the thin incorporation problem.

Issuing "Section 1244 stock"

If stock qualifies as "Section 1244 stock," a subsequent loss on that stock is treated as an ordinary, rather than a capital loss, to the extent of $25,000 ($50,000 on a joint return) in one year. The losses can be realized on the sale or exchange of the stock, on the stock becoming worthless, and on the liquidation of the company. A loss in excess of income can be the basis of a net operating loss carryback.

To qualify as "Section 1244 stock," the following rules must be met: (1) The stock has to be voting or nonvoting common stock of a corporation organized in the United States. (2) The stock is issued under a plan adopted by the corporation and the stock is not issued more than two years after the adoption of the plan. (If there is a prior plan in existence to offer Section 1244 stock, that prior plan must be ended before the new plan is adopted. (3) The stock must be issued in return for money or property; but the property cannot consist of other stocks or securities. (4) The company cannot be predominantly an investment company rather than an operating company. For its five most recent years (or its entire period of existence where it has been in existence less than five years) more than half its gross receipts must come from sources other than royalties, rents, dividends, interest, annuities, or gain from the sale or exchange of stock or securities. (5) The company does not issue more than $500,000 of Section 1244 stock and its equity capital including this stock is not more than $1,000,000.

Limitations on loss. In addition to the $25,000 ($50,000 on a joint return) annual ceiling on the amount of ordinary loss, there are other limitations: (1) The loss is available to only an individual or partnership. Trusts and estates are not considered individuals, nor can they be partners for this purpose. (2) The loss is available only to the individual or partnership to whom the stock was originally issued. If Section 1244 stock is issued to A, who later sells it to B, B cannot get an ordinary loss on a subsequent sale of the stock. (3) There is a special basis rule limiting the amount of loss on the sale of Section 1244 stock. If you transfer property to a corporation in a taxfree exchange for Section 1244 stock and the basis of the property is higher than its value, then the basis of the Section 1244 stock if you later sell the stock at a loss is the old basis of the property exchanged, less the excess of basis over value. What this does is to lower the basis of the Section 1244 stock and avoid the situation where a stockholder puts a loss asset into a corporation, gets Section 1244 stock, and sells the stock, getting an ordinary loss instead of the capital loss he would have gotten had he sold the asset directly.

EXAMPLE:

You transfer equipment to your corporation that has a basis to you of $10,000 but is worth only $6,000. In exchange, you get back stock from the company that qualifies as Section 1244 stock. You and your co-stockholders who have also transferred property to the corporation at that time own the necessary 80% of the stock to make the transaction taxfree. The basis for your stock is $10,000 under the taxfree exchange rules. Some time later, you sell your stock for $2,000. You have an $8,000 loss. But only $4,000 of that loss is deductible as an ordinary loss. Your actual $8,000 loss less the $4,000 by which your basis for the stock exceeded the market value of the equipment you transferred to the corporation. The remaining $4,000 loss is a capital loss.

Adoption of the plan. The adoption of the plan to issue Section 1244 stock should be at a meeting of directors or stockholders if their authorization is required. The plan should be in a formal written statement, such as a resolution or the minutes. It should be dated, contain a statement in dollars of the maximum amount that can be received for the Section 1244 stock, and the time period the offer for the stock remains open. Two years from the date of adoption is the longest the offering can continue. So it is wise to set a date that is a few days or even weeks less than two years.

Computations to substantiate the two limitations listed in rule (5) above should be set out in the plan, supported by adequate records. It is not enough to follow the form in the written plan. You must be careful not to exceed the limitations when the stock is finally issued. You may be required to show that what was contained in the plan was *in fact* the blueprint for what was finally carried out.

You should include in your plan a statement that any prior offerings of stock are revoked. According to Treasury regulations, "an offer is outstanding unless and until it is withdrawn by affirmative action prior to the time the plan is adopted. Stock rights, stock warrants, stock options or securities convertible into stock, which are outstanding at the time the plan is adopted, are deemed to be prior offerings." So, if any of these are outstanding, your ability to use Section 1244 stock is hampered.

Preservation of records by the corporation. Aside from the written plan itself, these records should be kept by the corporation: (1) Which stockholders the stock was issued to, and a description of the amount and type of consideration received by each; (2) If the consideration was property, the basis in the hands of the stockholder and the market value of the property when received by the corporation; (3) Which certificates represent stock issued under the plan; (4) The amount of money and the basis in the hands of the corporation of other property received after June 30, 1958, and before the adoption of the plan for its stock, as a contribution to capital, and as paid-in surplus; (5) The equity capital of the corporation on the date of the adoption of the plan; and (6) Information as to any taxfree stock dividend made with respect to stock issued under the plan and any reorganization in which stock is transferred by the corporation in exchange for stock issued pursuant to the plan.

Preservation of records by the stockholder. If you are claiming an ordinary deduction on your Section 1244 stock, you must attach to your tax return for that year a statement showing: (1) The address of the corporation that issued the stock; (2) How you acquired the stock, and the kind and amount of consideration you gave for it; and (3) If you acquired the property in a nontaxable transaction in exchange for other property other than money, give the type of property, its fair market value on the date of transfer to the corporation, and its adjusted basis on that date.

A corporation whose only class of stock outstanding is Section 1244 stock may elect to get the benefits of Subchapter S.

Uses of Preferred Stock

Preferred stock stands midway between common stock and bonds. Although the preferred stockholder shares with common stockholders the risk that there may be no profits with which to pay dividends, he is assured that any dividends must be paid to him before common stockholders receive theirs. Thus, in a sense, he assumes the risks of an owner but enjoys to a limited degree the preferred status of a creditor.

The preferred stock may be voting or nonvoting. It may be redeemable or callable at the will of the corporation, and it may contain a conversion feature, allowing the stockholder an option to convert the preferred stock into another class of stock, such as common.

Preferred stock can be used to implement corporate financial policy and tax saving plans. It can be used to attract additional equity capital into the corporation without diluting the voting control by issuing nonvoting preferred stock. Preferred stock can also provide you with the flexibility needed for income splitting, bailing out corporate earnings, providing incentive for key employees, retaining an investment interest in your business if you someday decide to sell your controlling interest, planning for retirement, and keeping down your estate taxes.

Before organizing a corporation with preferred stock, you should consider its consequences on a Subchapter S election. One of the requirements for a valid Subchapter S election is that the corporation have only one class of stock. Since the most frequent use of the election is in the beginning years of a corporation's life (to allow the passthrough to stockholders of operating losses) you may decide to forego the tax planning benefits of preferred stock until the election is no longer required. At that point, you can terminate the Subchapter S election by recapitalizing the corporation with common and preferred. If, however, the new preferred is received in a taxfree distribution such as a stock dividend or recapitalization, by persons also holding common stock, the penalty rules of "Section 306 stock" which are discussed below may apply.

Tax Planning Uses of Preferred Stock

Income splitting. By issuing preferred stock in your children's names, the dividends they receive are taxed at lower rates resulting in an overall tax saving for the family. You can do this without relinquishing voting control by making the preferred nonvoting. If the stock is given at the organization of the corporation, there is little or no gift tax involved. Also, preferred stock issued at the inception of the corporation is not 306 stock.

If you do not wish to give preferred stock to the children now, you can give it to them by way of gifts at some later time. However, at that time, the increase in the value of the corporate stock may give rise to a gift tax.

Bailing out corporate earnings. You can issue the preferred stock to your wife. Later, when the business has grown and has accumulated earnings, she terminates her interest in the corporation in a redemption of all her stock, paying capital gain on the redemption profit. The redemption of stock initially issued to your wife can be, for tax purposes, more readily redeemed than stock given to her by you after the corporation is in existence.

Providing stock for key employees. Key employees may want an interest in your corporation but they may not be able to finance the purchase of common stock. If the value of the common stock is too high, a recapitalization issue of preferred stock would decrease the value of the common. In this way the common can be placed within the reach of the key employees. At the same time, your substantial interest in the business is reflected by the preferred held by you.

EXAMPLE:

> Jones owns all of the capital stock of his corporation. It has a book value of $200,000. Recapitalizing, the company issues 1,500 shares of $100 par, 6% preferred to Jones. This provides him with preferred worth $150,000 and common worth $50,000. He can then enter into an agreement under which the key men can buy the common at book value.

Saving estate taxes. You can reduce the size of your estate by shifting from common stock to preferred. For example, if you foresee increased earnings and appreciation in value of the business, you can recapitalize the business, issuing the new common to your children and holding on to the new preferred. In this way, all the future appreciation in the business is reflected in the common stock. By residing voting power in the preferred, you retain managerial control of the business.

Retaining an investment interest in your business. If you anticipate selling your business to outsiders, but want to retain an investment interest to guarantee an income in your retirement years, you can accomplish this by selling the voting stock and retaining nonvoting cumulative preferred (or common). Whether the buyers of your business will concede to this arrangement depends, of course, on the strength of your bargaining position.

Prohibited Uses of Preferred Stock—Section 306 Stock

Assume your business has accumulated earnings that would be taxable as dividends if distributed to you directly. You conceive a plan to withdraw these earnings at capital gain rates. You cause your corporation to issue a stock dividend of preferred stock. You then negotiate with a third party to purchase the preferred stock from you, which would be followed by a redemption of the preferred by your corporation. The hoped-for result would be a capital gain to you on your profit from the sale, and a depletion of the corporate earnings and profits account when it redeems the stock from the third party. In effect, you have gotten out earnings and profits at the cost of a capital gains tax. However, Congress has provided an effective bar to this type of maneuver by treating such preferred stock as "Section 306 Stock," which, when sold or redeemed, produces ordinary income instead of capital gain. Section 306 stock retains its undesirable "taint" until sale, redemption or prior death of the stockholder. Thus, if the corporation issues a taxfree dividend of preferred stock, whether voting or nonvoting, and certain other conditions exist (discussed below), the preferred stock in Section 306 stock.

What is Section 306 Stock?

Section 306 stock is generally preferred stock issued as a stock dividend to holders of common stock at a time when the corporation has earnings and profits. (The effect of the 306 taint is explained below in the discussion on sale and redemption).

Section 306 stock can also result in a taxfree reorganization, including a spin-off, split-off and split-up, if the effect of the transaction was substantially the same as the receipt of a stock dividend, or if the stock was received in exchange for other Section 306 stock.

If the corporation has no earnings and profits at the time the stock is distributed, there can be no Section 306 stock. Thus, you can issue preferred stock at the time of incorporation without worry of Section 306.

If you are planning a preferred stock issue in a corporation which has no earnings and profits, keep precise records and any other evidence available to convince the Treasury in some later year when you dispose of the tainted stock that there were in fact no earnings and profits at the time of the dividend declaration. A dollar of earnings is sufficient to taint all the preferred stock as 306 stock.

The taint of 306 stock is not cleansed by giving the stock to another party.

EXAMPLE:

You own all the common stock of a corporation and cause it to issue as a dividend 100 shares of preferred stock. There is no tax on receipt of the dividend, but the preferred stock is 306 stock. You give the preferred to your son. The preferred stock remains Section 306 stock in your son's hands.

Stock rights are treated as stock for purposes of determining whether the stock later received upon exercise of the rights is Section 306 stock. The stock received on exercise is treated as having been received at the time the rights were received.

The 306 taint can be removed by exchanging the tainted stock for common stock in the same corporation. For this purpose, it does not matter if there was a conversion privilege contained in the Section 306 stock. But if you received *common* stock containing a privilege of conversion into stock other than common, then that new stock is not treated as common stock. Thus, if you exchange Section 306 stock for common stock containing the privilege to convert into other preferred stock, the newly-acquired common remains Section 306 stock.

Sale of Section 306 Stock

When 306 stock is sold, the Treasury will claim that all or part of the amount received from your purchaser is taxed as a dividend. The taxable dividend element is the dividend that would have resulted if cash equal to the fair market value of the stock dividend was received instead at the time of the distribution of the stock. The corporation's earnings and profits at the time of the stock dividend are allocated among all the common stock outstanding at that time. However, the dividend cannot exceed the lower of the stock's fair market value at the time of the distribution or the ratable share of earnings and profits. If the sales proceeds exceed the amount treated as a dividend plus the basis of the stock sold, the excess is capital gain.

EXAMPLE:

You sell for $100 a share of 306 stock having a basis of $20 and a fair market value of $75 at the time the stock was originally distributed.

(1) If your ratable share of the earnings and profits of your corporation at the time of the stock distribution was $60, you have a dividend of $60 and a capital gain of $20.

(2) If your ratable share of the earnings and profits of your corporation at the time of the stock distribution was $95, you have a dividend of $75 (lower of earnings and profits or fair market value) and a capital gain of $5.

On the death of a stockholder, the Section 306 taint disappears from his stock.

If you sell your entire interest in the corporation, that is, your entire ownership interest including the tainted stock, the preferred stock is not subject to dividend treatment. An important condition on this rule is that the sale must not be to a person whose stock ownership is attributed to you (*see* pages 165-166). Similarly, if the redemption in which you turn in your tainted stock completely terminates your interest in the corporation, you get capital gain treatment. In figuring whether your interest in the corporation is completely terminated, all of the rules stated at pages 168-170, including the 10-year "look-forward" and "look-backward" rules must be satisfied.

Redemption of 306 Stock

A redemption of Section 306 stock is treated as a distribution of cash or property from the corporation and is governed by the general rules governing corporate distributions.

EXAMPLE:

Smith is the sole stockholder of X Corporation. On December 31, 1966, when the corporation's earnings and profits account is $1,000, it issues a dividend of preferred stock to Smith. On July 1, 1967, X Corporation redeems the preferred stock for $10,000. In 1967 there were $10,000 of current and accumulated earnings and profits. The whole $10,000 is treated as a dividend to Smith.

The major difference between a sale and a redemption of 306 stock is that in a sale the corporation's earnings and profits account *at the time of the distribution of the stock* determines ordinary income tax treatment. With a redemption, the tax year of the corporation in which the redemption takes place is crucial.

In the example above, if Smith had made a sale of his preferred stock, receiving $10,000, then only $1,000 would have been taxed as a dividend, since there was only that amount of earnings and profits in the corporation at the time of the stock distribution.

Capital gain treatment is also available to 306 stock in a partial or complete liquidation of the corporation.

If you exchange 306 stock in a nontaxable transaction such as a taxfree reorganization, "taxfree incorporation," or a gift, the exchange does not give rise to immediate tax consequences on the 306 stock.

Avoiding 306 Taint by Proving No Tax Avoidance Motive

If you can show to the satisfaction of the Treasury that the distribution of the preferred stock and the later sale or redemption of the stock was not part of a plan to convert corporate earnings to capital gain, then you get capital gain treatment. The usual procedure for establishing lack of tax avoidance motive is to obtain an advance ruling from the Treasury.

To get a favorable ruling, you must show the following: (1) The stock of the issuing company is widely held; (2) the Section 306 stock is not redeemable for at least five years from the date of issuance; and

(3) you represent under penalties of perjury that there will in fact be no redemption of the Section 306 stock for at least five years.

If, prior to or simultaneous with the disposition of the preferred stock, there was a redemption or other disposition of the underlying common stock, the disposition of the preferred stock is presumed not to be part of a plan of tax avoidance.

Gifts of 306 Stock

The 306 taint may not be a serious drawback if the stock is to be used as gift property in an income-splitting plan. A gift is not a taxable disposition for income tax purposes. The stock, however, remains tainted in the hands of the donee and will be taxed at ordinary rates if the donee sells prior to the death of the donor. However, if the donee holds on to the preferred stock for ten years, he may get capital gain treatment on a redemption of his entire interest in the corporation, since he would then qualify under the 10-year "look-backward" rule (page 168). He could not while the donor was alive *sell* the stock after 10 years and hope for capital gain treatment, since the attribution rules apply to a sale even though it completely terminates the seller's interest in the corporation.

Charitable contributions. The Treasury allows a charitable contribution deduction for Section 306 stock. For a stockholder in an over-50% tax bracket, such a gift may provide him a better economic return than if he had sold the stock or received a dividend.

CHAPTER IV

Buying a Business

Do NOT WAIT until after you have bought your business to consider how much you will pay in income taxes after your purchase. Tax planning should begin before you buy, even though you are not liable for income taxes on the initial purchase. The time for paying taxes will arrive soon enough, perhaps within a few months and no later than a year after the purchase. It will then be too late to undo the purchase, if you discover that you have bought along with the business tax liabilities.

When you consider buying a new business, you should estimate the tax that will be due on the income earned from the business. Does it carry tax disadvantages, such as a low basis for figuring depreciation? Decide whether your manner of making the purchase gives you tax advantages. Can taxes be reduced by leasing rather than by purchasing? Or if you are buying property owned by a corporation, would a purchase of the corporate stock place you in a better tax position than a direct purchase of the property? These and other problems are discussed in the following pages.

If you are buying an interest in a partnership, the price paid for the partnership interest may reflect the current market price, but it may be higher than the basis for the assets on the partnership's books. You may "step up" the basis of your share of the partnership's assets to reflect the purchase price you paid. (See page 162)

How to Buy Assets Owned by a Corporation

Are you planning to buy assets owned by a seller's corporation? The purchase can be arranged in one of two ways. You might buy the corporate stock or the assets directly from the corporation. If you buy stock, you can continue the operation of the property in its present corporate form, or you can liquidate the corporation in order to put the assets into another business form or new company.

In making your decision, consider these guides:

1. How does the seller's price compare with the tax basis of the property on the books of the corporation? If the purchase price is more than its tax basis, try to buy the assets directly. Then your tax basis for the property will be the price you pay.

2. If you buy the stock, you may be held to low book values, unless you meet the special taxfree liquidation rules explained below, under which you can buy the corporation's stock, liquidate the corporation and then set up the assets at the price you paid for the stock.

3. If the purchase price is lower than the tax basis, try to buy the stock. In this case, the corporation's basis for the property will give you larger depreciation deductions. And if you sell the property later at a profit, you can cut the gain or even get a book loss with the use of the higher basis.

4. Does the corporation hold depreciable property which is subject to recapture rules? If you buy the stock and the corporation later sells the asset, it may incur ordinary income on the sale. If the ordinary income element is large, you may want to avoid a purchase of stock and insist on a purchase of the assets directly. On your purchase, the seller will incur tax on the ordinary income, not you. Or, as an alternative, you buy the stock but at a discounted price that reflects the amount of ordinary income you will realize on a later sale.

5. What tax benefits of the seller can you get if you continue the same corporate form? Compare the advantages of what you can elect by starting your own business with the seller's accounting methods, methods of computing depreciation, depletion or amortization, carryback or carryforward of capital losses.

Problems to Avoid If You Decide to Buy Stock

See if the corporation has unknown, hidden, or contingent liabilities, especially unpaid tax bills, for which you may be liable. Protect yourself by getting a warranty from the seller, covering you for any

loss you may suffer from these liabilities. See if it has unfavorable contracts or restrictions such as burdensome contracts with unions, officers, or pension plans.

Plan your transaction to avoid paying a tax on part of the purchase
price. Assume you agree to buy corporate stock. Assume, too, that
your price of the stock reflects the higher market values (as compared
with corporate costs) of real estate, etc. When these assets are sold,
both the corporation and you, when dividends are distributed, will pay
tax on a book profit. This is in part a return of your capital. Make sure
your buying plan does not include this penalty. Try to buy assets, or
plan a liquidation which leaves the corporation untaxed and gives you
a cost basis reflecting market value. Otherwise, get an adjustment for
the penalty you are assuming.

How to Liquidate Seller's Company for its Assets

Suppose the seller will sell only his stock, but you want to buy only
the property of a corporation. You do not want the stock because the
cost basis of the property acquired will then be less than your purchase
price, that is, the market price of the stock is more than the depreciated cost of the asset to the company. For example, the owner may
have paid $100,000 for property put into his company in 1950, and
that property has been depreciated to $30,000. But the asset may now
be worth $150,000, which is also the fair market value of the owner's
stock in his company. How can you pay $150,000 for the stock and
still get an asset basis for continued depreciation of $150,000?

When the stock purchase is made by your corporation, your corporation can liquidate the purchased corporation and then pick up the
property at the price at which the stock was bought. To do this:

1. The corporation must buy 80% or more of the stock during a
period of not more than 12 months.

2. A plan to liquidate the purchased corporation must be adopted
within a period of not more than two years after the stock purchase.
(See page 241 for further discussion.)

Allocating the Purchase Price When Assets are Purchased Instead of Stock

Bargaining between you and the seller will fix the final purchase price. But once the price is set, make sure you spell out its terms, especially for items you can recover as tax deductions or realize later as capital gains.

Are you buying several assets from the same buyer? Make certain that you specifically allocate the portions of the purchase price applying to each asset and that you can recover a greater part of your investment through depreciation. Although an arbitrary allocation will be rejected by the Treasury, you and the seller do have some leeway in setting the value of each asset. Generally, the Treasury will accept allocations fixed between a buyer and a seller in an arm's-length transaction. Recognizing that an ideal allocation is rarely attainable, here are the values a buyer generally wants depending on his tax position:

Buildings, building improvements, elevators and escalators and machinery, equipment of long life: Value high because you get depreciation to recover the cost, and loss on sale or abandonment is fully deductible. Also try to allocate a higher value to assets with short useful-lives so that you can get larger depreciation deductions earlier.

Land: Value low, because no depreciation is allowed. Any gain on a later sale would be a capital gain.

Stocks, bonds and securities: Value low, because gain on a later sale would be taxed at capital gain rates.

Goodwill: Value low, because the cost is recovered only through eventual sale of the business.

Generally, your interests as buyer in fixing asset values are directly opposed to those of your seller. For example, in the case of depreciable equipment, the seller wants the lowest possible price fixed on depreciable assets to cut down the ordinary income he realizes from depreciation recapture. Likewise, with goodwill, he wants a high allocated value, since it is a capital asset. Your relative bargaining positions often determine what the final result will be.

Allocations between covenants not to compete and goodwill. You will want to allocate as much as you can to an agreement not to compete and as little, if anything, to goodwill. You can deduct the cost of a covenant not to compete over the period of the covenant. So, if you pay $100,000 for a seller's agreement not to compete for 10 years, you deduct $10,000 a year. On the other hand, if you buy goodwill, you get no deduction. You recover the cost of goodwill only when you sell the business.

The seller, of course, wants the opposite. Payments for a covenant not to compete are ordinary income to him. But payments for goodwill give him a capital gain.

In court decisions, the amounts allocated to a covenant not to compete have been approved when: (1) The covenant was separable from the other assets. (2) It was bargained for between the parties. The fact that a covenant is stated separately in the contract with a price allocated helped the buyers establish that there was a separate covenant bargained for. (3) There was a real business need for the noncompete agreement. There was a real possibility that without the covenant the seller would go into competition and hurt the buyer. In other words, the allocation was not arbitrarily arranged to give a tax deduction to the buyer.

Evidence that the price for the covenant is unreasonable exists where the price set for the covenant is extremely high in comparison to the total price of the business. However, the courts may uphold a high allocation where both parties are before the court and it can examine both sides of the argument. Where only the buyer is before the court, the court will likely take the position that an extremely large allocation to the covenant is unreasonable. In one case, the Tax Court agreed that an allocation to the noncompete covenant of $142,000 out of a total sales price of $147,000 was reasonable where both parties were before the court. The court implied that it might have held otherwise were only the buyer before it.

Purchase of Partnership Interest

When you purchase an interest in a partnership, the price you pay for the interest generally represents the fair market value of your share of the partnership property. This price becomes your basis for your partnership interest. However, the partnership may have a low basis for its assets. If no adjustment is made to the partnership's basis of its appreciated assets in your favor, the portion of the appreciation attributable to your interest in the partnership may be taxed twice.

EXAMPLE:

Adam-Baker-Cane partnership has $450 cash, and machinery with a basis of $1,200 but worth $1,500. Adam, Baker and Cane each have a one-third interest in the partnership with a basis of $550. Adam sells his interest to Doe for $650. Adam realizes a $100 profit on the transaction. Thereafter, the Baker-Cane-Doe partnership sells the machinery for $1,500, resulting in a $300 gain to the partnership. This gain would be divided proportionately among the three partners. $100 of the gain is attributable to each, Baker, Cane and Doe. Doe's tax situation with respect to the gain would be the same as his partners despite the fact that the purchase price of $650 for his partnership interest reflected the $100 appreciation of the machinery. Furthermore, Adam has already paid a tax on the $100 profit realized from the sale of his one-third partnership interest to Doe. The $100 gain now attributable to Doe as a result of the sale of the machinery by the partnership duplicates the tax paid by Adam.

To avoid such double taxation, the basis of the partnership property can be adjusted to account for the difference between the partnership's basis for your proportionate share in the partnership property and the basis for your partnership interest. The adjustment must be by election. Failure to elect leaves the partnership's basis for its property unchanged.

The adjustment is based on the difference between the basis for your interest and the partnership's basis for your proportionate share of the partnership property. The resulting adjustment increases or decreases the partnership's basis for its property. But it is attributable only to your interest.

The partnership makes the election, even though it is for your benefit, by filing a written statement with the District Director with whom the partnership returns are filed. The election is effective for the year in which made and for all later years until revoked. Sometimes the election can work to your disadvantage, especially if you pay less for your partnership interest than your share of partnership assets.

EXAMPLE:

A is a member of partnership ABC in which the partners have equal interests in capital and profits. The partnership has made the special election relating to the optional adjustment to the basis of partnership property. A sells his interest to P for $22,000. The balance sheet of the partnership at the date of sale shows the following:

ASSETS	Adjusted Basis Per Books	Market Value	LIABILITIES AND CAPITAL	Adjusted Basis Per Books	Market Value
Cash	$ 5,000	$ 5,000	Liabilities	$10,000	$10,000
Accounts			Capital—		
receivable	10,000	10,000	A	15,000	22,000
Inventory	20,000	21,000	B	15,000	22,000
Depreciable			C	15,000	22,000
assets	20,000	40,000			
Total	$55,000	$76,000	Total	$55,000	$76,000

The amount of the adjustment to the basis of the partnership assets is the difference between the basis of P's interest in the partnership and his share of the adjusted basis of partnership property. The basis of P's interest is $25,333 (the cash paid for A's interest, $22,000, plus $3,333, P's share of partnership liabilities). P's share of the adjusted basis of partnership property is $18,333, i.e., $15,000 plus $3,333. The amount to be added to the basis of partnership property is, therefore, $7,000, the difference between $25,333 and $18,333. This amount will be allocated to partnership properties whose values exceed their bases in proportion to the difference between the value and basis of each.

Even though the partnership basis is stepped up for the appreciated properties, this step-up applies only to the purchasing partner.

EXAMPLE:

A, B, and C form partnership ABC, to which A contributes land worth $1,000 (property X) with an adjusted basis to him of $400, and B and C each contributes $1,000 cash. Each partner has $1,000 credited to him on the books of the partnership as his capital contribution. The partners share in profits equally. During the partnership's first taxable year, property X appreciates in value to $1,300. A sells his one-third interest in the partnership to D for $1,100, at a time when the special partnership election to step-up basis is in effect. The adjusted basis of the partnership property is increased for D by the excess of his basis for his partnership interest, $1,100, over his share of the adjusted basis of partnership property, $800 (⅓ of $2,400, the total adjusted basis of partnership property). The amount of the adjustment, therefore, is $300 ($1,100 minus $800), which is an increase in the basis of partnership property with respect to D only. This special basis adjustment will be allocated to property X since that is the only appreciated asset. If property X is sold for $1,600, the gain to the partnership is $1,200 ($1,600 received, less the adjusted common partnership basis of $400 for property X). Thus, each partner's distributive share of the gain on the sale is $400. However, D's recognized gain is only $100 (his $400 distributive share of the gain, reduced by $300, his special basis adjustment with respect to property X). If D purchased his interest from B or C, the partners who contributed cash, D's adjustment would also be $300, computed in exactly the same manner as in the case of a purchase from A.

Purchase of a Corporate Business

You can buy the stock of the corporation and thereby acquire the control of its assets, or you can buy the assets from the corporation.

Buyers generally prefer to acquire the assets. Sellers generally prefer to sell stock, *see* page 225. In buying assets, you need not be concerned with any possible contingent or undisclosed liabilities the corporation may have. If you buy stock and the corporation later turns out to owe taxes or other undisclosed or unanticipated liabilities, the corporation will be liable even though ownership of the stock has changed hands. You can protect yourself with guarantees or insist that part of the purchase price be put in escrow for a period of time. But these devices may entail litigation or be unacceptable to the seller. Consequently, from your viewpoint, the "cleanest" deal is a purchase of assets.

When you buy assets, the purchase price becomes the basis for the assets. You can figure depreciation on that value. On a later sale of any of the assets, gain or loss will be figured in terms of the adjusted basis, using the purchase price as the starting point. However, if you buy stock, the corporation remains intact. Its basis for its assets does not change merely because the stock ownership has changed. However, if the basis of the assets is below fair market value, you may want to liquidate the corporation within two years in order to step up the basis of the corporate assets (see below).

EXAMPLE:

Assume the corporation you are buying has depreciable assets shown on the books with an adjusted basis of $10,000 but currently worth $20,000. It also has inventories which cost it $15,000 and which are now worth $20,-

ooo. You are willing to pay $40,000 for the company, the value of its assets. And you do so by buying all of its stock for $40,000. If nothing further is done, the corporation retains the same basis ($25,000) it had before. It can take depreciation deductions based on its $10,000 basis for its depreciable assets and if it sells its inventories, its profits will be based on the extent the selling price exceeds $15,000. So, you would get no tax benefit from the $15,000 in excess of book value that you paid for the company.

Finally, to the extent you acquire equipment, you may be entitled to an investment credit. If you buy stock, no investment credit is available.

How to Step Up the Basis of Assets in an Acquired Corporation

To step up basis, the stock of the corporation being bought should be purchased by your corporation. Your corporation has to buy at least 80% of the stock within a 12-month period. Then, if the corporation whose stock was bought is liquidated pursuant to a plan of liquidation adopted within a two-year period beginning on the date the stock ownership requirement was met, the assets received in the liquidation take as their total basis the basis of the purchased stock. The basis of the stock is allocated among the assets received in the liquidation in proportion to their market values.

EXAMPLE:

Facts of the example above except you organize A Corp. in order to acquire all the stock of B Corp. And using the figures used above, B Corp. has depreciable assets worth $20,000 with an adjusted basis of $15,000. B Corp. also has inventories worth $20,000 which cost it $15,000. A Corp. buys all the stock of B for $40,000. Then, shortly after the purchase, B Corp. is liquidated and A Corp. receives all of assets of B Corp. Since A Corp. paid $40,000 for the B stock, it can now allocate that $40,000 over the assets it acquired in the liquidation. Since the depreciable assets and the inventories each have an equal market value, $20,000 will be allocated to the depreciable assets and $20,000 to the inventories. Thereafter, A Corp. will be able to compute its depreciation deductions using $20,000 as its adjusted basis for its depreciable asset. And when it sells the inventories, only amounts received in excess of $20,000 will be treated as profits.

How an Individual Buyer Can Step Up the Value of the Assets When He Buys Stock

Suppose you want to run the business you are buying as a sole proprietorship or partnership. But to buy the business, you have to buy stock. This presents no problem. You can step up the basis of the assets even though you buy the stock. After you buy the stock, liquidate the corporation. Normally, when a corporation is liquidated, the stockholders are taxed on their gain, the difference between the market value of what they receive in the liquidation and the basis of their stock. In this case, when you bought the stock, the price you paid reflected the market value of the corporate assets. So, when you liquidate the company, the value of the assets you receive will equal the basis for the stock you just bought. Although this is technically a taxable liquidation, there is no gain to tax. And, in a liquidation of this type, the market value of the assets received becomes your basis.

Do not buy the stock personally if you intend to run the new business as a corporation. As indicated above, if you organize a corporation first and it buys the stock and then liquidates the purchased company, you can step up the basis of the assets acquired. But if you personally buy the stock first, then transfer that stock to your corporation, and then liquidate the purchased corporation, you will not get that result. *Reason:* The corporation which owns the stock at the time of liquidation must be the purchaser of that stock. In this case, your corporation will have acquired that stock from you in a transfer, a taxfree exchange, not a purchase.

You will not be any better off if you buy the stock personally, liquidate the purchased corporation and then transfer the assets to your own corporation. *Reason:* The purchase by you, the liquidation of the purchased company, and the transfer of the assets to your corporation will be viewed by the courts as step transactions adding up to a taxfree reorganization. In this type of taxfree reorganization, there is no step-up in the basis of the assets.

Buying a Company with Its Own Funds or Earnings

The purchase of the business may be transacted by letting the buyer pay for the business in part with the company's own funds or future earnings. Before you buy the stock of a corporation holding substantial cash, you can agree with the seller that he will receive part of the price from the company. You then buy from the seller only a portion of his stock. The corporation redeems the balance of the stock from the seller with the cash it has. Because all of the seller's interest in the corporation is being redeemed, he realizes a capital gain on the redemption instead of a fully taxable dividend. As you have the remaining stock, the only outstanding stock, you are in full control of the purchased corporation. (See page 172 for further discussion.)

Using the company's future earnings. You can organize a new corporation to make the stock purchase, paying in installments. Now, your corporation, not you, owes the seller the purchase price. Your corporation, on acquiring the stock, can liquidate the corporation it has acquired, receiving all of its assets. Since the profits earned by the purchased business will now be in the corporation that owes the purchase price, these future profits will help pay for the purchase of that business.

Buying a Loss Corporation

A corporation may incur substantial losses over a period of years. These losses are available as carryovers to offset the profits of future years; an operating loss may be carried back three years and carried forward five years. However, if the company is incapable of generating future profits, its losses will remain unused. In these circumstances, another company may want to take over the corporation to use its losses.

Because of the desirability of acquiring losses, a heavy traffic in loss companies developed. Congress decided, however, that transfers of losses from company to company should not be freely available and set down a number of rules governing the transfer of carryover losses. In addition, the Treasury and the courts have laid down further rules in this area that restrict the availability of accumulated losses as carryovers when a loss business is acquired. Nevertheless within these boundaries, it is still possible to acquire carryover losses.

Methods of Acquiring Loss Companies

There are two methods of acquiring the losses of an existing corporation:

1. *Purchase of stock.* You acquire control of the loss company by purchasing its stock. The company continues its existence as before. This type of acquisition is practical when you have a profit-making business to add to the acquired corporation to utilize its losses.

2. *Taxfree reorganization.* If the acquisition is effected by using certain types of taxfree reorganizations or liquidations, the combined company can then continue to use the carryover losses. But certain rules must be followed, including a requirement that the stockholders of the loss company acquired in a taxfree reorganization must continue to be at least 20% stockholders in the acquiring corporation. For every percentage point under 20%, the company loses 5% of its carryover loss. This rule is further explained below.

Even if you follow one of the two routes detailed above, the Treasury will bar the use of the loss carryovers unless you can show that your principal purpose in acquiring the corporation was not to avoid taxes by the use of the losses. This may be shown by demonstrating a good business purpose for the acquisition and by showing that the purchase price of the stock did not reflect the value of the losses. Examples are: Buying out your principal competitor, purchasing a corporation to acquire its plant, inventory and personnel, diversifying your line, or expanding your geographic market. Note that the use of losses may be disallowed even where you can show a good business purpose if the Treasury proves that the *principal* motive behind the acquisition was tax avoidance.

In the following sections, the rules for stock acquisitions and taxfree reorganizations, and allied problems are discussed in detail.

Stock Purchase of a Loss Corporation: The 50 Percentage Point Rule

Your corporation will forfeit the use of prior operating losses if: (1) during the period from the beginning of the prior taxable year to the end of the current year, any one or more of the 10 stockholders owning the greatest percentage of the fair market value of the stock of your corporation buys at least 50 percentage points more stock (in terms of fair market value rather than number of shares) than they owned at the beginning of the two-year period; (2) the corporation has not continued substantially the same business as before the two-year period.

A purchase of stock includes not only an outright purchase of stock but also a purchase of stock of a corporation owning stock of the loss corporation and a purchase of an interest in a partnership or trust owning stock in the loss corporation. It also includes the increase in percentage points of stock resulting from a redemption of stock of any other stockholder (except where the redemption qualifies as a redemption to pay death taxes). Purchase does not include stock received as a result of a gift or bequest or in a taxfree reorganization or liquidation.

In determining the 10 stockholders, the constructive ownership rules are applied. A husband and wife whose stock is attributed to one another are considered one stockholder for purposes of determining the 10.

Stock means all shares except nonvoting stock which is limited and preferred as to dividends.

Note that the test refers to percentage points, rather than "percent."

EXAMPLE:

You own 20 of the 100 outstanding shares of a corporation, which is 20%. You purchase 40 shares from the owner of the remaining 80. You now own 60 shares. Even though you have increased your holdings in the corporation by 200%, your percentage point holding has only increased by 40. You do not fall within the 50 percentage point rule. If you had purchased 50 shares (or if your wife had purchased 10 shares in addition to your 40), your holdings would have increased by 50 percentage points.

An outright purchase of 100% of the stock of a loss corporation fits within the above rules, so in order to avoid the disallowance of the loss carryover, you must carry on substantially the same business that existed before your purchase. What constitutes carrying on substantially the same business is not easy to define. The Treasury has issued extensive regulations, and the courts have not always sided with the Treasury view. Evidence that will be relevant on whether there has been a substantial change of business is changes in the corporation's employees, plant, equipment, product, location, customers and similar items. A change of location may be acceptable to the Treasury if you can show that after the move you are selling substantially the same products to substantially the same customers, or that your salesmen are working the same geographical area.

The Treasury regulations allow you to discontinue a minor part of the old business, as long as that part did not generate the operating losses. You also may add a new business without falling afoul of the "same business" requirement. But you cannot continue a minor part of the old business and then add a new one. Carrying a minor portion only, according to the Treasury, does not meet the requirement of carrying on the business substantially the same as before.

EXAMPLES:

1. *Adding a new business.* X Corporation, a calendar year taxpayer, manufactures and sells electrical appliances and has sustained substantial net operating losses. On June 30, 1968, Y Corporation purchases 100% of X Corporation's outstanding stock. During 1969, X Corporation continues substantially undiminished its activities in the manufacture and sale of electrical appliances and also acquires a cement manufacturing plant. The addition of the cement manufacturing business by X Corporation does not of itself constitute a failure to carry on substantially the same trade or business even though net operating loss carryovers attributable to the electrical appliance business are used to offset profits of the cement manufacturing business.

2. *Discontinuing the loss business.* X Corporation, a calendar year taxpayer, is engaged in three separate businesses, A, B, and C. Approximately half of X Corporation's total business activities (measured in terms of capital invested, gross income, size of payroll, and similar factors) relates to business A, 30% to business B, and the remaining 20% to business C. On December 31, 1968, X Corporation has substantial net operating loss carryovers all of which arose from business C. On June 1, 1969, Y Corporation purchases at least 50% of X Corporation's outstanding stock and during 1970 X Corporation discontinues business C. As of December 31, 1970, X Corporation has not continued to carry on substantially the same trade or business as that conducted prior to the increase in ownership.

3. *Discontinuing a profit business.* Assume the same facts as in example (2), except that all of X Corporation's net operating loss carryovers come from business A and that the capital released by the discontinuance of business C is used to revitalize business A. Since discontinuing business C does not result in the use of net operating losses attributable to one business to offset gains of an unrelated business, discontinuing that business does not of itself add up to the failure to carry on substantially the same trade or business as was conducted prior to the increase in ownership.

4. *Change of location.* X Corporation, a calendar year taxpayer, is engaged in the business of manufacturing in State A and has sustained substantial net operating losses. On June 30, 1968, Y Corporation buys all of

X Corporation's outstanding stock. During 1969, X Corporation transfers its operations to State B, several hundred miles away. X Corporation disposes of its plant and a large portion of its machinery in State A. The distance between State A and State B makes it necessary for the majority of the employees of X Corporation to terminate their employment with X Corporation. During 1969, X Corporation resumes its manufacturing activities in State B and continues to make the same product and to serve substantially the same group of customers. However, by reason of the changes in location, employees, plant, and equipment, the Treasury view is that X Corporation, on December 31, 1969, is not carrying on substantially the same trade or business as that conducted before the change of ownership.

5. *Change of location.* Y Corporation, a calendar year taxpayer, operates a department store in city A. On June 30, 1968, Z Corporation purchases all of the outstanding stock of Y Corporation. During 1969, Y Corporation transfers its operations to town B, a suburb of city A. Y Corporation disposes of its interest in the building formerly occupied by it in city A and also substitutes new equipment for a major portion of the equipment formerly used by it in city A. After the change in location, Y Corporation continues to sell substantially the same products to substantially the same customers or to customers drawn from substantially the same area and retains substantially all of the employees formerly employed in city A. Under such circumstances, the Treasury says that the change of location does not result in a failure to carry on substantially the same trade or business.

6. Z Corporation, a calendar year taxpayer, operates a retail liquor store in town M. It has 10 employees. On June 30, 1968, individual A purchases all of the stock of Z Corporation. During 1969, Z Corporation transfers its operations to town O, a distance of five miles from its former location. Z Corporation disposes of its interest in the premises formerly occupied by it and also disposes of the license and franchise issued by town M. During 1969, Z Corporation tranfers its inventory of liquor to its new location and resumes its retail liquor activities under a license and franchise issued by town O. Z Corporation continues to employ five of the 10 employees formerly employed in town M, but the corporation does not serve substantially the same customers or customers drawn from substantially the same area. Under these circumstances, according to the Treasury, the change of location results in a failure to carry on substantially the same trade or business.

The courts will not always go along with this Treasury view that change of location and customers is not carrying on substantially the same business. In one case, a business moved twice but retained the same business name, dealt with the same type of customers although most of its old customers were lost and new ones added, expanded its line of products, and added retail sales outlets (it was originally in the wholesale business only). Nevertheless, said the court, it continued to carry on substantially the same business.

If you buy a corporation in the service business and after the purchase you continue the same type of service but different individuals render the service, the Treasury says you are not continuing the business substantially as before.

EXAMPLES:

1. X Corporation, a calendar year taxpayer, is engaged in the business of selling real estate and insurance primarily through the services of individual A as broker. On June 30, 1968, individual B purchases all of the stock of X Corporation, and individual A retires from the business. During the latter part of 1968, X Corporation is engaged primarily in rendering the brokerage services of individual B in the sale of insurance and real estate. On December 31, 1968, the corporation has not continued to carry on a trade or business substantially the same as that conducted before the change of ownership.

2. Y Corporation, a calendar year taxpayer, is engaged in the business of operating a beauty salon with 10 employees under the supervision of individual A, who owns all of the stock of Y Corporation and who is held out to the public as the corporation's principal beauty consultant. However, the quality of the services rendered by each of the 10 employees is primarily responsible for attracting the corporation's clientele. On June 30, 1968, individual B purchases all of the outstanding stock of Y Corporation and individual A retires from the business. During 1969, Y Corporation continues to operate the beauty salon in the same location and continues to serve substantially the same group of customers with substantially the same employees under the supervision of individual B, who is held out to the public as the corporation's principal beauty consultant. On December 31, 1969, Y Corporation has continued to carry on substantially the same trade or business.

Reactivating a Dormant Corporation

Sometimes a corporation with a large carryover loss may have become dormant. If you then buy it and reactivate it in the same line of business as it was before it became dormant, you might argue that you are continuing the same business. But the Treasury says reactivating a dormant company is *not* the continuation of substantially the same business as before.

EXAMPLES:

1. X Corporation is engaged in the business of manufacturing and selling machinery. On January 1, 1968, the corporation suspends its manufac-

turing activities and begins to reduce its inventory of finished products because of general adverse business conditions and lack of profits. During the period between January 1 and September 1, 1968, the business of the corporation remains dormant. On September 1, 1968, Jones purchases 100% of X Corporation's outstanding stock. On October 1, 1968, the corporation begins to manufacture the same type of machinery it manufactured before January 1, 1968. The reactivation of the corporation in the same line of business as conducted before January 1, 1968, does not constitute the carrying on of a trade or business substantially the same as that conducted before the increase in stock ownership.

2. Y Corporation is engaged in the business of manufacturing machinery. On January 1, 1968, the corporation suspends its manufacturing activities because of a fire which disrupts the operation of its plant. During the period between January 1 and June 1, 1968, substantial efforts are made to reactivate the business of the corporation by reconstructing the damaged plant. On June 1, 1968, Jones purchases 100% of Y Corporation's outstanding stock. On July 1, 1968, the corporation resumes its normal manufacturing activities. The fact that the corporation's normal activities are temporarily suspended at the time of the increase in ownership does not of itself add up to a failure to carry on a trade or business substantially the same as that conducted before the increase in stock ownership.

In considering the "dormant corporation" rule, the Tax Court has upheld the Treasury. But the court has held that a corporation which leases all of its operating assets for a period of time during which it takes steps to pull itself out of financial trouble, is not dormant. So, after the lease period, where that corporation is bought and continues in the same manufacturing business that it followed before the leasing period, the "same business" requirement is satisfied.

How Reorganizations or Taxfree Liquidations Affect Carryover Losses

Where one corporation acquires another corporation through a tax-free reorganization (other than a so-called "B" reorganization where stock of the company being acquired is exchanged solely for voting stock of the company doing the acquiring, see page 187), the carryover losses of the acquired company become available to the acquiring company.

Similarly, where a parent corporation (one owning at least 80% of the voting stock of its subsidiary) causes the subsidiary to be liquidated so that the parent acquires the subsidiary's assets, the subsidiary's carryover losses become available to the parent.

In order for the carryovers to be fully allowed, the stockholders of the acquired loss corporation—as a result of the reorganization—must own at least 20% of the stock of the acquiring corporation. For each percentage point below 20%, the acquiring corporation permanently forfeits 5% of the total carryover losses. Thus, if the acquired corporation's stockholders receive only 18% of the acquiring corporation's stock in the reorganization, only 90% of the carryover will be allowed to the acquiring corporation.

Where a parent corporation liquidates its newly-acquired subsidiary in the special liquidation described at page 59, it does not get the benefit of the subsidiary's loss carryovers. (On page 203: discussion of what corporate attributes—such as losses, earnings and profits, etc.— are carried over in a liquidation or reorganization.) The rule against a subsidiary liquidation within a two-year period cannot be circumvented by merging the two corporations, since in this case the merger will be treated as a liquidation of the subsidiary into the parent.

Other Means of Blocking Use of an Acquired Loss

Transaction		*Loss Carryover is*
Stock purchases		
1. 50% change in ownership	and change in business	barred
2. Less than 50% change in ownership	and change in business	not barred
3. 50% change in ownership	and no change in business	not barred
4. Acquisition of control	and tax avoidance purpose	barred
Taxfree reorganizations (except stock-for-stock)		
5. Less than 20% stock ownership by loss corporation's stockholders after the reorganization		barred (partially or fully)
Adoption of plan of liquidation of subsidiary into parent corporation		
6. Within two years of purchasing stock		barred
7. After two years from purchasing stock		not barred

Although the seven transactions cover a wide area, their scope is far from complete. Take, for example, the following case:

EXAMPLE:

X Corporation operates a hardware business at a loss. A owns a new real estate corporation and transfers its ownership to X Corporation in return for X Corporation preferred and an interest in the future profits of the combined corporation. The amount of preferred received by A is less than 50% of the total outstanding stock of X Corporation. Since the hardware business is continued, there is no substantial change in the business of X Corporation. Thus, the transaction does not fall within 1, 2 or 3 of the above table. Also, because A did not acquire control of X Corporation, 4 does not apply. It is also apparent that 5, 6 and 7 have no application to this transaction. The Treasury nonetheless refused to allow the losses from the hardware business to be applied against the income earned by the real estate division. It said that for the loss to be applied against profits, the income must be earned by the same entity as suffered the loss. Although one court agreed with the Treasury, its reasoning was finally overturned by an Appellate court.

However, in another case, a different result was reached:

EXAMPLE:

B, an individual, owns 58% of Y Corporation, a clothing store. After several years of operating in the red, B acquires the stock of Z Corporation, engaged in the identical business. After merging the two corporations, B winds up with 95% of the stock of the combined corporation. His attempt to offset the profits of the combined corporation with the pre-merger losses of Y Corporation is disallowed by the Treasury, using the same reasoning as in the previous example. This time the Treasury position was upheld, that the post-merger income was not earned by the same entity that suffered the losses. The court however admitted that it reached its decision with reluctance and said that it would welcome clarification of this area by the Supreme Court (which, to this date, has not been done).

Present Treasury policy is not to contest loss carryovers in cases (other than those which fall subject to the statutory rules) where there has been less than 50% change in the beneficial ownership of the loss company, or where there has not been a substantial change in the business. The ownership test is not based entirely on stock ownership, but includes shifting assets, interest in future profits and other valuable rights.

In cases where there has been more than 49% change in ownership or where there has been a change in the business, you will have the burden of proving to a court that the resulting taxable entity is the same entity that suffered the loss.

Expenses of Investigating a New Business

Before buying a new business, investigation costs may be incurred such as: Costs of traveling to look at property, accounting, legal and business counsel fees, even the cost of training special personnel to take over a new type of business operation. These expenses are not deductible because they are not incurred in the business at the time of the investigation; they are incurred in preparation for going into the business if the prospects are considered good.

If, after investigation, you decide to go ahead with the business, the investigation costs become part of the cost of the business. The business itself, whether it is a proprietorship, partnership, or corporation, cannot write this cost off over any period of time. The cost is recovered only if the business is sold or abandoned.

EXAMPLES:

1. Two men were interested in buying a newspaper or radio station. In searching for and investigating prospective businesses, they incurred traveling, telephone, telegraph, and other expenses. Of the many propositions made to them, they did not find any in which they were willing to invest. They attempted to deduct the costs of searching for the business, but a court disallowed the deductions. *Reason:* They merely investigated businesses. They entered into none; so no abandonment resulted on which they could base their deduction.

2. A corporation spent over $53,000 to train its staff to run a television station prior to actually obtaining its TV license. Since it was not in the business of operating a TV station at the time it incurred its expenses, they were denied as deductions. And they were not recoverable over any ascertainable time because, even though technically a TV license runs for only three years, the Federal Communications Commission usually renews almost all licenses. This made the life of the license indefinite.

If the business is actually started and operated and then abandoned, the resulting loss is deductible. For example, in one case, after tentatively satisfying himself that a mine could be profitably operated, a man advanced some funds, had the mine reopened, equipment repaired, and actually operated the mine for a month. Then, he determined that his original opinion was wrong, that the mine could not be profitably operated. In that case, the Internal Revenue Service conceded that he could deduct his loss when he abandoned the venture.

Forming a Corporation to Investigate Business Opportunities

Setting up a corporation before going ahead with the investigation of a new business may make it easier to establish the loss. To do this, it is important that the stock issued on setting up the corporation qualify as "Section 1244 stock" (qualification requirements, *see* page 47). If, after the investigation you decided not to go ahead with the new business, the corporation's assets will have been reduced by the amounts spent in investigating the new business. If at that time the corporation is liquidated, the stockholders will receive back less than they paid in for their stock. This loss, because they took the precaution of setting it up as Section 1244 stock, will be an ordinary loss to the extent of $25,000 per stockholder ($50,000 on a joint return) even though normally losses on liquidations of corporations are treated as capital losses.

Promoters Get Ordinary Deductions for Investigating New Businesses

Investigating and looking for a new business is treated as a business activity for a promoter of new businesses. Compare these two cases:

(1) A business promoter traveled looking for businesses, took on some and if they were not profitable, dropped them. His deduction for travel, hotel, entertainment, auto hire, office rent, and assistants' pay was approved.

(2) After selling his car agency, Day searched around for a new agency to buy. In his investigations, he incurred travel, food, hotel and telephone expenses which he deducted as business expenses. But these were disallowed. For this period, Day was not in a trade or business. In searching for business property he was not carrying on a business. In the first case, looking for new businesses was the promoter's business.

CHAPTER V

How Subchapter S Corporations and Their Stockholders Are Taxed

THE SUBCHAPTER S CORPORATION ELECTION allows a business to operate in corporate form and yet not pay tax as a separate entity, thus, generally eliminating the double tax feature of corporate operations.

The Subchapter S election is not limited to a corporation with small or moderate income. There is no income limitation on a Subchapter S corporation. However, there is a limit on the number of stockholders.

Each stockholder of a Subchapter S corporation is taxable on his share of the corporation's income whether or not distributed to him. Similarly, each stockholder reports his share of the corporation's ordinary losses and deducts them on his personal tax return. Long-term capital gains also pass through to the stockholders. Corporate short-term capital gains become part of the corporate ordinary income and pass through as such. However, corporate net capital losses do not pass through. They remain in the corporation as carryover losses.

You will generally make a Subchapter S election when your personal tax rates do not exceed the corporate tax rates, when you cannot take sufficient money out of a corporation without subjecting some or all of it to the double tax, or when a special advantage is offered by a Subchapter S election. In the early years of a corporation's existence when losses are expected, an election may be useful to pass through the losses to the stockholders who have substantial other income against which to offset these losses.

A Subchapter S election can facilitate family income shifting. You can make gifts to children through gifts of stock without confronting the problems accompanying similar arrangements in family partnerships. Income can be shifted even after it has been earned. For example, a gift of stock in a Subchapter S corporation made on December 30 shifts tax on a dividend declared and paid on December 31.

An election can also facilitate the timing of income to stockholders. An electing corporation operating on a taxable year differing from yours can time income distributions to cover two tax years. For example, an electing company reports on a fiscal year ending January 31. Its stockholders report on a calendar year. By December 31, 1968, it has earned $60,000. If it doesn't distribute any of the $60,000, the entire amount is taxable to the stockholders in 1969. The stockholders prefer to have the income spread over the years of 1968 and 1969 rather than to have all of it in 1969. They can accomplish this result by having the company distribute $30,000 on December 31, 1968. Thus, $30,000 is taxable income in 1968 and $30,000 in 1969. Undistributed corporate income on January 31, 1969, when the corporate year ends, is only $30,000 because of the previous distribution of $30,000 in 1968.

If a corporation must accumulate working capital and at the same time you do not personally need corporate income, it may be advisable not to elect Subchapter S.

If the election is being considered in an existing corporation which has an operating loss carryover, an election may not be advisable. The loss may not be used by the stockholders so that its tax benefit is forfeited. Each year the election is in force counts as a year in figuring the carryover period. This is true even though the loss is not utilized.

Can Your Company Qualify for Subchapter S Status?

Your corporation can elect Subchapter S status if it meets *all* the following tests.

Stock test. The company is a domestic corporation and has:

1. No more than 10 stockholders, all of whom must agree to elect Subchapter S. A husband and wife owning stock jointly, or as community property, are counted as one shareholder. Each minor owning stock held by a custodian is counted. For example, Jones is custodian for several children who are stockholders; each child is counted as a stockholder.

2. Stockholders who are either individuals or estates of a deceased

person. The election is not available if a trust, voting trust, partnership or another corporation owns stock in your company. Stock may be held by a custodian for an individual.

3. No nonresident alien stockholders.

4. One class of stock. For example, you cannot make the election if your company has common and preferred stock. Only outstanding stock is counted in determining whether there is one class of stock. Treasury stock or unissued preferred stock of a different class does not disqualify the election.

Debt obligations may be treated by the Treasury as a class of stock. However, this Treasury position, when taken, has been generally rejected by the courts. Treasury regulations state that loans that are made pro rata by the stockholders and that do not change their control and claims against the corporate profits and assets will not be considered a second class of stock. However, the regulations warn that a change in a shareholder's proportionate share of stock or debt through a sale or redemption or other transfer may lead to determination that there is a second class of stock. This warning may be interpreted as requiring a stockholder to treat his stock and loans as a unit, so that if he transfers the stock he must also transfer the debt. Conformity with Treasury's pro rata requirement for debt for purposes of Subchapter S could lead to "thin capitalization" problems if the corporation loses the election. At that time, if the debt is considered equity capital, the interest deduction may be disallowed and the repayment of the loan considered a dividend.

Class A voting common and Class B nonvoting common with dividend rights and liquidation preferences being equal are treated as two classes. But where the same class of common is owned by several groups of stockholders with each group having the right to vote for a number of directors proportionate to its stockholdings, there is only one class of stock.

The right to corporate election was lost where inactive stockholders granted irrevocable proxies to the active stockholders to vote their shares. These proxies amounted to the creation of two classes of stock which disqualified the election.

A stockholder election cannot be made by a corporation which has qualified for FHA mortgage benefits and has issued a nominal amount of preferred stock to the FHA. The stock held by the FHA is considered a second class of stock.

5. Has no relationship to another corporation that makes it part of an affiliated group and so eligible to file consolidated returns. But a corporation with an inactive subsidiary can make the election as long as the subsidiary is inactive and has no taxable income.

Income test. A company cannot make an election if it has gross annual receipts of more than:

1. 20% from "passive income" such as rents, royalties, dividends, interest, annuities, and sales or exchanges of securities. Stockholders of most personal holding and real estate companies cannot take advantage of the election.

Rents of a hotel, motel, garage or parking lot or of a share-farming arrangement where the landowner actively participates in the farm are not treated as rents under this rule. Rent received for leasing equipment where important services such as handling and repairs are also rendered is also not considered as rent here.

There is an exception to the rule that a corporation is disqualified from Subchapter S status if its "passive income" exceeds 20% of its gross receipts. The "passive income" may exceed 20% of gross receipts without losing Subchapter S status if the passive investment income over 20% is earned during the first or second year in which the corporation is in business, *and* it does not exceed $3,000. This rule applies for taxable years ending after April 14, 1966. In certain circumstances, the corporation can get permission to apply this exception to the 20% rule for years beginning after 1962 and ending before April 14, 1966.

2. 80% from sources outside the United States.

How and When to Make the Subchapter S Election

To elect Subchapter S status, the corporation makes the election by filing Form 2553 with the District Director of the district in which the corporation files its tax return. Statements from all of the stockholders consenting to the election are attached to Form 2553.

Make sure the form is filed on or before the end of the first calendar month of the taxable year you want the election to be effective. You cannot get an extension of time to make an election.

EXAMPLE:

Your corporation reports on a calendar year. You want the election to be effective in 1968. File Form 2553 and the statements of the stockholders' consents on or before January 31, 1968. The earliest you can file these papers is the month before the first calendar month—in this case, December 1967.

An election made before a corporation is legally in existence is invalid.

If stock is owned by a minor, his legal or natural guardian must make the consent. The Treasury has ruled that a custodian holding stock for a minor under the Uniform Gifts to Minors Act or the Model Gifts of Securities to Minors Act cannot consent to an election as custodian. He may consent only if he is also the minor's legal or natural guardian.

Newly organized corporation. Usually, the first tax year of a newly organized corporation will be for a period of less than 12 months. An election can be made for this short first tax year. If the short tax year begins after the first day of a month, the term "calendar month" means the period beginning on the first day of the corporation's tax year and ending with the day preceding the numerically corresponding day of the next month. If a "calendar month" should begin on the 31st and there is no corresponding day in the succeeding month, the last day of that month closes the period.

The first month of a tax year of a new corporation does not begin until the corporation has shareholders, acquires assets, or begins doing business.

When a new stockholder enters the company, his consent to the election must be quickly obtained. If he does not consent the election will automatically terminate. If an election has been made before the first day of the corporation's taxable year, a new shareholder entering the corporation on or before this first day must file his consent not later than the last day of the first calendar month of the tax year. If the new stockholder enters the corporation after the first day of the taxable year for which an election is effective, his consent must be filed within a 30-day period beginning on the date he became a stockholder.

When a stockholder dies and his stock passes through his estate, the executor or administrator of the estate must file a consent to the election within the period of 30 days beginning with the day on which the estate becomes a stockholder. This rule, however, is eased by Treasury regulations. The 30-day period starts from the day the executor or administrator qualifies under state law. But the period cannot begin later than 30 days following the close of the company's tax year in which the estate became a stockholder.

The Treasury will not consider requests for extensions to file consents unless they are made by new shareholders or a husband or wife who owns shares jointly or as community property. The following conditions must also be met: (1) The corporation has filed a timely election, or the election is in effect for the corporation and stockholders in the year the extension is requested; (2) good cause is shown for the extension; (3) the Treasury's interests are not jeopardized; and (4) all other stockholders who previously filed consents file new consents.

To insure the election, it may be advisable to provide a restrictive clause or agreement which would require new stockholders to consent to the election as a condition of becoming a stockholder. The restrictions might also be made part of the corporation's charter.

How the Subchapter S Election is Lost

The Subchapter S election does not have to be renewed each year. But it can be revoked or automatically terminated under any one of these conditions:

1. All stockholders agree to revoke the election by filing a statement of revocation. If made before the close of the first month of the corporation's taxable year, the revocation is effective for that year. If made after that date, the revocation is not effective until the year following the year in which the revocation was filed.

2. A new stockholder enters the corporation and does not consent to the election.

3. The company no longer meets the stock or income tests, *see* pages 79-81. For example, a company receives more than 20% of its gross receipts from dividends or rents or stock is issued to a nonresident alien or to a trust.

Where the corporation's Subchapter S status automatically terminates because either item 2 or 3 applies, the termination is effective for the year in which the disqualifying act occurs. For example, The Greenway Corporation elected Subchapter S status in 1960 and has maintained that status since then. It is a calendar year corporation. In November 1968, Green, one of the stockholders transfers some stock to a trust. Since a trust cannot be a stockholder in a Subchapter S corporation, the corporation's status as a Subchapter S corporation is terminated effective for the entire year 1968 even though the stock transfer to the trust took place in November.

When the election is revoked or terminated, you cannot make another election until the fifth year following the year in which the election was revoked or terminated. But you might get it sooner with Treasury permission. Permission during the waiting period will usually be denied unless the cause of the termination was not reasonably within the control of the corporation or the stockholders controlling a substantial interest. A 50% change in new stock ownership may be grounds for permission.

How Subchapter S Income is Taxed

The Subchapter S corporation pays no tax. The stockholders report their shares of the corporation's income on their personal tax returns.

Determining and planning the distribution of corporate income to stockholders presents the major tax problem of an operating Subchapter S corporation. The rules are somewhat complex and must be understood if full advantage of the election is to be secured.

The corporation's annual taxable income is computed in the same way any other corporation figures taxable income, except that neither deductions for net operating losses nor the dividends received deduction are taken. The shareholders are taxable on their share of this taxable income whether distributed or not. It is treated on their tax returns as dividend income except that it is not subject to the $100 dividend exclusion. (The reporting of capital gains is discussed at page 90.)

Distributions made during the year are deemed to be paid out of current earnings and profits. Distributions made within the first 2½ months of the corporation's taxable year are treated as distributed in the previous year. If all of the taxable income is not distributed, the balance is treated and taxed to the stockholder as if it had been distributed on the last day of the corporation's taxable year in proportion to each stockholder's shareholdings on that last day. Because he is treated as if he actually received the distribution on that day, each stockholder reports his share of the undistributed taxable income on his return in his taxable year in which the corporation's taxable year falls.

Stockholdings on the last day of the corporate taxable year determine how the corporation's undistributed taxable income is to be allocated. Thus, if you acquire stock a day before the end of the corporate year, you can be taxed on the full year's corporate income attributed to your shares.

Undistributed taxable income reported by the shareholders becomes *previously taxed income* on the company's books. This *previously taxed income* can be withdrawn taxfree only after cash distributions in a year exceed current earnings. That portion of a current distribution which exceeds the current year's taxable income but does not exceed the current year's earnings and profits is also a dividend.

A corporation may have current earnings and profits in excess of current taxable income as when, for example, it has nontaxable income such as tax-exempt interest or life insurance proceeds. Furthermore, it may have nondeductible expenses or losses. Treasury regulations make it clear that a Subchapter S corporation cannot reduce its earnings and profits by these expenses. Examples of nondeductible expenses include life insurance premiums where the corporation is beneficiary, capital losses in excess of capital gains, and percentage depletion in excess of cost depletion.

Distributions that exceed current earnings and profits are treated as distributions of previously taxed income.

Distributions exceeding previously taxed income are considered as coming from the surplus existing at the time the corporation was not subject to an election. Of course, this type of account does not exist if the corporation from the start of its existence was subject to the election.

Distributions in excess of accumulated earnings are treated as a return of capital. They reduce stockholder's basis for his stock; if they exceed basis, the excess is treated as capital gain.

With the consent of all stockholders, a corporation can elect to make a distribution a taxable dividend instead of a distribution of previously taxed income. This might be done where stockholders have large current losses against which ordinary income can be offset.

EXAMPLES:

1. AB, Inc. was formed on January 1, 1966 and immediately made a Subchapter S election. It had two stockholders, A and B, each a 50% stockholder. The corporation and the stockholders are calendar year taxpayers.

For 1967, the corporation had taxable income of $30,000. During 1967, distributions of $5,000 each were made to A and B. So, at the end of 1967, the corporation had undistributed taxable income of $20,000 ($30,000 taxable income less the $10,000 of cash distributions). A and B each report $15,000 of income ($5,000 of distributions plus $10,000 as his share of the undistributed taxable income).

In 1968, the corporation's taxable income amounts to $24,000 and in July 1968, it distributes $10,000 cash each to A and B. Although the distributions made in July 1968 equal the previous year's undistributable taxable income, the distributions are fully taxable to A and B and are not treated as distributions of previously taxed income. Reason: The 1968 taxable income was $24,000; so the full $20,000 distribution in July is treated as distribution of the current income. A and B each report $12,000 of income ($10,-000 distribution plus $2,000 as his share of the $4,000 undistributed taxable income for 1968).

At this point the total undistributed taxable income is $24,000 ($20,000 in 1967 and $4,000 in 1968) with each stockholder having a claim to half of it.

2. Same facts as above but assume that the total taxable income for 1969 is $20,000. In May 1969 the corporation distributes $15,000 in cash each to A and B. Of the $15,000 distribution each stockholder receives, $10,000 is taxable and $5,000 is a payment of previously taxable income. Reason: The first $10,000 each receives is deemed to be a distribution of the corporation's current year's taxable income of $20,000. Distributions in excess of the current year's income are treated as distributions of previously taxed income. Since the full taxable income for 1969 was distributed before the end of the year, the corporation had no undistributed taxable income for 1969 and so each stockholder's total taxable income from the corporation that year is the $10,000 taxable portion of the distribution received.

Undistributed Income May Set a Tax Trap

A potential tax trap lodges within the previously taxed income. You can treat a distribution as being previously taxed income only if at the time of the distribution the corporation is still a Subchapter S corporation. If all the undistributed taxable income is not distributed when the corporation ends its status as a Subchapter S corporation, the remaining undistributed taxable income (which has already been taxed to the stockholders) becomes part of the corporation's regular earnings and profits and is "locked in." That is, any subsequent distribution to the stockholders will be treated as an ordinary dividend and be subject to tax again. So, it becomes important to make distributions of all corporate earnings (current or previous years' undistributed taxable income) before the corporation ends its Subchapter S status.

Also keep in mind that previously taxed income is computed separately for each stockholder. So, if a stockholder sells or gives away part of his stock at a time when not all of the undistributed taxable income on which he was taxed has been distributed to him (that is, he still has previously taxed income in the corporation), the new stockholder does not "inherit" his share of the previously taxed income and cannot get these funds out of the corporation taxfree.

Distributions Made During First 2½ Months of the Year

If the corporation loses its Subchapter S status, a serious problem is created when there is undistributed taxable income that is "locked in." However, the risks of a lock-in are reduced by a recent law that treats distributions of money made by the Subchapter S corporation within 2½ months after the close of its taxable year as made on the last day of the previous year.

The throwback rule is automatic, not elective. A distribution made not later than the 15th day of the third month after the close of the taxable year, is automatically treated as made the previous year. (It is also possible for corporations to elect to have this throwback rule applied to distributions made before April 15, 1966 by filing an election and consents of the stockholders according to rules prescribed by the Regulations.)

The throwback rule applies only if the distribution was made to a person who was a shareholder at the close of the preceding taxable year and only to the extent that this distribution does not exceed his share of his undistributed taxable income at the end of the corporation's previous taxable year.

EXAMPLES:

1. A Subchapter S corporation uses a fiscal year ending March 31. The corporation's undistributed taxable income for the year ended March 31, 1968 is $50,000. It has two stockholders, A and B, each using the calendar year. On May 1, 1968, the corporation distributes $25,000 in cash to each of the two stockholders. The corporation makes no further distributions through December 31, 1969. Its taxable income for the year ending March 31, 1969 is $60,000.

Assuming that the automatic distribution rule was not effective, the result would have been as follows: On their 1968 returns, A and B would each have picked up $50,000 made up of (1) each stockholder's share of the $50,000 undistributed taxable income as of March 31, 1968 ($25,000 each), and (2) the $25,000 distribution each received on May 1, 1968 (since these distributions did not exceed the corporation's taxable income for the full taxable year ending on March 31, 1969). On their 1969 returns, each stockholder would pick up $5,000 of income. The $60,000 of the corporation's taxable income for the year ending March 31, 1969 would be reduced by the May 1, 1968 distribution of $50,000 giving an undistributed taxable income on March 31, 1969 of $10,000 (with each stockholder picking up $5,000). But with the throwback distribution rule in effect, this is the actual result: Each stockholder reports $25,000 of income in 1968 and another $30,000 each in 1969. The corporation's undistributed taxable income on March 31, 1968 is $50,000. The May 1, 1968 distribution of $50,000 is treated as having been made not later than March 31, 1968 (because it was made within 2½ months of March 31, 1968). So the stockholders treat the distribution as having been received by March 31, 1968 and that eliminates any undistributed taxable income to be passed on to them. Hence, they merely pick up the $25,000 distributions on their 1968 returns. On their 1969 returns, each stockholder picks up half of the $60,000 corporate taxable income as of March 31, 1969. The distributions on May 1, 1968 are treated as having been made by March 31, 1968 and do not reduce the corporation's taxable income for the year ending March 31, 1969. Thus, the corporation's undistributed taxable income for the year ending March 31, 1969 is $60,000.

The total income picked up by each stockholder for the two years 1968-1969 is $55,000. Without the throwback distribution rule, $50,000 would have to be picked up in 1968 and only $5,000 in 1969. Under the throwback rule, the $55,000 is divided $25,000-$30,000 and unfair "bunching" of income in one year is eliminated.

2. A Subchapter S corporation using the calendar year has two 50% stockholders, Black and White. For the year 1967 it has $10,000 of undistributed taxable income. On February 1, 1968, Black sells his stock in the corporation to Grey who does not file a consent to continue the corporation's Subchapter S status. Consequently, the corporation is no longer a Subchapter S corporation for 1968. On February 28, the corporation distributes $5,000 each to White and Grey. If there were no throwback rule,

White and Grey would each have had a $5,000 taxable dividend in 1968. White's previously taxed income of $5,000 would have been "locked in" in the corporation because the corporation had lost its Subchapter S status. Grey, of course, had no previously taxable income because he was not a stockholder on December 31, 1967. With the throwback rule in effect, this is the result: Although the corporation is no longer a Subchapter S corporation, the February 28 distribution is treated as having been made in 1967. Hence, White has no income. As for Grey, since he was not a stockholder in 1967 and has no previously taxed income, the distribution to him does not meet the automatic distribution rule; the distribution to him is treated as having been made on February 28. He therefore has a taxable dividend.

How Property Distributions Are Handled

A distribution of property does not reduce undistributed taxable income. Current year's earnings and profits are allocated between the property distribution and the undistributed taxable income as illustrated in the following examples.

EXAMPLES:

1. Assume in one year a corporation has taxable income and earnings and profits of $10,000. The corporation has no accumulated profits from prior years. During the year, the corporation distributes property (other than cash) with a basis of $10,000 and a fair market value of $20,000. The undistributed taxable income of the corporation is $10,000 because property distributions do not reduce taxable income. But the current earnings and profits are allocated between the property distribution and the undistributed taxable income in proportion to their relative values (taking the property at its fair market value). So, $6,667 of earnings and profits is allocated to the property distribution and $3,333 to the undistributed taxable income. The stockholders still report $10,000 of income—$6,667 as a dividend received in property and $3,333 as a constructive distribution of undistributed taxable income at the end of the year.

2. Assume the same facts as above except that in addition to the current earnings and profits of $10,000 the corporation also had accumulated earnings and profits of $20,000 at the beginning of the year. Now the full $20,000 property dividend and the full $10,000 undistributed taxable income are taxable to the stockholders. The current year's earnings and profits are allocated as in Example 1. That leaves $13,333 of property dividends and $6,667 of undistributed taxable income not covered by the current year's taxable income. But these amounts (total of $20,000) are fully covered by the accumulated earnings and profits of prior years. So, the $20,000 is also taxable.

How Capital Gains Pass Through to the Stockholders

Net long-term capital gains of a Subchapter S company pass through to the stockholders, including gains from the sale of business property (Section 1231 property). However, the passthrough is limited by the corporation's taxable income.

Each shareholder reports his share of the corporation's long-term capital gains as if he had realized them as long-term capital gains. The total long-term capital gains reported by the stockholders in any one year cannot exceed the corporation's taxable income for that year. For example, the total long-term gains may come to $30,000, but the total taxable income of the corporation may only be $20,000. The long-term capital gains picked up by the stockholders are $20,000.

EXAMPLE:

> *Allocation of distributions.* A Subchapter S corporation has a taxable year ending June 30, 1968. Total taxable income for the year comes to $50,000, of which $5,000 is a long-term capital gain. Furthermore, the capital gain was realized in May of 1968. During the period from July 1, 1967 to December 31, 1967, the corporation distributed in cash to its stockholders $20,000. The stockholders, reporting on a calendar year basis, report the $20,000 of distributions as income in their 1967 returns. And at June 31, 1968, the corporation has undistributed taxable income of $30,000 ($50,000 less $20,000 distributed). The stockholders will also pick up this $30,000 of income, but in their 1968 tax returns. Because 10% of the total taxable income was long-term capital gain, 10% of every direct distribution out of that taxable income plus 10% of his share of the undistributed taxable income is reported by each stockholder as long-term capital gain. So, of the $20,000 of income reported in 1967, the stockholders report $2,000 as long-term capital gain. Of the $30,000 undistributed taxable income, they report another $3,000 of long-term capital gain. Note that it makes no difference that the actual capital gain was realized in 1968 while the $20,000 distribution was made in 1967; $2,000 of the 1967 distribution is nevertheless treated as capital gain.

This treatment of each distribution as being made up of pro rata shares of capital gain and ordinary income requires stockholders to file claims for refunds in some cases. When they report a distribution, they do not know that the corporation will have a long-term capital gain in May. So, when the capital gain is realized, the stockholder's tax return for the previous year may have already been filed with the entire distribution received in the prior year reported as ordinary income. When the stockholders learn that part should have been reported as long-term capital gain, they have to file a claim for refund.

Another result of the allocation rule on each distribution is that a former stockholder may benefit from a capital gain realized by the corporation after he sells his stock. For example, early in 1968, Jones, a stockholder in a Subchapter S corporation sells out his interest. Before the sale of the stock, he receives a distribution of $10,000 from the corporation as his share of the corporation's taxable income up to the time of his stock sale. Later in the year, the corporation realizes a $10,000 capital gain and its taxable income for the entire year is $100,000. Even though he was no longer a stockholder when the corporation realized the long-term capital gain, Jones still treats 10% of his $10,000 distribution (or $1,000) as long-term capital gain.

Short-term capital gains and capital losses. The passthrough of capital gains applies only to long-term capital gains. If the corporation has short-term capital gains, they become part of its ordinary income; they do not pass through as capital gains that might then be offset by the individual stockholder's personal capital losses.

Corporate capital losses can only be applied to offset corporate capital gains. Remaining losses are available to the corporation as carryovers for five years to be used to offset corporate capital gains. No part of the capital losses pass through to the stockholders as such.

Timing the capital gain. If possible, a capital gain transaction should not be entered into in a year where there is an ordinary operating loss. A capital gain in a loss year may be passed through as capital gain only to the extent that it exceeds the ordinary loss. The balance of the gain is wasted. If the gain is realized in a loss year, it may be advisable to decrease stockholders' salaries so as not to create or increase the ordinary loss.

"One-Shot" Elections for Capital Gain Passthrough Are Limited

Before 1966, an existing corporation that anticipated a substantial capital gain might elect Subchapter S to pass through the capital gain as a single tax at the stockholder level. It would elect Subchapter S status for the year it expected the gain and pass it through to its stockholders without having to pay a corporate capital gain tax. In the following year, it would commit a disqualifying act and lose Subchapter S status. This was known as the "one-shot" election. For taxable years beginning after April 14, 1966, this "one-shot" approach has been effectively blocked by taxing the corporation (even though it is a Subchapter S corporation) on that capital gain, and only the gain after deducting the tax is passed through to the stockholders. So a double tax is not avoided.

Two tests determine if a corporation is to be taxed on its capital gains: (1) A time test and (2) an income test.

The time test. If it has been a Subchapter S corporation during the current taxable year and the previous three taxable years, capital gains are not taxed. If it has not been in existence for less than three years, it will not be taxed on its capital gains if it has been a Subchapter S corporation during the entire corporate life. In other words, if the corporation "passes" the time test, it is not considered to be making a "one-shot" election. A provision prevents a Subchapter S corporation from picking up property in a taxfree merger with a corporation that cannot pass the time test and then selling the acquired property at a capital gain. In that case, the gain attributed to property acquired in the merger will be taxable to the Subchapter S corporation even if it itself does pass the time test.

The income test. The income test is applied where the corporation does not pass the time test. The Subchapter S corporation will not be taxed on capital gains if:

1. The net capital gain is not more than $25,000, *or*

2. The net capital gain is not more than half the corporation's taxable income, *or*

3. The taxable income is not more than $25,000.

If the corporation "fails" the time test and its capital gain and taxable income exceed the above limits, the corporation is taxed on its capital gain as follows: Two tax computations are made. The corporation pays the lower of the two:

1. Subtract $25,000 from the capital gain and apply a flat 25% tax to the balance.

2. Figure the tax in the regular way on the entire taxable income of the corporation, that is, 22% on the first $25,000 and 48% on the balance.

EXAMPLES:

1. A Subchapter S corporation that fails the time test has $30,000 of capital gain and $10,000 of ordinary income. Since its capital gain exceeds $25,000 and the $30,000 gain is more than half the $40,000 taxable income, and since the $40,000 taxable income is more than $25,000, it is subject to tax. Under the first computation, the $30,000 capital gain is reduced by $25,000, leaving $5,000 taxable at 25%, or a tax of $1,250. Under the second computation, the first $25,000 of taxable income is taxed at 22% ($5,500 tax) the remaining $15,000 at 48% ($7,200 tax) for a total tax of $12,700. The corporation pays the $1,250 tax.

2. A Subchapter S corporation that fails the time test has capital gains of $125,000 and deductions of $65,000. So, its taxable income is $60,000. The amount of its capital gain and taxable income make it subject to the tax on capital gains. Using the first computation, $25,000 is subtracted from the $125,000 capital gain, leaving $100,000 taxable at 25%, or a tax of $25,000. Under the second computation, the first $25,000 of taxable income is taxed at 22% (or $5,500), the remaining $35,000 is taxable at 48% (or $16,800) giving a total tax under the second computation of $22,300. Here, the second computation provides the lower tax.

Avoiding or Easing the One-Shot Capital Gains Tax

Assume that your capital gain transaction may be subject to the one-shot capital gains tax. Planning the sale to meet the installment election may avoid tax if the capital gain is kept below $25,000 per year (assuming there are no other capital gains). Once a corporation has been a Subchapter S corporation for more than three years, the amount of the capital gain realized is irrelevant and there may be no further need for the installment election or sale. However, note that where the installment election is made, at least 4% simple interest must be charged (or 5% interest compounded semiannually will be imputed), and it is possible that the interest income realized on the installment notes may invalidate the Subchapter S election.

If the installment election is not feasible, capital gains tax incurred by the corporation may not be as onerous under the election as it might be if the election was not made. Compare the tax that would be incurred if the election is made and the amount of tax without the election. Where the taxpayers are in a substantially high income tax bracket and the proceeds of the sale are to be distributed to them, the Subchapter S election will probably be less costly.

EXAMPLE:

You have a capital asset that would realize a capital gain of $200,000. If you elect Subchapter S to report its sale, here is the tax result assuming there is no other taxable income of the corporation for that year: The corporation pays a capital gain of $43,750 on $175,000 ($200,000-25,-000). As a stockholder, you pay an additional capital gains tax on $156,-250 ($200,000 less the tax paid by the corporation), or $39,062.50. The total tax is thus $82,812.50. Now compare the result where there is no Subchapter S election. The corporation pays a $50,000 tax on the sale (25% of $200,000); the remaining $150,000 is distributed to you as a dividend. Assuming this is your only income, and you have no deductions or exemptions, you are in the 70% bracket and your tax is $105,000. The combined taxes are thus $155,000, leaving you only $45,000. You save $72,187.50 by making the Subchapter S election.

Passing Through Losses

One of the advantages of Subchapter S is that the net losses of the corporation are passed through to the stockholders. Each stockholder reports his share of the corporate loss and applies it against any other income he may have. If the loss exceeds his other current income, he can use the loss as a carryback (for three years) and a carryforward (for five years).

Unlike the rule for passing through the corporation's undistributed taxable income, the corporation's net operating loss is not divided among the stockholders in proportion to their stockholdings on the last day of the corporation's taxable year; the loss is prorated on a daily basis. To arrive at a daily net operating loss, the loss for the entire year is divided by the number of days in the year. Each stockholder gets his share of each day's loss on which he was a stockholder. So, if stockholder A owned 30% of the stock for 200 days during the year, his share of the loss is 30% of the daily loss multiplied by 200. If another stockholder held 15% of the stock for 30 days, he gets 15% of the daily loss multiplied by 30.

Under this rule, an individual who is no longer a stockholder on the last day of the corporation's tax year is nevertheless entitled to deduct his share of the loss for the days during the year on which he was a stockholder. This is so, even though the entire corporate loss arose after he ceased being a stockholder.

The loss is deductible by each stockholder in his taxable year in which or with which the corporation's taxable year ends. For example, suppose the corporation in its taxable year ending March 31, 1968 has an operating loss. Stockholder A is on a calendar year; Stockholder B's taxable year ends January 31. A will pick up his share of the loss on his 1968 tax return; B, on his return for the taxable year ending January 31, 1969.

Since the death of an individual ends his tax year, it would seem that if a Subchapter S stockholder died before the end of the corporate year in which the company had a loss, he would lose his share of the loss. The reason: The corporate loss year would not end with or within his taxable year. And as for his estate, it would only be a stockholder from the time of his death to the end of the corporate taxable year; so its loss could be very small (since losses are prorated on a daily basis). *But there is a special rule for deceased stockholders which preserves their shares of the loss.* On the decedent's final income tax return his share of the corporate loss (computed on a daily basis up to the date of his death) is allowed as a deduction.

Limitations on losses. A stockholder's loss deduction cannot exceed the sum of the basis of his stock plus the basis of debts owed by the corporation to him. Unlike the partnership rule, he cannot get any disallowed loss of one year allowed in a following year by increasing his basis. If losses are imminent and there is insufficient basis for the stockholder to absorb the entire loss, he should consider buying additional stock, contributing to capital, or lending money to the corporation.

Basis is computed as of the last day of the taxable year if the stockholder is still a stockholder at that time. If stock has been disposed of during the year, basis is figured as of the day before the disposition.

When basis for stock and indebtedness is reduced because of losses, subsequent increases in basis (as when the corporation subsequently acquires undistributed taxable income) are all added to the basis of the stock. Once the basis for indebtedness is decreased or wiped out it is not later increased.

Losses and previously taxed income. A Subchapter S corporation's losses reduces the previously taxed income in the corporation. But the advantage of the loss and the availability of previously taxed income can both be enjoyed if the previously taxed income is distributed in the loss year.

Since there are no current earnings and profits in a loss year, distributions in that year where previously taxed income is available will be treated as distributions of the previously taxed income and hence will be taxfree. The full loss of that year will also be available to pass through to the stockholders. It is only if the previously taxed income is not distributed during the loss year that the loss of that year reduces or eliminates the balance of the previously taxed income for future years.

Dividend Payment Problems When Corporation is Short of Cash Funds

To prevent previously taxed income from being "locked in," it is preferable to make cash dividends equal to taxable income. If the distribution is not made, the stockholders run the risk that the underestimated income will not be withdrawn taxfree. However, if the corporation needs the cash, a problem arises if the cash requirements cannot be met by an outside loan. How can the corporation pay out the cash and have funds for business use? The corporation may make the distribution and the stockholders then loan the money to the corporation. This transaction may be attacked as having no substance or as creating a dividend in kind if notes are given for the loan, or the loan may be considered as creating a second class of stock.

Liquidation of Subchapter S Corporations

The election may facilitate the liquidation of a corporation at a single capital gains rate. The effect of the election is similar to the 12-month liquidation rules which provide a single tax route of liquidation. However, there are important differences. A Subchapter S election can permit the use of an installment sale election; a 12-month liquidation does not. On the other hand, the 12-month liquidation can provide capital gain on the bulk sale of inventory which under usual circumstances would result in ordinary income.

It is also possible to coordinate both the Subchapter S and the 12-month liquidation.

Unreasonable Compensation Paid to Stockholder-Employee

It is often thought that where Subchapter S election is in force, a reasonable pay issue will not be brought up by the Treasury. The reasoning is that it is immaterial to the Treasury whether or not the income is picked up by the stockholder as dividend or pay. This reasoning may be valid, but the Treasury could raise the issue to invalidate the funding of a profit or pension plan for the employee-stockholder. There is also another possible problem, as illustrated in this example:

EXAMPLE:

Jones and Smith are 50-50 stockholders in a Subchapter S corporation. Jones receives $40,000 salary, which the Treasury agrees is reasonable. But Smith receives $50,000 salary, $10,000 of which is held by the Treasury to be unreasonable. There are two possible results: (1) The excess $10,000 becomes undistributed taxable income and taxed $5,000 to Smith and $5,000 to Jones. Jones is taxed on $45,000 and Smith on $55,000. In other words, each stockholder is taxed on $5,000 more than he received. (2) The excess $10,000 is treated as a dividend to Smith; no undistributed taxable income is created.

Inadequate compensation. This issue generally arises in family corporations and is covered by Treasury regulations. Where there is inadequate compensation to one or more employee-stockholders, the Treasury will allocate dividend income among all the stockholders according to the value of each one's services. Where reallocation is made, the amount by which the underpaid employee's taxable income is increased is the amount by which the others' taxable incomes are reduced. Thus, there is no danger here of double taxation; just a shifting of income, presumably, into higher tax brackets. The Treasury regulations also say that a waiver of dividends by a family member will result in taxable income to him unless he can prove that he objected to the payment of the disproportionate dividends.

CHAPTER VI

How Partnership Operations Are Taxed

ALTHOUGH A PARTNERSHIP PAYS NO INCOME TAX, it must file a return informing the Government of its profit or loss. The responsibility for paying the tax rests on each partner who reports his share of the partnership profit or loss in his personal income tax return. This split of responsibility between the partnership, as an income reporting and computing unit, and the partners, as taxpayers for the partnership, is a common characteristic of partnership tax rules. In some cases, partnerships are treated as if they were separate and distinct units from the partners (like corporations). In others, partnership operations are handled through the partners in their personal capacities.

How Partnerships and Partners Report Partnership Income

On Form 1065, the partnership computes its taxable income or loss as if it were a separate tax-paying entity and allocates the income or loss and separate items to each partner according to the agreed profit-sharing ratio. Each partner reports his share of the partnership income or loss and his share of the other items and includes them on his own personal tax return, Form 1040. Each partner pays his own personal income tax based on all of his own income and deductions from all sources, including the amounts he picks up as his partnership share.

Partnership items separately distributed to each partner. Certain items are not included by the partnership in computing its net income or loss but are stated separately with each partner picking up his distinctive share of each item. These items are:

Short-term capital gains and losses

Long-term capital gains and losses

Gains and losses from sale or involuntary conversion of business property

Charitable contributions

Dividends on which an exclusion is allowable

Taxes paid to foreign countries and U. S. possessions

Partially exempt interest on U. S. obligations

Investment tax credit in depreciable property

First-year "bonus" depreciation deductions

Intangible drilling and development costs

Exploration expenditures

Income, loss, deduction, or credit subject to a special allocation that differs from the allocation among the partners for income and loss generally

Other items of allowable income, gain, loss, deduction or credit requiring separate treatment, such as recoveries of bad debts, refunds on taxes and the like.

EXAMPLES:

1. Hiram and Sam Jones are equal partners. The partnership, in addition to its ordinary income for the year, also has a long-term capital gain of $12,000. Hiram and Sam each picks up $6,000 of long-term gain on his own return. Hiram also has a $4,000 long-term capital loss on transactions into which he entered personally, while Sam has a $2,000 long-term capital gain on his own. On his return, Hiram will report a net long-term gain of $2,000 ($6,000 share of partnership gain less $4,000 personal long-term capital loss). Sam, on his return will report an $8,000 long-term gain ($6,000 partnership share plus $2,000 personal gain).

2. Smith personally contributed $400 to charities. The partnership of which he is a partner contributed $2,000 to charity. Smith's share of his partnership's contribution is $800. On his personal tax return, Smith will report a total of $1,200 ($400 + $800) in charitable contributions.

The character of an item of partnership income or deduction reported by each partner remains unchanged in his hands. Thus, a share of a gain realized by the partnership on the sale of depreciable business property reported by the partner is treated by him as the gain from the sale of depreciable business property. This can create unwanted tax results and may require timing of transactions by the partnership to accommodate the personal needs of the partners.

EXAMPLE:

Partnership AB sells rental real estate owned by the partnership at a profit of $10,000. Adam's share of the gain is $5,000. During the same year, he personally sells at a $3,000 loss an individually owned piece of rental realty. Because his share of the partnership gain retains its character in his hands, he must offset his share of partnership gain by his personal loss.

Partnership		Partner Adam	
Gain	Loss	Gain	Loss
$10,000	0	$5,000	$3,000
		(Attributed to partner)	(From rental property)

Result: Net long-term capital gain of $2,000.

Generally, on the sale of several pieces of rental or business property, a net gain would be a capital gain; a net loss, an ordinary loss. But here, because Adam's personal loss and his share of partnership gain must be aggregated, the tax saving that would result from reporting the gain as capital gain and the loss as ordinary loss is diminished.

This unwanted result can be avoided by proper timing of business sales. Adam's personal sale or the partnership sale should be postponed a year. Then, with each transaction falling in a different year, it would be possible to realize a full ordinary loss.

A partner's share of the gross income of the partnership is treated as his gross income. This rule must be considered in these cases:

(1) Filing of an income tax return. For example, a partner's only income for the year is his share of the partnership's net income, $100. But his share of the partnership gross income is $600. Although he has no tax to pay, he is required to file a tax return because he had at least $600 of gross income.

(2) *Statutes of limitation.* Where the six-year, rather than the three-year statute of limitations on tax assessments, may apply to a tax return filed by a partner. If more than 25% of gross income is omitted from a tax return, the six-year statute applies.

(3) *Income from Possessions.* Where a partner receives gross income from sources within a possession. If 80% or more of gross income comes from a possession, that income might not be subject to U.S. income tax.

When a Partner Reports Partnership Income or Loss

Each partner reports his distributive share of the partnership's income or loss on his tax return for the year in which or with which the partnership year ends. For example, if both the partnership and the partner use the calendar year as their taxable years, on his 1967 personal tax return, the partner will report his share of the partnership income or loss for the partnership year ending December 31, 1967.

Where a partner and partnership have different taxable years, the partner reports on his return the partnership's full year's income or loss in his taxable year within which the partnership taxable year ended. So, if the partnership has a taxable year that ends March 31, 1967, the partner who uses the calendar year as his own taxable year will pick up his share of the partnership income or loss for that full partnership taxable year on his own 1967 return. Thus, the partner will be filing in April of 1968 a tax return which includes partnership income that was earned by the partnership in a taxable year that occupied nine months of 1966 and three months of 1967.

Partnerships must get Treasury permission to choose a taxable year other than that of a principal partner.

A partner reports his distributive share of the income whether or not actually distributed to him.

Guaranteed payments. A partner may receive guaranteed payments, a specified return on his capital investments or "salaries" before profits are computed. These guaranteed payments are deductible by the partnership and reportable by the partners who receive them as income. Regardless of his method of accounting, the partner reports guaranteed payments received by him in his taxable year in which ended the partnership year during which the payments were made.

EXAMPLE:

Green, a partner in Green and White, reports on a calendar year basis; the partnership uses a fiscal year ending May 31. During the partnership year ending May 31, 1968, Green received guaranteed payments totaling $1,200, at the rate of $100 a month. So, of that $1,200, Green received $700 during the months of June-December, 1967 and $500 during the months January-May, 1968. Although he is a cash-basis taxpayer, Green reports the entire $1,200 in his 1968 tax return, the partnership year of payment that ended within his taxable year.

If after making the guaranteed payment to the partner, the partnership ends up with a net loss, the partner picks up the guaranteed payment as income and also his share of the net loss. Assume partner Green is to get a $10,000 guaranteed payment for services plus 30% of taxable income or loss of the partnership (after deducting the $10,000 payment to him) and the partnership then ends up with a $9,000 loss. Green will report $10,000 of income and $2,700 of the loss. Where a partner's actual share of profits is less than his guaranteed payment, only the excess of the payment over his distributive share is treated as a guaranteed payment. This rule must be followed even if the partnership agreement may require that the entire amount of guaranteed payment is to be treated as a business expense in figuring partnership profit and loss.

An allocation between capital gain and loss is sometimes required. Assume the partnership in the example has no ordinary income and a $30,000 long-term capital gain. After paying Green his guaranteed payment of $10,000, the partnership has an ordinary loss (since it deducts the guaranteed payment) of $10,000 and the $30,000 capital gain. In that case, Green reports his salary of $10,000 as income and also 30% of the $10,000 loss ($3,000) and 30% of the $30,000 capital gain ($9,000).

Limitation on Deductible Losses

Losses from partnership operations are generally treated in the same way as partnership gains. Each partner reports his share of partnership loss on his personal tax return. It can be deducted from his other income and if the loss is greater than his other income, he can use the excess as a net operating loss carryback or carryover.

A partner's loss can never be more than the basis of his partnership interest. If it is more than his basis, the excess loss cannot be deducted on his return until additional capital is invested to cover the loss, later partnership earnings cover the loss, or his basis is increased by some other means, as, for example, by the partnership's incurring of liabilities.

EXAMPLE:

On January 1, 1967, the capital accounts of partners Young and West show the following: Partner Young, an original contribution of cash of $1,000. Partner West, an original contribution of cash of $1,000 plus $2,000 accumulated taxed earnings that West has not withdrawn. In 1967, the partnership suffered a loss of $3,000. Each partner's share of the loss was $1,500. West's partnership basis is $1,000. He can deduct only $1,000 of the partnership loss on his individual tax return. In 1968, each partner's share of income is $600. Young can now offset his 1967 unused loss of $500 against the $600. He will report taxable income from the partnership of $100. West will report the full $600 income.

Figuring the Tax Basis of a Partner's Interest in the Partnership

A partner needs to know his basis to compute gain or loss on the sale of his partnership interest and to determine the tax consequence of certain partnership distributions.

The starting point is the basis for the original investment. If only cash was contributed, the partner's basis is the amount of cash contributed. If property was contributed, the partner's basis is his basis (not the value) of the property contributed. If he also contributed cash, the cash is added to the basis of the property contributed. Where the property transferred to the partnership is subject to a mortgage or other indebtedness taken over by the partnership, the contributing partner is considered to have received a distribution from the other partners for the portion of the debt allocable to them. So, if the amount taken over by the other partners is more than the contributing partner's basis for the contributed property, the contributing partner ends up with a taxable gain.

EXAMPLES:

1. Jones acquired a 20% interest in a partnership by contributing property. The property had a fair market value of $10,000, an adjusted basis to Jones of $4,000, and was subject to a mortgage of $2,000. Payment of the mortgage was assumed by the partnership. The basis of Jones' interest in the partnership is $2,400.

Adjusted basis to Jones	$4,000
Less portion of mortgage assumed by other partners which must be treated as a distribution to Jones (80% of $2,000)	1,600
Basis of Jones' interest	$2,400

2. Assume that in Example 1 the property contributed was subject to a mortgage of $6,000, then the basis of Jones' interest would be zero, computed as follows:

Adjusted basis of property	$4,000
Less portion of mortgage assumed treated as a distribution (80% of $6,000)	4,800
	($ 800)

Jones' basis cannot be less than zero. The $800 in excess of basis is considered a distribution of money and taxed as capital gain from the sale or exchange or a partnership interest.

If the partnership interest is purchased from another partner, the purchaser's basis for the partnership interest is what he paid for it. If the partnership's basis for its assets do not reflect increased values for which the purchaser paid in buying his interest, it is possible to increase the partnership's basis for the assets (but only as to the purchasing partner's interest) by having the partnership make the necessary election. See page 62.

If the interest was inherited the basis of the partner acquiring the interest is its fair market value at the deceased partner's date of death (or the alternative value at optional valuation date if that is elected by the estate).

If the interest is received as a gift, the donee partner's basis is the donor partner's basis increased by any gift tax paid.

Increase in basis. The original basis is increased by: (1) Further contributions to the partnership. (2) Partner's share of the undistributed partnership's taxable income (including capital gains). (3) Partner's share of any tax exempt income of the partnership. (4) Deductions for depletion to the extent they exceed the basis of the partner's interest in the depletable property. (5) Partner's share of any increase in partnership liabilities. When a partner contributes property subject to liabilities, his basis is decreased by the portion of those liabilities that are allocable to the other partners. (See examples above.) But his own basis is not increased by the portion of those liabilities allocable to his share of the partnership.

Decrease in basis. Basis is reduced by: (1) Partner's share of the partnership's losses (including capital losses). (2) Partner's share of partnership expenditures which are neither deductible nor chargeable to capital. (3) Money distributed to the partner by the partnership and the partner's basis of any other property distributed to him by the partnership.

Where it is not practicable for a partner to compute his basis under the above rules, he may be allowed to use an alternative method. His basis for his partnership interest is his proportionate share of the tax basis of the assets in the hands of the partnership. Use of this alternative method is permitted where the result will not differ substantially from that of the usual method.

How to Use the Partnership Agreement to Solve
Future Tax Problems

The partnership agreement is a vital instrument that should not only present and preserve the partners' intentions on how the business is to operate but also how certain tax problems are to be treated when they arise. In the absence of such provisions, the tax law may supply rules differing widely from the partners' intentions. Thus, it is important to anticipate these difficulties and resolve them in the partnership agreement. Tax problems that should be anticipated by agreement are discussed below.

Each partner's share of special income or loss items. Generally, a partner's share of partnership income or loss or any other item of income, deduction, or credit is fixed by the partnership agreement. If the partnership agreement covers only the profit-and-loss sharing ratio, it will be presumed also to govern the division of such items as capital gains and losses, contributions, tax exempt interest, and dividends.

EXAMPLE:

Jones and Green agree to share profits and losses equally. At the end of the year the partnership has a net profit from operations of $12,000 and a long-term capital gain of $4,000. Nothing is said about how capital gains are divided. Then each partner reports $2,000 as his share of capital gains from the partnership, the same ratio they use to divide operating profits and losses.

Partners can agree to any division of income, deduction, or credit items if the special ratio is not motivated by a tax avoidance or evasion scheme and the allocation has a substantial economic effect independent of the tax consequences. For example, special allocations can permit (1) a partner who is a Puerto Rican resident to receive a percentage of the income derived from Puerto Rican sources that is greater than his distributive share of partnership income; and (2) a partner to receive all of the partnership's tax-exempt income while the other partner receives all of the partnership dividend income, provided, however, that the partner to whom the tax-exempt income is being allocated bears the economic risk of the presence or absence of tax-exempt income and similarly with the partner receiving the dividend income.

Arrangements can be set aside for lack of economic effect. The Treasury will not recognize an allocation under an agreement that allocates all partnership loss on the sale of depreciable property used in trade or business to one partner, or allocates a greater part or all of foreign tax payments to one partner, while simultaneously allocating to the other partner or partners an equivalent amount of partnership loss or a deduction of a different nature.

Depreciation, and gain or loss on sale of contributed property. A partner, instead of investing cash, may contribute property to the partnership. If, however, there is a difference between his cost or basis for the property and its present market value, his fellow partners may be burdened with tax costs they never bargained for. Assume that in forming the AJ partnership, Adam invested $30,000 in cash and Jones a warehouse that cost him $15,000 but which is now worth $30,000. The tax basis of the warehouse to the partnership is $15,000 (Jones' tax basis) even though, for nontax purposes, Jones is credited in his capital account with a $30,000 investment. The disparity between bases creates the following drawbacks: If the property is sold shortly thereafter for $30,000, the partnership has a $15,000 gain and Adam would be taxed on half, or $7,500, patently unfair to him. He is taxed on a gain that really belongs to Jones. Even if the property is not sold, depreciation has to be figured on the lower tax basis of $15,000, depriving Adams of the larger depreciation deduction he would normally expect. To overcome these inequities, the partnership agreement can provide for leveling-out adjustments.

EXAMPLES:

1. Frost and Smith form an equal partnership. Frost invests $10,000 in cash. Smith contributes machinery which cost him $4,000 but which is now worth $10,000. The partnership intends to depreciate the machinery at a 10% rate. Without provision for adjustments, the depreciation deduction of $400 (10% of $4,000) would be divided equally between Frost and Smith. But they agree to attribute to Smith his potential gain of $6,000 on the machinery—the difference between his tax cost of $4,000 and the fair market value of $10,000 at the time of contribution. The agreement then considers that Frost, by investing $10,000 in cash, has bought a one-half interest in the machinery for $5,000 (one-half of its fair market value at the time of contribution). Thus, the partnership allocates to Frost an annual depreciation deduction of $500 (10% of $5,000). But because the

total depreciation that can be allowed to the partnership is $400 (10% of its $4,000 tax basis), only $400 of the depreciation deduction can be allocated to Frost's interest. Smith, by not getting any of the depreciation deduction, actually realizes a portion of the potential gain of $6,000.

2. Frost and Smith also agree to the following: If the machinery is sold, the excess of its fair market value at the time of contribution (less depreciation figured on that value) over its tax basis (less depreciation figured on that value) is to be reported as gain by Smith. A year later, when the machinery is sold for $8,000, the partnership realizes a gain for tax purposes of $4,400 (the $8,000 sales price less its adjusted basis of $3,600— the $4,000 original basis less one year's depreciation of $400). Under the agreement, the entire amount is reported by Smith. He is taxable on any gain realized on the machinery up to $5,400 in the second year of partnership. That is $9,000 (the excess of the fair market value of $10,000 less $1,000 depreciation) over the tax basis of $3,600. This way, Smith is taxed on the appreciation that existed on the property before he contributed it to the partnership. However, if the gain was more than $5,400, then the excess would be allocated equally between Frost and Smith since the provision has no effect on appreciation realized while the machinery was held by the partnership.

Recapture of depreciation. Each partner's share of partnership's ordinary income realized on the recapture of depreciation should be fixed by the partnership agreement. If the agreement provides for the allocation of the total gain from a sale of property, but does not provide for the allocation of recaptured depreciation, the allocation of the income realized on the recapture is made in the same proportion as the total gain. However, if the partnership elects to make certain special adjustments to reflect the difference between the basis of a partner's interest in the partnership and his proportionate share of the adjusted basis of partnership property, the adjustments must be taken into account. If a partner receives a distribution of property, other than money, within two years after acquiring his interest in the partnership, he may, even though no election was made, be able to compute his income as if such an election has been made.

A contribution of depreciable property by a partner to a partnership generally does not result in recapture of depreciation to the contributing partner, and the basis of the property in the hands of the partnership is the same as its adjusted basis to the partner contributing it. If the property is subject to a mortgage which is assumed by the partnership, however, the contributing partner may be required to report ordinary income on account of depreciation.

EXAMPLES:

   1. Jones contributes property to a new partnership in which he holds a one-half interest. The property has a fair market value of $10,000, an adjusted basis in Jones' hands of $4,000, and depreciation after 1961 of $3,000. No ordinary income is required to be reported by Jones on the transfer and the basis of the property to the partnership is the same as its adjusted basis to Jones, or $4,000.

   2. Assume the same facts as in (1) above, except that the property is subject to a $9,000 mortgage which is assumed by the partnership. Jones is treated as receiving a distribution in money of one-half of the $9,000 liability assumed by the partnership, or $4,500, and thereby realizes a gain of $500 ($4,500 less his adjusted basis of $4,000). Taxable ordinary income is limited to the amount of gain otherwise includible in income. Therefore ordinary income taxable to Jones is limited to $500.

Ordinary income will not result to the partnership if, at some later date, the contributed property is distributed back to the contributing partner.

Instead of contributing the recapture property to the partnership, you might consider leasing it. This would give the partnership a rent deduction and would relieve it from the burden of holding recapture property. An added advantage to the partnership is the larger deduction for rent than it normally would get for depreciation on that equipment, since its basis for the contributed property is the same as it was in the hands of the contributing partner (usually less than fair market value).

Interest and salary payments to partners. Partners' salaries and interest payments on capital can be treated in one of two ways: As distributions of profits or as guaranteed payments. The partnership agreement can determine which method is to be used.

Elections to Make When Organizing a Partnership

Although the partnership is not a taxpaying entity, nevertheless any election affecting the computation of taxable partnership income has to be made by the partnership. Each partner is governed by that partnership election. An election that may benefit one partner may not benefit another. Therefore, partners should understand the effect of elections and agree among themselves which elections will be made. Some elections have to be made right away; others in the future. The following are the more important elections the partnership will have to deal with at the outset:

Accounting methods. Should the partnership use the cash or accrual method of accounting for tax purposes? Whatever choice it makes will govern the calculation of the partnership's taxable income which is then divided into the distributive shares picked up by each partner. Each partner reports his distributive share whether or not actually distributed to him. Thus, if the partnership uses the accrual method and therefore computes a partner's distributive share by that method, that partner has to report his share of the income in his taxable year in which the partnership year ends even though he, personally, is on the cash method of accounting. (Note that the partnership may use an accounting method that differs from the method used by any or all of its partners.)

The partnership has to observe the usual limitations on choice of accounting method. So, if inventories are a substantial income-producing factor, the partnership will have to use the accrual method of accounting.

Depreciation methods. Various methods of depreciation are available to a taxpayer, and the partnership will have to decide which to employ. A partner with substantial income from other sources may prefer accelerated depreciation methods that give higher writeoffs in the earlier years. He wants to keep his share of the partnership income as low as possible. Another with insignificant outside income would prefer straight line depreciation in order to level out income. The partners will have to get together and decide on the methods to be used. Of course, the depreciation methods chosen by the partnership do not have to coincide with the methods used by the partners individually on other depreciable property they may own personally.

Bonus depreciation. On newly-acquired nonreal estate property, each partner can get a special deduction equal to 20% of the portion of the cost of the property allocated to him, with a maximum deduction of $2,000 ($4,000 on a joint return). However, the partnership has to elect to take the bonus deduction by choosing the properties to which it is to apply.

Partnership taxable year. Each partner reports his share of the partnership income or loss in his taxable year in which the partnership taxable year ends. Thus, if the partnership year is different than the partners' years and if it ends early in the partners' years, there is an effect of tax deferral. A partnership year that ends January 31, 1969 falls 11/12 in 1968; nevertheless each partner using the calendar year reports his share of the partnership income in his 1969 calendar year return. To prevent the use of the partnership year for such purposes, a partnership generally cannot adopt a different partnership year from that used by all of its principal partners. (A principal partner is one who has an interest of 5% or more in partnership capital or profits.)

It *is* possible to adopt a partnership year that differs from the one used by all of the principal partners if permission is first secured from Treasury. Permission will usually be granted if a good business reason is shown. One good business reason is the adoption by the partnership of a "natural business year."

Inventories. Whether inventories are to be valued at cost or lower of cost or market, whether the retail inventory method should be used where permissible, whether the FIFO or LIFO method should be used in determining cost are all important decisions that can affect the amount of taxable income in any given year. These decisions have to be made by the partnership.

Installment sale election. Sales by a dealer, or occasional sales of real estate or other property for more than $1,000, may be reported under the installment method (spreading income over period of collection) or by regular method of accounting.

Bad debts. These may be deducted as they arise or by setting up a reserve for bad debts.

Research and development costs. These may be capitalized or written off over 60 months if certain requirements are met.

Involuntary conversions. Gain may be reported when it arises or postponed by reinvesting the proceeds in appropriate property.

Intangible drilling and development costs. These may be capitalized or written off immediately.

Dealings Between the Partnership and Partners

A partner who deals with his partnership otherwise than in his capacity as a partner is treated as though he were an outsider. The treatment of guaranteed payments for services is an example.

Gain or loss from the sale or exchange of property between a partner and his partnership is reported as if the transaction were between strangers. But deductions for losses are not allowed on a sale or exchange of property between a partnership and a controlling partner. A controlling partner is one who has *more* than a 50% interest in either the capital or profits of the firm. To find if he meets the "over-50%" test, the partner is considered as owning the interest of the other members of the partnership who are related to him—his wife, children, grandchildren, parents, grandparents, brothers, and sisters.

EXAMPLE:

Adam Brown and his brother John are partners in firm AB. Each partner has a 50% interest in the firm profits. AB sells equipment to Adam at a loss of $8,000. As Adam and John are related partners, the ownership of each is attributed to the other. So Adam is treated as owning a 100% interest. The total $8,000 loss is denied to the partnership.

A similar result follows and no loss is allowed to a controlling partner who sells property to the partnership or on a sale between two partnerships having the same controlling partners. The disallowed loss need not be permanent. On a later sale of this property to an outsider, any gain realized is reduced by the amount of the disallowed loss.

EXAMPLE:

Firm AB sells merchandise to firm AF at a net loss of $6,000. Adam Brown has a 60% interest in both firms. AB cannot deduct the $6,000 loss on its partnership return. The sale was between two partnerships having the same controlling partner. AF Company sells this merchandise to outsiders, realizing a profit of $9,000 of which it has to report only $3,000, the excess over the amount of the loss previously disallowed to AB.

In addition to the rule disallowing losses, another rule converts capital gain into ordinary income. Ordinarily, there is no tax avoidance problem on the sale of property at a gain between a partner and his partnership. The gain is treated as if the sale were made by or to the partnership by an outsider. But there is possible tax avoidance where the seller realizes capital gains on the sale, and the related purchaser gets a deduction against ordinary income. To block this device, the seller must treat gain as ordinary income where the property in the buyer's hand is held for sale to customers, or is used in his business.

This rule applies only if the partner has over 80% interest in the capital or profits of the partnership. Here, too, the same rules for determining partnership ownership apply as in the loss situation.

EXAMPLE:

John sells real estate which he held for investments to IJ Company at a gain of $2,000. John has an interest of 90% in partnership profits of IJ Company. IJ is in the real estate business and buys the property for purpose of resale in the ordinary course of its business. John reports the $2,000 as ordinary income. Assume the only partnership transaction is the sale of the property at a loss of $1,000. John's share of the partnership loss is $900 (90% of $1,000), which is fully deductible.

The rules governing the dealings between a partner and his partnership do not apply to contributions of property to the partnership by the partner. There is no tax effect when a partner contributes property to a partnership. It is considered a taxfree exchange of property for a partnership interest. The result is the same whether the contribution is made to a new or an existing partnership.

How to Use a Family Partnership

By making family members partners, you can reduce the overall family tax burden by shifting income from your higher tax brackets to the family members' lower brackets. If you look upon your family as one unit, a family partnership permits you to retain more after-tax income than you otherwise would.

When You Can Set Up a Family Partnership

You can create a family partnership if capital is a material income-producing factor in the business. Where the partnership is essentially a service business, real estate or insurance, for example, a gift of a partnership interest to a family member will not shift partnership income unless the donee actually performs services for the partnership.

Gift or Sale of Partnership Interest to Family Member

A gift of a partnership interest is subject to Treasury examination. If your partnership is examined, it may require you to show: (1) You are mentally competent to make the gift. (2) The donee is competent to accept the gift. (3) You transferred title and control absolutely. (4) The donee accepted the gift.

Sharing partnership income. Generally, partnership income can be shared any way the partners decide. However, where there is a gift of partnership interests, or any sale to a spouse, ancestors, or lineal descendants (and any trusts for the primary benefit of those persons), these restrictions apply: (1) The partner-donor (or seller) of the partnership interest must get "reasonable" compensation out of profits before any profits are distributed. (2) Sharing of the net profits by the new partner is after the deduction for compensation to the donor or seller and can be no greater than the ratio of the donated or sold share to the entire partnership capital.

EXAMPLE:

A father sells a nonworking son 25% of the capital. He can give the son only a 25% share of the profits, after the compensation allowance to the father.

That the purpose of a gift or a sale of a partnership interest is to cut the family's taxes is not important. But the transfer of the partnership interest must be real. No sham ownership will split the family taxes.

The Treasury will examine a purchase of a partnership interest to see if the purchase has "reality." Otherwise, the transaction will be treated as a gift. A gift may be found where the purchase price of the partnership interest is to be made out of partnership earnings. For example, the new partner buys his interest from the partnership, giving his notes, and pays off his notes from his share of the partnership.

A purchase meets the Treasury tests of "reality" even if financed by loans or credit extended by a family member directly or indirectly if *either* of the following two tests is met: (1) The purchase meets the usual tests of arm's length purchase—price of the interest, terms, due date of payment, collateral put up for loan, credit standing of purchaser, and capacity of purchaser to incur a legally binding obligation. (2) Even though you cannot prove an arm's length purchase, there was a business purpose in getting the buyer into the partnership. Bringing him into the business or by adding his credit to those of the other partners would contribute to the success of the business.

Retained control. If you make a gift of a partnership interest but then retain such controls over it that are inconsistent with the gift, the gift of partnership interest will not be recognized and you will be taxed on the partnership income allocable to that partnership interest.

Following are factors that indicate you have retained the control that may prevent the recognition of the gift of the partnership interest: (1) You control the distribution of income (but an agreement by the partners for retention, or an agreement by the partners that there be a managing partner or partners who will decide on distributions is not evidence that you retained control). (2) There are limitations and restrictions on donee-partner's right to liquidate or sell his partnership interest. (3) You personally control the assets needed by the partnership (for example, you own the assets and lease them to the partnership). (4) You control management decisions inconsistent with normal relations among partners.

Minors as Partners

It is often necessary to make minors partners in order to obtain the income tax benefits from a family partnership arrangement. No tax savings are available if you make your wife your partner since you will probably file a joint return with her and the distributable partnership shares of both would be included therein. But the overall family tax bill can be cut by making your children partners.

A minor child will not be recognized as a partner unless (1) he is competent to manage his own property and participate in partnership activities. (This might be the case if he is 19 or 20 years old, although the Treasury's Regulations do not set any age limits.) Or (2) his property interest is managed by a guardian who is supervised by a court.

Use of trusts. Instead of having a guardianship, you can have a trust, which need not be only for minor beneficiaries. It is advisable to employ a trustee who is not the donor of the partnership interest and is independent of the donor. If the trustee is the donor, or someone over whom he has influence, the trust will be examined to see that the trustee is acting to represent the interest of the beneficiaries in partnership affairs and does not give preference to his own interests in the partnership (or to those of the donor).

Limited Partnerships as Family Partnerships

A family partnership can take the form of a limited partnership.

Some partners can be general partners subject to the liabilities of the laws as to general partners.

Wives or children can be limited partners, each limited partner to be entitled to a fixed percentage of the profits and losses from the operation of the business. Or the liability of each limited partner can be expressed not to exceed the value of his capital contribution.

Upon liquidation, the distributive shares of the partners can be in proportion to their partnership interests.

General partners can be given limited authority to determine whether any part of the annual profits are needed for additional working capital, to be used for improvements, alterations or additions to the plant, or to be withheld for expansion or develpment. General partners can be given complete management and control. Special partners can be denied a voice in the management and operation of the business.

When an Unincorporated Business May Be Taxed as a Corporation

An unincorporated business such as a *limited* partnership can be taxed as a corporation. For federal income tax purposes, a corporation is not limited to the artificial legal entity commonly known as a corporation, but includes other business organizations with more corporate than noncorporate characteristics. If your unincorporated business is held for tax purposes to be a corporation, it is subject to the corporate tax provisions. This can result in having distributions taxed as dividends, losses that would otherwise have been deductible on your personal return deducted by the business, and income taxed at higher corporate rates than if the income were taxed directly on your return.

Whether your unincorporated business has characteristics of a corporation is a question of fact. If the problem arises, the Treasury takes into consideration the six major characteristics that distinguish a corporation: (1) Associates; (2) carrying on a business for profit-sharing among its owners; (3) continuity of life; (4) centralized management;

(5) limited liability for debts; and (6) free transferability of owner's interest.

An unincorporated business will be taxed as a corporation if it has more corporate than noncorporate characteristics. Since the first two characteristics, associates and carrying on a business for profit-sharing among its owners, are essential elements of all organizations engaged in business for a profit (with the exception of sole proprietorships) they may be disregarded. You must determine, however, how many of the remaining four characteristics apply to your unincorporated business. If at least three of them apply, then your business is taxed as a corporation. An unincorporated business with two or less corporate characteristics will not be considered a corporation for tax purposes.

Continuity of life. An unincorporated business has continuity of life if the death, withdrawal, bankruptcy, retirement, resignation or expulsion of any member will not cause a dissolution of the organization. An agreement which provides for the continuation of the business by the remaining members in the event of the death or withdrawal of a member will not establish continuity of life if, under local law, the death or withdrawal of any member is deemed to cause a dissolution of the organization.

Centralized management. Where a person or group of persons (not including all the members of the organization) has continuing, exclusive authority to make the management decisions necessary to conduct the business, the corporate characteristic of centralized management exists.

Limited liability for debts. Limited liability is present when no member of the business is personally liable for the debts or claims against the organization. However, the member of the organization who is personally liable for the obligations of the business may make an agreement whereby another person assumes the liability or agrees to indemnify. Limited liability is not established if under local law, the member, despite the agreement, remains personally liable to creditors.

Free transferability of owner's interest. When a member of an organization, without the consent of the other members, may transfer his interest to a person not a member of the organization and confer upon this outsider all the attributes of his interest in the business, the corporate characteristic of free transferability is present. If, under local law, the transfer of a member's interest results in the dissolution of the old organization and the formation of a new organization, there is no free transferability of interest. If a member of an organization can transfer his interest to an outsider only after having offered his interest to the other members at its fair market value, a modified form of transferability exists.

EXAMPLE:

A group of 25 persons forms an organization to invest in real estate. Each member has the power to dissolve the organization at any time. The management of the organization is vested exclusively in an executive committee of five members elected by all the members, and under the applicable local law, no one acting without the authority of this committee has the power to bind the organization by his acts. Under the applicable local law, each member is personally liable for the obligations of the organization, at the same time that he has the right to transfer his interest to a person who is not a member of the organization. He must, however, first advise the organization of the proposed transfer, and give it the opportunity, on a vote of the majority, to purchase the interest at its fair market value. While the organization does have the characteristics of centralized management and a modified form of free transferability of interests, it does not have the corporate characteristics of continuity of life and limited liability. Therefore, it is not taxable as a corporation.

However, change some of the facts in the above example. If the liability of each member for the obligations of the organization to paid and subscribed capital is limited, a different result would ensue. The organization would have the characteristics following corporate central management, limited liability, and a modified form of free transferability of interests. It would be subject to taxation as a corporation.

Professional corporations. Because corporate employees can get fringe benefits (including inclusion in pension and profit-sharing plans) which sole proprietors and partners cannot get (or can get only to a much more limited extent), many professionals—doctors, lawyers, accountants—who, by law, are not permitted to incorporate, sought to have their unincorporated businesses qualify as corporations under the rules set forth above. But they were usually unable to meet these Treasury rules.

To help them, many states passed laws permitting professionals to incorporate. But even in corporate form, the Treasury refuses to recognize them as corporations.

CHAPTER VII

How Multiple Corporations Are Taxed

THE CORPORATE INCOME TAX consists of a normal tax of 22% and a surtax of 28%. The first $25,000 of corporate taxable income is exempt from the surtax; thus, each corporation is said to have a surtax exemption. There is an obvious tax saving if a business can be divided into more than one corporation to give each a surtax exemption. If one corporation has $100,000 of income, the first $25,000 is subject to a 22% tax or $5,500, while the remaining $75,000 is subject to a 48% tax, or $36,000, a total of $41,500. If the same business can be divided into four corporations each with $25,000 of income, each would pay a tax of $5,500 or a total of only $22,000, a saving of $19,500. There is also the advantage that each corporation has its own surplus accumulation exemption, thus allowing more income to be accumulated.

Because of these advantages provided by multiple corporations, the tax law has set up several restrictions on their use. In certain cases, an additional 6% tax is imposed on the first $25,000 of income, raising the rate to 28%. In addition, the Treasury may have the authority to treat all of the corporations as one, thereby restricting the corporate set-up to one surtax exemption and one surplus accumulation exemption.

This chapter discusses the tax rules applicable to multiple corporations, whether they file as separate units or together in a consolidated return.

An Additional 6% Tax is Imposed on Multiple Corporations

To reduce the tax benefit available to multiple corporations, an additional 6% tax is added to the 22% tax rate for the first $25,000 of taxable income earned by each corporation that is a member of a controlled group not filing a consolidated return. This extra tax is not a serious discouragement to the use of multiple corporations.

The application of the law follows these steps:

1. Only one surtax exemption is allowed to members of a controlled group. For purposes of this discussion, assume your corporations are a controlled group. For example, you own all of the stock in A which in turn owns stock in B, C and D; or you own all of the stock in A, B, C and D. Only one surtax exemption is permitted among the four corporations. However, the corporations can divide the exemption among themselves, or they can choose the election described in (2) below. A division of the surtax exemption might be made under the following circumstances. Assume A earns taxable income of $1,000; B, $2,500; C, $2,500; D, $21,000. The exemption would be allocated $1,000 to A, $2,500 to B, $2,500 to C and $19,000 to D. Without an allocation, the Treasury would insist that the exemption be allocated evenly, that is, $6,250 to each company. As a result, part of the exemption would be wasted in companies A, B and C.

2. If you do not want to restrict your group of corporations to one surtax exemption of $25,000, the corporations can elect to claim a surtax exemption for each corporation subject to the payment of an additional 6% on the first $25,000 of income. This increases the normal tax from 22% to 28% for each corporation.

The dividing line between electing a single surtax exemption and multiple surtax exemptions plus the 6% penalty tax is around $32,-500. If the taxable income is less than this, a single surtax exemption is advisable. If the income of the group is equal to or above $32,500, it is advisable to elect multiple surtax exemptions plus the 6% penalty tax.

The election may be made retroactively. It can be made at any time within three years after the date that the income tax return is required to be filed for the taxable year of the component member of a controlled group whose taxable year ends first on or after the December

31st for which the election applies. Thus, each corporation's return can be filed without the election, and without claiming more than one surtax exemption for the entire group. If later an audit of the return increases the income of the members of the group, the election can then be made. A retroactive election must include all years succeeding the first year for which the election is thus retroactively made.

The election may be revoked. However, after a revocation you cannot again elect multiple surtax exemptions until after a five-year waiting period.

Tests Determining What is a Controlled Group

A controlled group is either a parent-subsidiary or a brother-sister arrangement. A parent-subsidiary group is one or more chains of corporations where a common parent corporation owns at least 80% of the total combined voting power or 80% of the total value of the shares of one of the other corporations in the group and each of the other corporations' stock is held by other members of the group to an extent that meets either of the two 80% tests. For example, Corporation A owns all the stock of Corporation B. Corporation B owns 75% of the voting stock in Corporations C and D, while Corporation C owns 25% of the voting stock in Corporation D and Corporation D owns 25% of the voting stock in Corporation C. A, the common parent, meets the 80% ownership test of Corporation B; and C and D are also owned at least 80% (actually 100%) by other corporations in the group.

A brother-sister controlled group is two or more corporations where at least 80% of the total voting power or at least 80% of the total value of the stock in each corporation is owned by one individual, estate, or trust. Ownership here is direct or indirect, so although an individual may own less than 80% of the required stock in his own name, by application of attribution rules he may own the required 80%.

The attribution rules. An individual is deemed to own stock which (1) he has an option to acquire; (2) is owned directly or indirectly by a partnership in which he is a partner in proportion to his partnership interest; (3) is owned by an estate or trust of which he is a beneficiary in proportion to his actuarial interest of at least 5%; (4) is owned by a corporation in which he has at least a 5% interest in proportion to his interest in that corporation; (5) is owned by his spouse unless he does not own any stock in the controlled group corporations directly and meets other tests of nonmanagement and the corporation is not engaged in passive investments to the extent of more than 50% of its income; (6) is owned by his minor children, or if he is a minor, by his parents—but if he owns directly, or via other attribution rules, more than 50% of the stock, then he must include the stock owned by his children, regardless of age, his grandchildren, parents, and grandparents.

When controlled group status is determined. Because various corporations in a group may have different taxable years, the status of a group of corporations as a controlled group is determined every December 31. If on that December 31, the corporations make up a controlled group, the rules apply to each of the corporations involved for its taxable year in which that December 31 falls. However, even if a corporation falls within a controlled group on a December 31, it will not be included in the group for the taxable year which precedes that December 31 if in that year it was not a member of the group for at least one half that taxable year. On the other hand, even though a corporation is not a member of a controlled group on a December 31, it can still be considered a member of that group for the taxable year which began before that December 31 if it was a member of that group for at least one-half the number of days in that taxable year.

When Multiple Corporations May be Challenged by the Treasury

Even if you elect the 6% tax, the Treasury may attempt to limit your entire multi-corporate structure to one surtax exemption of $25,-000. There are several avenues of Treasury attack:

1. It can argue that tax avoidance was a principal purpose in acquiring or setting up the additional corporations. And if you cannot show a good business reason that outweighs the tax avoidance motive, the surtax exemptions and accumulated earnings credits of those additional corporations are disallowed.

2. It can argue that all your corporations comprise an association taxable as one corporation. Thus, the entire group of corporations may be restricted to one surtax exemption.

3. It can apply a provision of the tax law that prevents a newly-

formed or acquired corporation from claiming a surtax exemption or accumulated earnings credit. The law applies where an existing corporation transfers property other than money to a new or dormant corporation or where five or fewer individuals in control of a corporation transfer property other than money to a new or dormant corporation. If a major purpose in setting up the new corporation or reviving the dormant one is to get an additional surtax exemption or accumulated earnings credit, the Treasury has the power to disallow all or part of either or both of them. Control is defined as at least 80% of vote or value of the new corporation's stock, or where five or less individuals set up a second corporation, they must in addition to the 80% stock test, pass a special 50% test. The Treasury warns that it will review a corporate ownership over a period of years, not just in one year, to see if a tax avoidance scheme is being implemented. Treasury regulations provide this example of such a review.

EXAMPLE:

Jones and Smith each own 50% of X Co. stock. In 1966, Jones transfers property to Y Co. (which was newly created by Jones for the purpose of acquiring the property) in exchange for all the Y stock. In 1968, Smith buys 50% of Jones's Y stock. Now Smith and Jones have identical holdings in both corporations. The Treasury might disallow all or part of Y's surtax exemption and accumulated earnings credit or allocate one between the two corporations. It can continue to do this each year if the stock ownership percentages remain the same. Furthermore, if the Treasury finds there was an agreement between Smith and Jones, dating back to 1966, it can go back to 1966 to disallow the exemption or credit.

4. It can allocate income and deductions between controlled companies. Using this method, income is shifted between corporations to remove it from the shelter of the surtax exemption. For example, A corporation sells merchandise for cash to its brother corporation, B, at less than an arm's length price. A reports taxable income for the year of $25,000 and B reports $25,000, resulting in a combined tax of $11,000 (22% of $50,000). In such a case, the Treasury increases the taxable income of the selling corporation, A by $10,000, reflecting market price. At the same time, B's taxable income is reduced by $10,-000, as a compensating adjustment. A's tax on $35,000 income is $10,300. B's tax on $15,000 income is $3,300, for a combined tax of

$13,600, a 23.6% increase over the unadjusted tax of $11,000. By shifting the $10,000 of income, $10,000 of B's surtax exemption goes unused and the same $10,000 is taxed to A at a 48% rate.

The Treasury will often combine several or all of the above attacks in one case.

Business purpose. In opposing all of the above attacks, you have to be prepared to show a good business reason for the additional corporations. Even if you succeed in proving business purpose, you may have to show that the dealings between the various corporations were at arm's length. Otherwise the Government may allocate income or deductions between the corporations.

Examples of Good Business Purpose for Multiple Corporations

1. Operator of freight terminals began to construct a new terminal for a related motor freight company. Before financing, the bank insisted that the new terminal be put into a separate corporation.

2. A partnership in the retail food business set up 20 separate corporations. Each corporation covered one retail store with the manager of each store a 50% stockholder in that corporation only. In this manner, a manager of one store would not be subject to liability problems arising in the other stores. If there had been one corporation, a matter originating in any one store would affect the entire corporation.

3. Two divisions of an existing company were divided into two corporations and a third corporation was set up to own the real estate. This action put the constantly warring managers of the two divisions into separate companies. The principal stockholder was then able to sell the operating divisions to his employees while the real estate corporation gave him a source of retirement income.

4. An existing company in the food processing business acquired a franchise in the frozen food distribution business. The franchiser insisted that it would not grant the franchise unless the new business was put into a separate corporation.

When multiple corporation arrangements have been attacked. Given evidence of substantial tax avoidance, courts may disregard business reasons for a transaction. For example, you can have business reasons for forming a development company to buy and subdivide land, a construction company to build houses on the land, and a sales corporation to sell the houses. However, a court can strike at it if transactions within the controlled group are rigged for tax savings. Take this case. A developer owned a construction company, a sales company, and nine development companies. The Treasury, with court approval, disallowed the surtax exemption of one of the development companies on the grounds that the controlling stockholder had fixed all transactions with that company so that it never earned more than $25,000 a year. Consequently, the court held that the corporation was being used for tax avoidance and was not entitled to the surtax exemption.

In another case, the court disregarded the separate corporate structures of 16 development corporations, and attributed their income to a controlling management corporation. Here are the facts: A management group organized a corporation to develop a tract, with the corporation arranging the subdivision and financing. After construction was begun, 16 additional corporations were organized and controlled by one or more members of the management group. The first corporation then conveyed 15 lots to each of the new corporations, and each corporation contracted with a contractor to construct houses. A separate broker, who handled the sales of the houses, advertised the entire development as owned by the management group. All the corporations were located in the same office, and shared a common staff. However, separate books were kept for each corporation. Following the sale of the houses, each of the 16 corporations was dissolved, and its profits were distributed to the management group. The Tax Court supported the Treasury's charge that the 16 corporations were not tax entities, and that their income was taxable to the managing corporation. It was held that there was no business purpose for each corporation despite management's argument that they were using the separate corporations to void a general claim against the entire project and limit its liability, and to ease the handling of mechanic's liens. The court answered that insurance and workmen's compensation could meet the first two problems, and that the third claim was not real.

In ruling against the developers, the court made these points, which can stand as warnings of what not to do with multiple corporations: The corporations were involved in developing one tract. They did not perform different functions. The costs of the land charged to each corporation were not based on actual values. The major corporation controlled the distribution of the profits, according to a prearranged plan. None of the 16 corporations had its own independent employees.

Holding corporate meetings, adopting by-laws, electing officers, and keeping separate books were not substantial income-producing activities sufficient to support a separate tax status for each corporation.

Note the different tax approach in the two cases. In the first case, the corporate structure of the one developing company was not ignored. Nor was its income attributed to another controlled company. However, the tax advantage of incorporation was nullified by the loss of the surtax exemption. In the second case, the court simply refused to recognize the existence of the 16 corporations.

Allocation of income and deductions between corporations. The Treasury has the authority to determine true taxable income in cases where controlled companies do not deal at arm's length. It will correct improper bookkeeping entries between separate but controlled entities.

To avoid Treasury allocation, be sure that the entities are separated legally, and in operation, each with its own books and records clearly reflecting its own income and deductions. The importance of avoiding a Treasury allocation cannot be overemphasized.

Prices and payments between controlled groups should be similar to those arranged in the open market. That is, the tax consequences of the transaction should not be different from what they would have been if the transaction between the controlled persons had been at arm's length. Poor accounting methods between corporations can also bring on an allocation dispute even where there has been no intent to avoid tax by shifting income or deductions.

Other allocations attempted by the Treasury include reducing the lessee's rental deductions and, conversely, increasing the lessor's rental income on leases between family members or controlled groups. Do not permit a family member to occupy leased premises without any rental payment. On the other hand, interest is allowed even if the creditor is the sole stockholder of the lending corporation—but the interest must be reasonable.

To summarize: (1) You may organize separate corporations to perform distinct business functions such as development, sales and construction. But, to be recognized for tax purposes, the transactions among the corporations must be bona fide. Sales prices must be similar to what parties in an arm's length transaction would bargain for. You must be ready to establish that no artificial diversion of income is being made from one corporation to another. Where the transactions have been manipulated to shelter income from high tax brackets, the Treasury may either disallow the corporation surtax or reallocate income and deductions. If the Treasury recognizes the corporations as bona fide taxpayers, then you must decide whether you will allocate one single $25,000 exemption, or elect a surtax exemption for each company at the price of a 6% added tax. As pointed out above, the election is usually advisable. In developing a single project, you cannot organize several corporations to perform one business transaction, such as subdivision and development of the tract. The Treasury will disregard these corporations for tax purposes.

Using a Dummy Corporation to Avoid Corporate Tax

The need for limited liability often dictates the use of a corporation. This may especially be true with real estate where the individuals who really own the property want to avoid liability on the mortgage. But their individual tax rates, plus the availability of depreciation and other deductions that they can use to offset personal income, make it desirable for the income and deductions of the property to be taxable to them. One solution is a Subchapter S corporation (Chapter 5). But that type of corporation cannot be used where rent income makes up more than 20% of the corporation's gross receipts.

Court authority has held that a dummy corporation is not a taxpayer. Its income is taxed directly to its stockholders who, for tax purposes, are treated as the actual owners of the realty held in the name of the corporation. Under the present uncertain state of the law, the use of dummy corporations is hazardous. You may still find it difficult to keep a dummy corporation free of corporate tax. The tax neutrality of a dummy corporation depends on its inactivity. Current court decisions indicate that any kind of corporate activity, except that of holding title, will subject a dummy corporation to tax. Dummy corporations have been taxed for negotiating mortgage loans and leases, and for collecting rents.

The attitude of the courts can be gauged by the following cases:

1. Five investors decided to buy a vacant building, repair and renovate it, get tenants and to sell when the building was operating profit-

ably. To eliminate legal complications on the death of any of the associates, and also to limit personal liability, they organized a corporation to take title to the building. They claimed that the rental income and a later sale of the building were to be taxed to them, and not to the corporation, which was merely their agent. Nevertheless, the Tax Court and an appeals court decided that the dummy corporation was subject to tax because the cash down payment used to buy the building was first contributed to the corporation. It, not the associates, then completed the purchase and obtained title to the building. The corporation, not the associates, assumed liability for payment of the purchase money mortgage. The associates had no agreement between themselves and the corporation (or even among themselves) showing the corporation to be merely their agent. The corporation made repairs using funds which it got from capital contributions made by the associates. Leases were made in the corporation's name. Rentals were deposited in the corporation's bank account and used for additional improvements to the building. When two of the associates were bought out, the transaction was consummated through a transfer of the corporation's stock. When the building was finally sold, the corporation signed the deed for the property, as authorized by the associates through a formal corporate resolution.

2. A dummy corporation was organized to hold real estate previously owned by a trust. The stockholders wanted to avoid title transfer difficulties such as might arise on the death of the sole life income beneficiary. The land held by the corporation was leased to a tenant, who paid the corporation rents which were then deposited in a bank to the accounts of the stockholders. The lease was a net lease, in which the lessee assumed the usual duties of ownership. The corporation had only a statutory office; its mailing address was in care of its attorneys; and expenses were limited to bank charges, small legal fees and state franchise taxes. Its only income was from rent, and its only activity was collecting the rent and distributing it to the shareholders. It executed documents relating to corporate formalities, ratified the lease once at the request of the lessee, adjusted the notes for increased interest due to increased rent, and held some ten directors' meetings. The Tax Court held that the corporate entity should be ignored, since the corporation was merely a dummy for holding of title. An appeals court

reversed, on the grounds that the corporation had engaged in business activities by having full ownership rights over the land and by collecting rent.

Filing Consolidated Returns

A consolidated tax return is a single return filed by a parent corporation and all its subsidiaries and other corporations within an affiliated group. For example, you own Corporation P, which in turn owns all or most of the stock of Corporations Q, R, and S, and Corporation S in turn owns all or most of the stock of Corporation T. If certain percentage-of-ownership requirements are met within this corporate complex, it qualifies as an "affiliated group," which may elect to have a consolidated tax return filed by the parent corporation, P.

Advantages of consolidated return election. (1) Dividends received by an affiliated corporation from another are not taxable. (2) The current losses of affiliated companies may be used to offset the current gains of others. If total losses exceed total gains, the resulting net operating loss may be carried back to pre-consolidation tax years of the parent corporation. To some extent, losses of subsidiaries in pre-consolidation years can be carried forward to offset current net income of the group if the multiple surtax exemption was not elected in the year of the loss after 1963, and the subsidiaries were part of the group during the year of loss. (A parent, which is a loss corporation, can acquire one or more subsidiaries and offset its losses against their gains in the current year by using a consolidated return.) (3) Capital losses are consolidated against capital gains. (4) You may get a greater benefit from the investment credit on business property and from the foreign tax credit if you have income from foreign operations. (5) The parent company is the agent for all the member companies for all tax purposes. This saves accounting and administrative costs. (6) Deferral of gain is available in sales between affiliated companies.

Disadvantages of consolidated return election. (1) It may be difficult to terminate the election in a later year (see below). (2) Corporations filing consolidated returns may only take *one* surtax exemption for the entire group. (3) A previous election to take multiple surtax exemptions on separate returns is terminated when the affiliated group files a consolidated return and may not be reelected for five years. (4) You cannot file a consolidated return unless *all* affiliated companies make the election. Sometimes this can be a considerable factor in deciding whether to make the election. For example, one corporate member of the group may have been operating at a profit in former years and in the year the consolidated return election is contemplated, it suffers an operating loss. If it filed a separate return, the current operating loss could be carried back to the three prior years to get a large tax refund. Assuming there are companies in the affiliated group with current earnings, a consolidated return election would use up the operating loss. You would then have to do the arithmetic to see which way results in the larger tax saving for the group. (5) Accounting periods and methods of all except those on 52-53 week year must correspond to those of the parent. (6) In the year the consolidated return election is terminated, there may be a bunching of previously deferred income, such as the deferral of tax on gain from intercompany sales of inventory.

Consolidated returns are filed by corporations substantially affiliated (at least 80% stock ownership) with one another. The affiliated group may consist of a parent and one or more corporations. (For specific details of necessary stock ownership rules, see Treasury regulations.)

How to make the election. If you have not filed a consolidated return before, you have until the time required for the parent corporation to file its income tax return, including extensions to file, to make the election. In making the election, the group agrees to be governed by the Treasury regulations. The election is made by each subsidiary on Form 1122, to be attached to the parent's consolidated return for the group. In addition, each subsidiary must file a duplicate 1122 with the district director in the district it would have filed a separate return but for the consolidated return election. The parent must also attach a Form 851 (Affiliations Schedule) to its 1120. After the first consolidated return is made, there is no further need to go through this process. The parent simply files an annual consolidated return.

Election to terminate consolidated returns. You must get permission from the Treasury to discontinue filing a consolidated return. The application must be made by the parent no later than 90 days before the next consolidated return is due (including extensions to file). The application is made to the Commissioner of Internal Revenue, Washington, D.C. 20224. Permission for discontinuance is granted only in certain cases: (1) You show that new tax laws or Treasury regulations taking effect in the current tax year have a substantial adverse effect on the consolidated tax liability as compared to tax liability using separate returns. (2) Old tax laws or regulations first take effect in the current year and have a substantial adverse effect on tax liability. (3) Laws other than tax laws or change or situation of the group will create substantial hardship on the affiliated group filing a consolidated return. (4) In addition, the Commissioner may, under certain conditions, grant permission to a whole group or class of corporations to file separate returns. (5) The group dissolves.

A group is considered as remaining in existence if the common parent corporation remains as the common parent and at least one subsidiary remains affiliated with it, whether or not the subsidiary was a member of the group in a prior year and whether or not one or more corporations have ceased to be subsidiaries at any time after the group was formed.

EXAMPLE:

Assume you form Corporation P. P acquires 100% of the stock of Corporation Q on January 1, 1965, and P and Q file a consolidated return for 1965 and 1966. On May 1, 1967, P acquires 100% of the stock of Corporation R and on July 1, 1967, P sells the stock of Corporation Q. The group (consisting originally of P and Q) remains in existence since P has remained as the common parent and at least one subsidiary (now Corporation R) remains affiliated with it.

Operating as a Single Corporation

There may be advantages in setting up a single corporation in which the separate units perform as branches or divisions. This way current losses from one branch offset current gains from another branch. Also, sales and other transactions between branches or divisions are not viewed by the Treasury with the same critical eye as are similar transactions between multiple corporations not filing a consolidated return.

When a corporation which has been a more-than-80% subsidiary for more than two years is merged into its parent, the parent acquires most of the tax attributes of the subsidiary, including its net operating loss carryovers. Thus, the prior losses of a former subsidiary, now a branch, may be used by the parent against its current year's gain. There are more stringent limitations on the use of prior losses when an affiliated group of corporations elect to file a consolidated return.

CHAPTER VIII

Corporate Problems in Paying and Receiving Dividends

AN IDEAL CORPORATE SITUATION for withdrawing current earnings is where the payments to stockholders can be in the form of deductible expenses, such as pay or interest. But as explained earlier, there are limits to the use of these methods of withdrawing corporate profits and when reached, further distributions in the course of the company's operational existence will probably be dividend payments which the corporation cannot deduct and which are fully taxable to stockholders.

This chapter explains how to determine when your company is paying a taxable dividend.

How to Determine When a Dividend is Taxable

A dividend is taxable if the company has earnings and profits to distribute. Technically, this calls for an accounting of profits at two different periods:

1. Current earnings and profits as of the end of the current year. A dividend is considered always to have been made from earnings most recently accumulated. Current earnings and profits are figured under your corporation's method of accounting.

2. Accumulated earnings and profits since March 1, 1913 as of the beginning of the current year. When current profits are large enough to meet the dividend, you do not have to make this computation. Therefore, it is only when the dividends exceed current earnings (or there are no current earnings) do you match accumulated earnings against the dividend.

Current earnings are figured at the close of the year to determine the taxability of a dividend. The amount of profits earned up to the date of a dividend payment made during the year is unimportant. Such profits are not reduced by dividend payments made during the year to determine the earnings at the end of the year.

EXAMPLES:

1. Jones Co. had a $15,000 deficit at the beginning of 1968. In February, 1968, it pays a dividend of $15,000. On December 31, 1968, it figures that it has made a current profit of $15,000. The dividend paid in February is taxed, even though at the time of payment there were no earnings and profits. Furthermore, the current $15,000 profit is not applied first against the deficit but against the dividend. That there is a deficit of a prior year does not affect the taxability of the dividend as long as there are sufficient current earnings to meet it.

2. Smith Co. at the beginning of 1968 has $15,000 of accumulated profits. In March, 1968, it makes a $10,000 profit. In April, 1968, it pays a $25,000 dividend. However, during the latter part of the year, it suffers a $10,000 loss which eliminates its earlier profit. The stockholders have a taxed dividend of only $15,000 attributed to the accumulated profits at the beginning of the year. Though the dividend was paid when there were current earnings of $10,000, the existence of this amount at the time of the payment is unimportant in determining the taxability of the dividend. Current earnings are measured at the end of the year.

If the total of several dividend payments made during the year exceeds current earnings, then the proportion of each payment which the total current earnings bears to the total dividend payments is treated as out of current earnings. The remaining portion of each distribution is treated as a taxable dividend to the extent of accumulated earnings.

EXAMPLE:

Corporation A at the beginning of 1968 had $12,000 of accumulated earnings and profits. Its current earnings for 1968 were $30,000. However, during the year, it made quarterly dividend payments of $15,000 each. Of each of the four distributions made, $7,500 $\left(\frac{\$30,000}{\$60,000}\text{ of }\$15,000\right)$ is treated as paid out of current earnings. And of the first and second payment, $7,500 and $4,500 is treated as paid out of accumulated earnings, as follows:

	Dividend Payments	Paid Out of 1967 Earnings	Paid Out of Accumulated Earnings	Amount Taxed
March	$15,000	$7,500	$7,500	$15,000
June	15,000	7,500	4,500	12,000
September	15,000	7,500		7,500
December	15,000	7,500		7,500
				$42,000

If the corporation had no accumulated earnings at the beginning of the year, $7,500 of each distribution would still be taxed.

Note: As dividend distribution is always considered to have been made from earnings most recently accumulated, a corporation, unless in liquidation, cannot make a distribution from a nontaxable source, such as capital, paid-in surplus, or pre-1913 earnings until it has exhausted its current and post-1913 earnings. In addition, any distribution in excess of earnings does not create a negative earnings and profits account. The earnings and profits account remains at zero.

What Are a Corporation's "Current Earnings and Profits"?

Current earnings and profits are not necessarily the amount of taxable income reported on the corporation's tax return or current net income computed under corporate accounting methods. Items such as tax-exempt income, although not taxable, are treated as part of the earnings and profits account. If a sale is made on an installment basis, only that part of the gain taxed in the current year is included.

To determine the amount of current earnings available for dividends, the starting point is the corporation's taxable income.

Add to taxable income:

Net operating losses carried forward from prior years.

85% dividend deduction for dividends received from other corporations.

Life insurance proceeds received at the death of insured officer or employee.

Excess of percentage depletion over cost depletion.

Interest upon tax-exempt Federal, State, or municipal obligations.

Receipts of damages resulting from suit for injury to goodwill, libel or slander.

Forgiveness of indebtedness (other than gratuitous cancellations) which are not deemed taxed because the company was insolvent after cancellations. Cancellations that still leave the company insolvent are not taxed but may nevertheless increase earnings. Cancellations beyond that point are taxed unless you exercise the option to reduce the basis of your assets instead of reporting the income. If you exercise the option, there is no increase in earnings and profits. Income from gratuitous cancellations of indebtedness is generally a gift and not taxed. These cancellations might be increases to paid-in capital. But if not, they probably increase earnings and profits.

Refund of federal taxes. This includes refunds and credits resulting from renegotiated government contracts. The overpayment of taxes of a prior year offsets the reduction in earnings due to the reduction in the income of the prior years.

Recovered debts not taxed to you under the law because you did not get a tax advantage when they were written off. These are included in earnings and profits up to the amount of the prior write-off from earnings and profits. This rule does not affect companies using the reserve method.

Forgiveness as a result of a Bankruptcy Act proceeding. Note that the earnings and profits cannot be increased by the amount which the companies were supposed to reduce their basis of assets.

Subtract from taxable income:

Income taxes paid or accrued (after reducing the tax by any investment credit allowed).

Charitable contributions in excess of the limitation.

Penalty payments for Federal tax matters.

Litigation expenses which are not deductible, as those to reduce local benefit assessments.

Unreasonable or excessive compensation to officers or employees, not allowed in returns.

Net capital losses which were not allowed.

When, as a result of an audit by the Treasury, or the acceptance of an amended return, or for any other reason, a tax deficiency is assessed for any prior year. Then a corresponding adjustment must be made for the taxes in the earnings and profits as if the corrected amount of the tax had been used in the original computation for the tax year.

Amortizable bond premium on wholly tax-exempt bonds owned by a corporation otherwise than as a dealer in securities must be taken into account, together with the interest from the bonds, for each year in computing earnings and profits for that year. The full amount of the interest from the bonds for each year must be added to other earnings and profits for that year. The amortizable bond premium for the year must be subtracted.

Premiums paid to reacquire or redeem capital stock for purposes other than resale. Any excess or purchase price over par or paid-in value reduces earnings and profits.

Losses on wash sales (sale at a loss and then repurchase of substantially the same property) are not allowed as deductions in computing net income. Nor do they reduce earnings and profits. The basis of the reacquired stock is merely increased by the loss.

Depreciation in excess of the amount allowable for tax purposes does not reduce the amount of earnings available for dividends.

Distributions in partial liquidations or capital gain redemptions reduce earnings and profits to the extent the distribution exceeds the basis of the redeemed stock.

What Are a Corporation's "Accumulated Earnings and Profits"?

The tax term "accumulated earnings and profits" is similar in meaning to the accounting term "retained earnings" or "earned surplus." Both stand for the net profits of the company after deducting distributions to stockholders. However, though the law intends that earnings and profits should be calculated in accordance with acceptable accounting methods, it does not say that your earnings are necessarily the same as your book earnings. "Tax" earnings may differ for the following reasons:

1. Reserve accounts, the additions to which are not deductible from income for income tax purposes, are ordinarily regarded as a part of earnings. This is true whether or not the accounts are called reserves or surplus or whether or not they are carried as special accounts or

deducted from assets. The important factors are the nature of the reserves and the previous allowance granted for income taxes. While it might have been sound business practice to set up a reserve out of income to meet a future liability, the reserve is not deductible in determining net income. The tax law has never recognized reserves other than those for depreciation or bad debts as being deductible from income.

2. The following items do not affect earnings and profits: Book entries that have reduced or increased earned surplus as a result of appraisals, capitalization of earnings by transferring them to stock accounts or to any kind of surplus or to hidden reserves; prospective losses anticipated by reserves or reductions of assets, or capitalization or reduction of goodwill or any other type of asset representing the franchise of a going business. These and other normal adjustments commonly made in corporate practice are reversed in calculating the earned surplus.

How Earnings and Profits Are Adjusted for Dividend Payments

On the distribution of a dividend, earnings and profits are reduced by (1) cash distributed, (2) the principal amount of the corporation's bonds or other obligations distributed; or (3) the adjusted basis of any property distributed. The reduction may not be related to the amount of the dividend taxed to the stockholder.

EXAMPLES:

1. Corporation B distributes property with a value of $10,000 and a basis of $5,000. It has $12,500 of earnings and profits, which is reduced by $5,000, the basis of the distributed property, even though the stockholders are taxed on $10,000, the fair market value of the property.

2. Corporation C distributes property with a value of $10,000 and a basis of $15,000. It has earnings and profits of $20,000. This is reduced by $15,000, the basis of the distributed property, even though the stockholders are only taxed on $10,000.

Adjustments are also made for liabilities on the distributed property assumed by the stockholders, for gains recognized on the distribution, and, for distributions of appreciated inventory and unrealized receivables. No adjustments are chargeable for taxfree stock dividends and stock rights.

Where property is distributed and the corporation has outstanding a loan insured by the U. S., such as an FHA housing loan, earnings and profits must be increased by any excess of the loan over the basis of the property (not adjusted for depreciation, depletion, amortization or obsolescence) held as security for the loan. This provision blocks the practice of bailing out excess FHA mortgage money. Such distributions are taxed as ordinary dividends.

How Property Dividends Are Taxed to Individuals

In addition to paying dividends in cash or its own stock, a corporation may distribute other property. These distributions are usually called "dividends in kind" and when received by an individual stockholder are taxed at their fair market values.

EXAMPLE:
> You receive 10 shares of Acme, Inc. stock as a dividend from the Brown Co. of which you are a stockholder. At that time it had a market value of $1,500. You include $1,500, the value of the stock received in your taxable income.

Where the property is subject to a liability, the stockholder assumes the liability, the dividend is reduced by the amount of the liability, but not below zero.

The taxable dividend can never be more than the distributing corporation's earnings and profits unless the distribution consists of inventory assets or unrealized receivables.

EXAMPLE:
> Your corporation owns a building with an adjusted basis of $2,000. It is now worth $10,000. The corporation distributes the building to you. At the time, it has earnings and profits of $2,000. You have a taxable dividend of $2,000. The remainder or $8,000 is treated as a return of capital. But if the corporation's earnings and profits were $10,000, the taxable dividend would be $10,000.

Special rule for dividends of inventory or unrealized receivables. In the preceding paragraph, it was stated that a property distribution is a dividend only if and to the extent there are earnings and profits in the distributing corporation. The exception to the rule is where the distributed property consists of inventory or unrealized receivables. When such property is distributed, the corporation must make a special two-step adjustment to its earnings and profits account: (1) Increase earnings and profits by the excess of the property's fair market value over its basis. For example, Brown Co. distributes to its stockholder inventory worth $100 with a basis of $60. Earnings and profits are increased by $40. (2) Decrease earnings and profits by the *lesser* of: (a) fair market value of the distributed property, or (b) all the earnings and profits (after the increase in step (1)). Thus earnings and profits cannot drop below zero.

The effect of this two-step adjustment is to force dividend treatment to the recipient stockholder, even if there were no earnings and profits before the distribution. Thus, if earnings and profits were zero before the distribution, the amount of dividend would be the increase in step (1).

When a Corporation May be Taxed on Dividends it Distributes

The distributing corporation incurs no tax on payment of cash dividends. As a general rule, the distribution of appreciated property results in no tax to the distributing company. However, there are exceptions to this general rule. A tax may be incurred inadvertently when a corporation declares a cash dividend and subsequently decides to pay the dividend with appreciated property. Here the Treasury will contend the company paid off a liability, the dividends payable, with property and thus consummated a sale. A careful drafting of the corporate resolution declaring the dividend to be paid *in property* with no inference of payment in a dollar amount avoids the possibility of tax to the corporation.

Dividend distributions of depreciable property. A dividend or liquidation distribution of property subject to depreciation recapture also gives rise to taxable income to the corporation. This is true even though the distribution might otherwise be taxfree.

EXAMPLE:

A corporation distributes depreciable equipment to its shareholders as a dividend. The fair market value of the equipment is $3,100, and its adjusted basis to the corporation is $2,000. Depreciation claimed by the corporation after 1961 is $1,300. The corporation reports $1,100 as ordinary income as a result of depreciation recapture. This is the lower of $1,300 depreciation after 1961 or the $1,100 difference between fair market value and adjusted basis.

The basis of the distributed property to a noncorporate shareholder is its fair market value. No adjustment is made for the ordinary income reported by the distributing corporation. For a corporate shareholder, basis is the lower of the fair market value of the property or its adjusted basis in the hands of the distributing corporation increased by the taxable ordinary income.

Installment obligations. The corporation is taxed on the difference between the fair market value of the obligations at the time of the distribution and their adjusted basis. This gain may be taxed at capital gain rates if the property which was sold on the installment basis was a capital asset.

"Lifo" inventory. The corporation is taxed on the difference between the value of the inventory computed on a non-"Lifo" basis (such as "Fifo") and the "Lifo" method.

EXAMPLES:

Corporation A uses the "Lifo" method. It distributes 200 units of its inventory to its stockholders. Before the distribution it had 300 units:

Lot Order	Lifo Quantity	Lifo Valuation	Fifo Quantity	Fifo Valuation
a	100	$1,000	100	$ 4,000
b	100	2,000	50	2,500
c	50	1,000	50	2,500
d	50	2,000	100	6,000
	300	$6,000	300	$15,000

1. Basis of inventory figured on the "Fifo" basis:

Inventory before distribution	$15,000
Inventory after distribution (lot "d")	6,000
"Fifo" value of inventory distributed	$ 9,000

2. Basis of inventory figured on the "Lifo" basis:

Inventory before distribution	$ 6,000
Inventory after distribution (lot "a")	1,000
"Lifo" value of inventory distributed	$ 5,000

3. Difference between "Fifo" and "Lifo" valuation:

"Fifo" value of inventory distributed	$ 9,000
"Lifo" value of inventory distributed	5,000
Income realized on distribution	$ 4,000

Where distributed property is subject to a liability which exceeds its basis, the corporation is taxed on the difference between liability and basis, if the liability is assumed by the recipient stockholder.

EXAMPLE:

> Property with an adjusted basis of $100 is distributed to stockholders. The property is subject to a liability of $900. Its market value is $1,000. The distributing corporation has taxed gain of $800 ($900 — $100). If the property is a capital asset, the gain is taxed at capital gain rates.

Where the property is subject to a liability which is not assumed by the stockholders, the gain is limited to the excess of the fair market value of the property over its basis. So, in this example the taxed amount would be $900 ($1,000 — $100).

Planning Corporate Distributions

The previous pages have shown that distributions are taxable when the corporation has earnings and profits. From this fact, you can conclude, that for tax purposes the best time to distribute funds is when the corporation does not have earnings and profits. Logically this seems contradictory. If there are no earnings and profits, there are probably no funds to distribute. However, because of the way earnings and profits are figured, you may have a transaction that generates funds but does not give rise to gain includible in earnings and profits. Under such circumstances, a distribution may not be taxed as an ordinary dividend. For example, gain is realized on the involuntary conversion of property. An election is made to defer gain by purchasing new property financed by a substantial mortgage. When the election is made, the gain is not reflected in earnings and profits. Assuming that there was little or no earnings and profits before the conversion, the funds realized from the conversion could be distributed with little or no ordinary income resulting from the distribution. Similarly, the same result is possible by distributing funds borrowed from mortgaging property that has increased in value.

Property dividends. Dividends in kind can be, within the rules discussed in this section, a useful method of cutting down corporate taxes. If the corporation sells property and distributes the proceeds, the corporation pays a tax on the gain and the stockholders are taxed on the dividend received. But if it distributes the property directly to the stockholders they pay only the one tax. The total tax cost is much smaller. In planning such distribution, be sure your dividend is in the terms of property. Do not mention cash. If you do, you may be taxed as if a sale had been made to the stockholders. If the property is to be sold by the stockholders after the distribution, be sure not to negotiate the sale in the name of the corporation. The Treasury argues that the sale, in such case, was actually made by the corporation, followed by a distribution of the cash proceeds to the stockholders resulting in the unwanted double tax.

Hidden Dividend Problems in Close Corporations

In examination of a corporate tax return, the Treasury scrutinizes transactions between the corporation and its stockholders. Benefits accruing to the stockholders from the transaction can be categorized and taxed to them as dividends regardless of the lack of a formal dividend declaration by the corporation. Examples of the types of transactions likely to result in dividend treatment: (1) Excess payments to stockholders for salaries or rent on property owned by the stockholder. (2) Corporate purchase at an excessive price of property owned by the stockholder. (3) Loans to stockholders where there is no intention of repayment. (4) Bargain purchases of corporate property by stockholder. The taxed amount is the difference between what the stockholder paid for the property and its fair market value. However, if the purchasing stockholder is a corporation, the rule is different. Where the fair market value of the property equals or is more than its adjusted basis in the hands of the distributing company, the dividend is the excess of the adjusted basis over the amount paid for the property. For example, Brown Co., Inc. owned property with a basis of $25. Jones Co., Inc., a stockholder, bought the property for $20 when its fair market value was $100. Jones Co. has dividend income of $5 ($25 — $20). Also, Brown Co.'s earnings and profits available for dividends are decreased by the amount by which the basis of the property exceeds what was received for it. (5) Payments of stockholder's personal expenses or obligations made, unless the payments are bona fide advances which are to be repaid. (6) Illegal dividends, even when directors are required to reimburse the corporation to the extent of the amount improperly distributed. (7) Distribution of property to a shareholder who is not a corporation creates taxable income in the amount of cash plus the fair market value of property received, but this may not exceed the earnings and profits of the distributing corporation. (8) Dividends on corporate stock which are unqualifiedly made subject to stockholder's demand, but which have not been received, such as a bookkeeping entry, creating an account payable, without the transfer of property between the corporation and the stockholder. (9) Distribution in redemption of stock if the redemption is a distribution of earnings (*See* page 162). (10) Forgiveness of a stockholder's indebtedness. (11) Proceeds from sale of corporate property retained by a stockholder. (12) Rental value of a dwelling owned by the corporation and occupied rent free by a stockholder. (13) Insurance premiums on lives of certain stockholders where the stockholders as well as the corporation derive benefits.

Waiver of Dividends

Dividends paid by a corporation go pro rata to stockholders according to their holdings. If one stockholder wishes to waive his dividend, perhaps because of his high tax bracket, can he do so without being taxed?

If the waiver comes after the dividend is declared, the stockholder cannot escape tax; the waiver is merely treated as a contribution to capital of the corporation. If the waiver is made before the dividend declaration, the tax result will depend on whether there is a business purpose for the waiver and the waiving stockholder's relationship to the other stockholders. You can get an advance ruling from the Treasury on the consequences of the waiver. The Treasury will rule on a waiver if you show a bona fide business purpose for it, and your relatives are not in a position to receive more than 20% of the total dividends distributed to the non-waving stockholders. Relatives include spouse, brothers and sisters and their spouses, your children and their spouses, and your parents and grandparents. The ruling is effective for a three-year period unless there is a change of ownership (except as a result of death) that gives more than 20% of the dividends to non-waiving relatives.

In one Treasury ruling, a majority stockholder waived all his right, title and interest in future undeclared dividends for a certain period of time to increase the corporation's surplus so it could meet state law requirements for setting up a new business. There was no family or direct business relationship between the majority and minority stockholders. Also, his waiver would not increase his share in any future corporate distributions. The Treasury ruled that dividend payments to minority stockholders would not result in income to the waiving stockholder. It said that the arrangement was entered into for a valid business purpose. But in another ruling, waiver by the majority stockholder resulted in taxable income to him where the following facts existed: (1) His pro rata share of the dividends was paid in the form of increased dividends to his relatives and employees who were minority stockholders, and (2) the waiver resulted primarily in benefiting his relatives. The Treasury disregarded the claim of the waiving stockholder that capital was needed by the corporation to purchase new equipment and that the dividend was declared to meet the protests of the minority stockholders that they were not getting a return on their investment. It also disregarded the claim that it was done to maintain goodwill of the employees, though it did say that this might be a valid business purpose under other circumstances, such as where there are no relatives involved.

Stock Dividends and Rights

Dividends of cash or property such as inventory are taxed to the stockholder at ordinary tax rates if the corporation has earnings and profits. What happens, however, if the dividend consists of additional stock of the distributing corporation?

When a corporation makes a stock dividend (common or preferred) to its stockholders, or splits its already-existing stock, no tax is paid by the recipient stockholder. This rule has two exceptions. The stock dividend is taxed as any other dividend if: (1) New stock is given to discharge preference dividends for the taxable year of the corporation in which the stock dividend is made, or for the preceding tax year, or (2) the stockholder has an election to receive the dividend in corporate stock, stock rights, or other property.

Dividend Received Deduction
for Corporations

A corporation is allowed a deduction equal to 85% of dividend income received from other taxable domestic corporations (but not from preferred stock of public utilities). In other words, only 15% of its dividend income is taxed. Thus if your corporation is in the 22% tax bracket, it pays a tax of only 3.3% on its dividend income; if it is in the 48% bracket, only 7.2%.

Limitation on deduction: It cannot be more than 85% of the corporation's taxable income (less any partially exempt U. S. interest and before deduction for dividends received or the net operating loss deduction). However, the limitation does not apply if there is a current net operating loss. But if a current operating loss is offset by income from nonoperating sources, there is no "net operating loss" and the limitation does apply.

EXAMPLES:

1. Gross profit from sales	$150,000
Dividends from other corporations	100,000
Gross income	250,000
Less: Allowable expenses	170,000
Taxable income before deduction for dividends received	80,000
Less: 85% dividends received deduction	85,000
Net operating loss	($ 5,000)

Since there is a net operating loss, the corporation may take the full $85,000 dividends received deduction. If there had been no net operating loss, the dividends received deduction would have been limited to 85% of taxable income before the deduction, or 85% of $80,000 = $68,000.

2. Gross profit from sales	$150,000
Dividends from other corporations	100,000
Gross income	250,000
Less: Allowable expenses	160,000
Taxable income before deduction for dividends received	90,000
Less: 85% dividends received deduction	85,000
Taxable income after deduction for dividends received	$ 5,000

In this example, business expenses are $10,000 less, making taxable income $10,000 more, resulting in a net gain for the year of $5,000. Since there is no net operating loss as in Example 1, the 85%-of-taxable-income limitation applies, and the dividends received deduction is limited to 85% of $90,000, or $76,500. Thus, the final picture looks like this:

Taxable income before deduction for dividends received	$90,000
Less: Dividends received deduction (85% of $90,000)	76,500
Taxable income after deduction for dividends received	$13,500

Property Dividends Received by the Corporation

When a dividend in kind is received, the deduction for dividends received is limited to the lesser of 85% of: (1) The adjusted basis of the property to the paying corporation or (2) its fair market value. If paying company has a gain or loss on the distribution, then the property's basis is increased by the amount of gain recognized.

EXAMPLE:

X Co. pays a dividend to your corporation in property that has a basis of $2,500. The property now has a fair market value of $7,500. Your corporation has gross income for the basis of the property, $2,500. And its deduction for dividends received is only 85% of the $2,500. If the property had a fair market value of $1,000, only $1,000 would be reported. The dividend deduction would then be 85% of $1,000.

No deduction is provided for dividends from an exempt corporation, a foreign corporation, China Trade Act Corporation, a corporation whose income is from sources in U. S. possessions, certain corporations organized by the U. S., and certain preferred stock of public utilities. These are treated separately for a specially computed dividend deduction.

Also excluded from the deduction are dividends from: (1) Stock which has been held by your corporation for 15 days or less (90 days or less if the stock has preference as to dividends, and the dividends received with respect to such stock are attributable to a period or periods totaling more than 366 days); or (2) Stock, to the extent that your corporation is under an obligation (whether pursuant to a short sale or otherwise) to make corresponding payments with respect to substantially identical stock or securities.

CHAPTER IX

How to Avoid the Personal Holding Company and Surplus Accumulation Penalties

THAT THE CORPORATION is taxed at rates different from its stockholders makes it susceptible to tax-planning innovations varying with the ingenuity of the taxpayer and his adviser. To stop or neutralize these maneuvers, several tax laws provide penalty provisions, two of which are discussed in this chapter. They are: The tax on personal holding companies and the tax on accumulated earnings.

Personal holding companies. Two facts would tend to encourage the use of corporations to hold investment property. The tax rates for corporations may be lower than those imposed on their stockholders and corporations pay an effective tax rate of only 3.3% or 7.2% on dividends received from domestic corporations. To discourage the use of a corporation as an incorporated pocketbook, a corporation that meets the definition of a personal holding company is subject to a 70% tax on undistributed after-tax profits.

Unreasonable accumulations of earnings and profits. Here, too, because the corporate tax rates may be considerably lower than the individual stockholders' personal income tax rates, there is a strong attraction to accumulate earnings in the corporation rather than pay them out as dividends, assuming, of course, that the reasonable salary levels have already been reached. Dividends have to be paid out of after-tax earnings of the corporation and are again subject to taxes in the hands of the stockholder. To prevent corporations from accumulating earnings beyond the needs of the business, a corporation accumulating

earnings over a certain limit may be subject to a penalty tax of 27½%
or 38½%.

Personal Holding Company Penalty Tax

The 70% personal holding company tax presents no problem to a
company earning income from the operation of a manufacturing or
service business. The tax is primarily designed to discourage upper
bracket investors from "incorporating" their investments to shield
them from high personal income taxes. However, the personal holding
company rules are sufficiently broad in scope to penalize business corporations that also receive such passive income as interest and dividends. Here are two examples: (1) A manufacturing company is in
the process of liquidation. Its assets are sold on credit, but it is temporarily kept alive as a holding company. In the year after the sale, its
income substantially consisted of interest on the buyer's notes. The
penalty tax applies notwithstanding that there was no intention to shelter interest income in a corporate shell. (2) A manufacturing company had gross receipts of $1,000,000, cost of goods sold was $950,-
000, and dividend income from other corporations, $100,000. The
penalty tax applies since the dividend income meets the personal holding company income test: The dividend income was more than 60%
of the gross income of $150,000.

Real estate corporations are also especially susceptible to such danger. All that may be necessary to be liable to the penalty is for a real
estate corporation to have investment income that exceeds 10% of
gross rental income.

How a Corporation Becomes a Personal Holding Company

If a company meets two tests, it is a personal holding company. The
first test concerns the nature of the stock ownership of the corporation;
the second, the nature of a very large part of its gross income. Remember that both tests must be met for you to have a personal holding
company; one is not enough. Most closely held corporations meet the
stock ownership test; yet most of them are not personal holding companies.

Stock Ownership Test

Your company meets the stock ownership requirements, if, at some time during the last half of the tax year, more than 50% in value of the outstanding stock of the corporation is owned, directly or indirectly, by or for not more than five individuals. This stock ownership test is met regardless of whether the five individuals are citizens, residents, or non-resident aliens. And it makes no difference that a great many stock-holders own the remaining stock or that the stock is listed on a stock exchange.

"In value" here means the value of the entire corporate stock out-standing at the time not including Treasury stock. It may also mean a value determined upon the basis of the company net worth, earning and dividend-paying capacity, and appreciation of assets, together with other facts influencing the value of the stock. Where there are two or more classes of stock outstanding, the total value of all the stock is allocated among the different classes according to their relative values.

Stock owned "indirectly" is held to be equivalent to actual owner-ship. Generally, you are considered to own your proportionate share of the stock held by your corporation or partnership, as well as by an estate or trust of which you are a beneficiary. Also you have "con-structive ownership" of stock owned by your brother, sister, wife, hus-band, children, grandchildren, parents, and grandparents.

Most close corporations would find it difficult to avoid meeting the stock ownership test. A close corporation would have to have at least 10 unrelated stockholders, each holding an equal amount of stock, to escape the stock ownership test.

Income Tests

To fall within the gross income test, a corporation must receive 60% or more of its "adjusted ordinary gross income" in the form of personal holding company income. Income from security investments (dividend and interest) is personal holding company income. Rents may be if they are within certain percentages. You can keep rental income from being personal holding company income by keeping ad-justed rental income (net) at a level of at least 50% of the company's adjusted ordinary gross income and by keeping investment income such as dividends and interest to no more than 10% of the company's ordinary gross income. Both percentages must be met to prevent rental income from being treated as personal holding company income. Adjusted rental income, even if it is more than 50% of adjusted ordinary gross income, is personal holding company income as long as income from securities (and other types of personal holding company income not discussed here) is more than 10% of the company's ordinary gross income.

The term "ordinary gross income" is gross income less (a) all gains from the sale or other disposition of capital assets and (b) all other gains from the sale of property used in a trade or business and entitled to capital gain treatment. Gain subject to ordinary income treatment under the recapture rules is included in gross income.

Adjusted ordinary gross income for a typical real estate company is ordinary gross income less deductions taken for depreciation, amortization of a leasehold interest, property taxes, interest, and leasehold rents.

EXAMPLES:

1. A corporation owns securities earning annually $50,000 in dividends and a building returning annual gross income from rents of $50,000. Depreciation, interest and real property taxes allocable to the rents are $25,000. Under the 50% test, all of the corporation's adjusted ordinary gross income is personal holding company income, computed as follows:

	Adjusted Ordinary Gross Income	Adjusted Income From Rents
Gross income from rents	$50,000	$50,000
Dividends	50,000	
Gross income	$100,000	
Less: Depreciation, interest and real property taxes	25,000	25,000
Total	$75,000	$25,000

Since the adjusted income from rents of $25,000 is not 50% or more of adjusted ordinary gross income (50% of $75,000) the $25,000 adjusted income from rents constitutes personal holding company income. Since the $50,000 in dividends is also personal holding company income, 100% of the corporation's adjusted ordinary gross income ($75,000) is personal holding company income.

2. A corporation receives $40,000 in dividends and $150,000 of gross income from rents. It also realizes $10,000 in capital gain on the sale of securities. Deductions for depreciation, interest, and real property taxes allocable to the rents equal $100,000. Under the 50% test, the adjusted income from rents, $50,000 ($150,000 less $100,000) is 55.5% of adjusted ordinary gross income of $90,000 ($200,000 less the $100,000 of deductions and $10,000 of capital gains). Accordingly, the adjusted rental income meets the 50% test. However, other personal holding company income (the dividend income of $40,000) is more than 10% of ordinary gross income of $190,000 ($200,000 less $10,000 of capital gains). Therefore, even though the rental income meets the 50% test, it nevertheless is personal holding company income because the 10% test was met. Thus, all of the corporation's adjusted ordinary gross income is personal holding company income.

Another type of rent that may be personal holding company income is rent or other payments received for the use of the corporation's property at any time during the year from a person owning directly or indirectly 25% or more of the value of the corporation's outstanding stock. However, this item is not included unless the corporation has personal holding income from other sources (not including rents from other sources) of more than 10% of its ordinary gross income.

3. A corporation receives $250,000 in gross income from rents, $20,000 of dividends and $130,000 from its sole shareholder as rent for the use of a building owned by the corporation and leased to the shareholder. Depreciation, interest, and property taxes totalling $100,000 are allocable to the $250,000 of rents. The adjusted income from rents, $150,000 ($250,000 less $100,000), equals 50% of adjusted ordinary gross income of $300,000 ($400,000 less $100,000) and thus the 50% test is met. In addition, the corporation meets the 10% test since personal holding company income for the taxable year (excluding the rents for the use of the corporate property by the shareholder which is not considered personal holding company income for purposes of the 10% test), namely $20,000 of dividends, is not more than 10% of ordinary gross income of $400,000. Since the adjusted income from rents meets both the 50% test and the 10% test, the adjusted income from rents is not personal holding company income.

How to Avoid the Personal Holding Tax

To avoid the personal holding company status, you can distribute the excess of other personal holding company income over the 10%. Thus, what remains does not exceed the 10% limit. You avoid personal holding company status and you can shelter 10% of personal holding company income from the personal holding company tax. You can make the distribution of the excess as follows: (1) Dividends paid during the taxable year. (2) Dividends paid the following year but not later than the 15th day of the third month of the following taxable year. This "post-year" dividend cannot exceed either the undistributed personal holding company income for the taxable year, or 10% of dividends paid during the taxable year. (3) You can declare a consent dividend, that is, the stockholders report the income as if a distribution had been made. (See below.)

EXAMPLE:

A corporation receives $40,000 in dividends and $150,000 of gross income from rents. It also realizes $10,000 in capital gain on the sale of securities. Its deductions for depreciation, interest, and real property taxes allocable to the rents equal $100,000. Under the 50% test, the adjusted income from rents $50,000 ($150,000 less $100,000) is 55.5% of adjusted ordinary gross income of $90,000 ($200,000 less $100,000 deductions and $10,000 of capital gains). Accordingly, the adjusted income from rents meets the 50% requirement. However, other personal holding company income (the dividend income of $40,000) is $21,000 in excess of the allowable 10% of ordinary gross income $190,000 ($200,000 less $10,000). The adjusted income from rents is personal holding company income and, therefore, all of the corporation's adjusted ordinary gross income is personal holding company income. However, the adjusted income from rents is not treated as personal holding company income if the corporation pays a dividend of $21,000 to its shareholders during the taxable year. On the other hand, if the amount of the dividend paid by the corporation is less than $21,000, the adjusted income from rents is personal holding company income.

The above discussion has been written from the perspective of a company that receives only rental income and holds investments in securities. Consequently, before leaving the subject of personal holding companies, be aware that the personal holding company rules are more extensive and cover other types of income and corporations as well. Check the rules in Treasury regulations if your corporation receives the following types of income that may also be treated as personal holding income: (1) Royalties from copyrights, mineral and gas properties; (2) produced film rents; (3) annuities, to the extent they are taxable income; (4) income from estates and trusts; or (5) compensation for personal services, or gains from the sale of a personal service contract. Item (5) covers a contract under which the corporation collects for the services of a stockholder who owns 25% or more in value of the corporation's stock at any time during the tax year. However, the fee for services is included only if either a person other than the corporation has the right to designate who is to perform the services, or if a designation of the performing person is made in the contract.

Consent Dividends

If, for some reason, an actual dividend payment cannot be made, you may consent to be taxed as if an actual dividend had been paid. File a "consent" on Form 972 specifying the amount which you consent is to be taxed as a dividend. The consent must be filed not later than the due date for the corporation's tax return. For example, if a calendar year corporation is a personal holding company during 1968, the consenting stockholders must file their Forms 972 by March 15, 1969. In addition, the corporation must file a Form 973, showing by classes the stock outstanding on the first and last days of the taxable year, the dividend rights of such stock, and all the other information required by the form. The amount of the consent dividend is treated as a contribution to capital by the consenting stockholders and increases the basis of their stock.

To be eligible to file a consent, you must have been a common or participating preferred stockholder on the last day of the corporation's taxable year.

Deficiency dividends. If you contest the status of personal holding company but there is an eventual determination that the corporation is a personal holding company, the corporation has until 90 days after the final determination to pay a deficiency dividend. A determination is any of the following: (1) A Tax Court decision or final judgment by any other court, (2) a closing agreement made with the Treasury, or (3) an informal agreement between the corporation and the Treasury.

Paying a deficiency dividend does not avoid payment of any interest or other late filing penalties which accrued up to the time of the determination.

How the Penalty Tax is Assessed

Corporations are required to file a Schedule PH along with their regular corporate tax return (Form 1120) for the tax year involved, on which they calculate their personal holding company tax. Failure to do so subjects the corporation to any and all additional penalties applicable to failures to file a return. In addition, where no Schedule PH, Form 1120 is filed, interest is assessed on the penalty tax.

There is a special statute of limitations for failure to file the Schedule PH, Form 1120. The general statute of limitations runs three years; the rule for a personal holding company is six years.

When Personal Holding Company Status May Be Desirable

If you plan to sell your company's assets and put the proceeds into investments, you may avoid capital gain tax by continuing your corporation as a personal holding company and increase your investment yield. The corporation pays a tax on sale of the assets and invests the proceeds. You pay consent dividends each year to the extent of the corporation's personal holding company income, and the corporation continues to reinvest the investment income (See page 160).

Subchapter S and Personal Holding Company

Because of the receipt of passive income test, a personal holding company usually cannot make a Subchapter S election. However, there are certain situations in which a personal holding company may make the election and avoid the personal holding company penalty.

EXAMPLES:

1. The sole income of a corporation is from installment notes due on the sale of assets. The corporation reports interest income on the notes and long-term capital gain on the collections of notes that become due. If the interest income does not exceed 20% of total receipts, a Subchapter S election avoids personal holding company tax consequences.

2. Rent for personal holding company and Subchapter S purposes differ. Under the Subchapter S, rent does not include rent for use of property tied to performance of substantial services. For example, income of a motel would not be rent for purposes of the Subchapter S receipts test but it would be for a personal holding company.

3. A personal holding company which derives income from personal service contracts can also make the election.

Unreasonable Accumulations of Surplus

Before going into the discussion of how unreasonable surplus problems arise and how they may be defended, you should have a clear idea of the income base on which the penalty tax is applied. The penalty tax is applied on what is generally "current undistributed earnings" of a particular taxable year or years that are open to an assessment of tax. The existence of accumulated earnings from prior years may be evidence of an unreasonable accumulation; however, the actual penalty is not applied on the prior accumulations as such.

The penalty tax is imposed on accumulated earnings of a particular current year for which there is no reasonable business use anticipated. Technically speaking, the tax base on which the penalty tax is imposed is referred to as the "accumulated taxable income."

The first $100,000 of accumulated taxable income is taxed at 27½%, and any excess at 38½%.

Although the penalty tax is not restricted to use against small corporations, in practice it is. Large corporations can more easily justify accumulations than can smaller ones. If a large corporation is attacked by the Treasury, it is usually one with the majority of control within one family.

There are three ways of avoiding all or part of the penalty tax. The first, is to distribute surplus current earnings as dividends to stockholders. Accumulated taxable income is reduced by dividends paid. The second way is to show a reasonable business need for the accumulations. On page 158 is a list of business needs. The third way is to offset fully or partially the amount of unreasonable accumulations by an "accumulated earnings credit."

The function of the accumulated earnings credit. The income base on which the penalty is imposed as mentioned above is the corporation's accumulated taxable income, which is the taxable income of the year in question reduced for certain items such as income taxes paid on current earnings and dividends paid during the year (or during the two-and-one-half months of the following year) and by the accumulated earnings credit. If the accumulated earnings credit exceeds or is equal to the accumulated taxable income (after being adjusted), there is no penalty tax. (Other adjustments to taxable income are not explained here but can be found in Treasury regulations.)

There are two features to the credit. The credit can be the amount estimated as needed for the reasonable business needs of the corporation, or it can be a minimum credit provided by the law. The minimum credit is $100,000, which is first reduced by the amount of the surplus accumulated before the year that is being questioned by the Treasury. The credit finally applied is the larger of (1) the credit based on business needs or (2) the minimum credit. If the accumulation of prior years is $100,000 or over, the corporation cannot use the minimum credit and must rely on proof that the accumulated earnings of the year under examination were for reasonable business needs.

EXAMPLES:

1. A corporation had $40,000 of accumulated earnings as of December 31, 1967. In 1968 its "accumulated taxable income" is $125,000. The Treasury questions the accumulation. The stockholders cannot prove any of the accumulation was for reasonable business needs. They can claim a minimum credit of $60,000 ($100,000 less $40,000). Accumulated taxable income subject to penalty tax is $65,000 ($125,000 less the $60,000 minimum credit).

2. Assume in Example 1 above that $25,000 was needed for the business. The credit would remain $60,000 as it is larger than the $25,000.

3. Assume $85,000 was needed for business purposes. Since $85,000 exceeds the minimum credit of $60,000, the credit is $85,000. The accumulated taxable income subject to tax is $40,000 ($125,000 − $85,000).

Living With the Penalty Tax

Over the years, businessmen have learned to live with the presence of the accumulated earnings tax. It is an additional risk of doing business, but one which might be avoided. An accumulation may not be questioned, or if it is questioned, it may be defended. And if a penalty is imposed, its imposition may not negate the overall saving accrued by the accumulation. The penalty tax on corporations is relatively low, and hence it may sometimes pay to risk the tax. Individual tax rates run up to 70%. The combination of the tax of 27½% or 38½% on the undistributed profits and the 25% tax due on the eventual liquidation of the company might be less than the tax payable by the shareholder receiving the dividends. As a result, some stockholders may risk the tax, figuring the tax plus the cost of liquidation to be less than the cost of a dividend to them.

Evidence to prove reasonable accumulation. Accumulations for valid business purposes should be supported by written evidence of the reasons for the accumulation. Correspondence, minutes, building plans, records of contract negotiations are all evidence of a plan. The more complete your records, the better your chance of avoiding the penalty tax.

The absence of a formal plan is not necessarily fatal. Courts have recognized evidence such as oral testimony describing conferences among officers and directors of the corporation. Evidence of later decisions can support the existence of a prior plan.

When the expansion plan involves a build-up of inventory, later acquisitions of inventory may be proof of the plan. However, a court may look into the nature of a business to see if it was necessary to accumulate inventory.

Factors Looked for by the Treasury to Prove Unreasonableness

The Treasury will use as the reason for imposing the penalty tax the following facts among others:

Cash has accumulated over the corporation's present and reasonably anticipated requirements.

There have been transactions between the corporation and its shareholders involving stockholders' withdrawals, personal loans, or the expenditure of funds for their personal benefit.

There has been comparatively little dividend distribution.

Corporate investments are made in securities unrelated to the business needs.

Earned surplus from past years has accumulated in large amounts.

Expansion and improvements may have been intended but were not actually made. Your intention to expand should be substantiated with some documents such as architects' estimates.

Endowments and other high premium policies have been taken on the lives of stockholder-employees.

Income has been retained that is not taxable to the corporation, but that would have been taxed if distributed to the stockholders.

Reasons for Nonpayment of Dividends

There are legitimate reasons for not paying dividends. You can avoid the penalty for nonpayment if you fit into one of several broad categories. Court decisions indicate acceptance of nonpayment of dividends under these conditions:

You are worried about possible future losses. You must prove that the anticipated hardship is realistic and that the reserve you have set up for this contingency will in fact be used should the contingency occur.

You cannot finance needed improvements otherwise, except by borrowing.

Changing laws will bring about a need for more money for financing.

Earnings available for distribution are not fairly stated, in view of current replacement costs. When prices rise sharply, replacements require much more capital than a normal accumulated reserve for depreciation.

A small personal tax would have resulted to stockholders if dividends had actually been paid.

Acquisition of the assets or the bulk of the stock of a reasonably related business. Court cases have allowed reserves for commencing unrelated businesses.

Retirement of indebtedness created in connection with the corporation's business.

Retirement of preferred stock, provided the preferred is not held by shareholders in proportion to their holdings of common stock.

Additional working capital. Some courts have been using a rule of thumb that you can accumulate sufficient earnings to cover working capital needs for one year. This has been refined in one case to allow working capital needs for a single operating cycle if that cycle is greater than one year. An operating cycle, according to the court, is the time it takes to convert cash into raw materials, raw materials into salable products, the inventory into sales and accounts receivable, and the accounts receivable into cash.

Establishment or enlargement of reserves, for example, for bad debts or replacement costs, that is for specific hazards and contingencies.

What To Do If Your Retained Earnings Will Exceed the Accumulated Earnings Credit

Here are steps that may help you avoid the penalty tax:

1. Declare the dividend payable in a later year, if you do not have the immediate funds. Several cases (not dealing directly with the accumulation penalty) suggest that such declaration creates a creditor position for a stockholder, if surplus is reduced on the books and the debt to stockholders is set up. Paying a stock dividend, however, or in any way capitalizing earnings does not eliminate the accumulated earnings. For tax purposes, the accumulated earnings are there. On the other hand, the mere fact that the corporation did capitalize earnings is not in itself evidence that it accumulated unreasonable earnings.

2. Make up a complete written plan for expansion or equipment purchase, etc., which you *fully intend to carry out*.

3. Any impairment of capital must be restored before any earnings are available for distribution to the stockholders. In this situation, you may not be taxed for unreasonable accumulation. It is essential to ascertain whether you do have any real accumulated earnings and profits which can be used for distribution to the stockholders. Often older companies find they do not have the accumulation they assume.

4. Make sure your directors' meetings fully explain the accumulation by reports and records of the discussions that led to your failure to pay dividends. Have the directors approve the creation of actual reserves required to cover the possible liability or loss for which you are providing. Then set the reserves up. Again, make sure you can prove that the reserves will go for their expressed purpose.

5. See if your stockholders really would have additional income taxes by your payment of dividends. They might not. In that case, you are not avoiding the taxes for the individual stockholders and should not be penalized if you do not pay dividends.

Consent Dividends to Avoid the Penalty

If your corporation's problem is lack of cash to pay a dividend, remember that a consent dividend can be paid. The law grants a full reduction of income, subject to the penalty for all distributions paid the stockholder or assumed by him in the form of consent distributions. By this, the stockholder agrees to accept the tax without receipt of a money or property dividend. The consent dividend can apply only to common shareholders or fully participating preferred holders. Dividends must be pro rata to all of them, but it is not necessary that all stockholders consent. Those who do not consent must get a cash dividend no later than the fifteenth day of the third month after the end of the tax year. These cash dividends must be equal in rate to the consent dividends of all those who do consent. The consents must be filed with the corporation's tax return.

When a stockholder agrees to accept the "consent income," he increases the basis of his stock by the amount of the dividend, and includes the dividend in income as if he had received it in cash. The corporation treats the consents as paid-in capital.

The stockholder is allowed the dividend exclusion of up to $100 on the consent dividend agreed to.

If the corporation's lack of cash at year-end to pay the dividend is temporary, the dividend can be paid within two and half months after the close of the year and can then be treated as if paid during the preceding year.

How the Tax Liability is Proved

The Treasury can use only facts known at the close of the tax year, in questioning the reasonableness of an accumulation. If your accumulation was reasonable in view of the company's prospects at the close of the tax year, later facts prejudicial to your accumulation cannot be shown. This does not, however, prevent the Treasury from showing later facts to prove that you had no intention of carrying out your plans with the accumulated funds.

Your case may be settled with the Treasury by negotiation. But if it is not, you may want to go to the Tax Court for adjudication. Here are the rules on how the case must be proved:

1. The Treasury has the burden of proof when it sends you notification that it intends to assess a deficiency based in whole or in part on the accumulated earnings tax. Within 60 days after getting this notification, you submit a statement showing why your business accumulated its profits, with sufficient facts to back up your reasons. If you do this, and your facts are sufficient, then, in the Tax Court, the Treasury must carry the burden of proof. If the Treasury does not send you this notification, it still has the burden of proof, even though you need not now submit at any time a statement backing up your position. (Prior notification must be sent you, before you get the actual notice of deficiency.)

2. You have the burden of proof, however, if after getting the notification, you do not submit a statement substantiating your accumulation, or if your reasons are not sufficiently supported by the facts, or if your statement is not timely filed.

Although technically you can shift the burden of proof to the Treasury by submitting the statement referred to above, many tax practitioners do not advise this procedure. You may reveal your entire case prematurely, with no guarantee that the burden will shift. The Court may be reluctant to rule until after trial on the sufficiency of your statement. But in a recent decision, the Court made a pre-trial ruling shifting the burden. A 49-page statement was acceptable as documenting the company's persistent expansion efforts. It included descriptions of negotiations and efforts to develop new products and to acquire new businesses.

Subchapter S Election May Avoid Penalty

Where a corporation makes a Subchapter S election, it is not subject to Section 531 tax during the years the election is effective. A Subchapter S election can also allow a corporation to avoid the penalty for the tax year before the year of election.

CHAPTER X

How to Qualify Redemptions and Partial Liquidations for Capital Gains

As a STOCKHOLDER, it is to your advantage to convert potential dividend income to capital gains. Two methods frequently used to accomplish this are redemptions of stock by the corporation and partial or complete liquidation of the corporation.

A redemption is the corporation's acquisition of its stock from a stockholder in exchange for cash or property. A redemption occurs whether or not the stock acquired is cancelled, retired, or held as treasury stock. A liquidation is similar to a redemption except that the corporation's distribution of its assets in exchange for its stock is followed by a termination of all or part of its business.

To curb the use of redemptions and liquidations as a means of avoiding a dividend tax on a corporate distribution of earnings, a rigid structure of rules has been developed. To qualify as a bona fide redemption or liquidation, the distribution must meet certain tests. Failure to do so may often result in the entire distribution being taxed as an ordinary dividend.

Liquidations are discussed at page 225.

When Should a Redemption be Considered?

A stockholder may decide to terminate or reduce his stock interest in his corporation. He may want to retire or enter into a new business. There may have been a serious disagreement between stockholders, or, as is often the case, a stockholder dies and his estate must liquidate part or all of his interest in order to meet his funeral, estate tax and other administrative expenses. In all of these situations, the problem is to withdraw the stockholder's interest in the company at capital gain rate.

Underlying the redemption rules is the idea that a redeeming stockholder should not be allowed to withdraw his corporation's earnings and profits at capital gain rates, unless he can show that his investment relationship to the corporation after the redemption has been significantly changed. To take an example, assume that Jones is the sole stockholder of X Co. which has earnings and profits of $100,000. He has X Co. redeem 25% of his stock, worth $50,000. After the redemption, earnings and profits are $50,000, Jones's stock holding has been reduced by 25%, but his 100% control of X Co. has remained unchanged. In such a case, the distribution would not qualify as a redemption and Jones would have a dividend of $50,000.

There are four redemption tests provided for in the law, any one of which, if met, will allow the distribution to be taxed at capital gain rates. They are: (1) redemptions which are "substantially disproportionate"; (2) redemptions which terminate the interest in the corporation of the redeeming stockholder; (3) redemptions which are "not essentially equivalent to a dividend"; and (4) redemptions to pay death taxes.

Substantially Disproportionate Redemptions

A redemption qualifying as a disproportionate redemption is treated as a sale or exchange. Thus, any gain or loss on the redemption is treated as a capital gain or loss by the stockholder. A redemption is "substantially disproportionate" if it meets the following tests which involve somewhat complicated percentage calculations:

1. Immediately after the redemption, the redeeming stockholder owns *less than* 50% of the total combined voting power of all classes of stock outstanding after the redemption.

2. Immediately after the redemption, the redeeming stockholder owns a percentage of the voting stock then outstanding that is *less than* 80% of the percentage of voting stock owned by him immediately before the redemption. For example, if Brown owned 60% of his corporation's voting stock before the redemption, he must own less than

48% (80% of 60%) of the remaining shares after the redemption.

In determining the number of shares that must be redeemed to meet the 80% test, there are two methods. The first is trial and error, which is naturally not the more desirable. As an alternative, use the following formula: $X = \dfrac{NT}{(5T - 4N)}$. Let X equal the number of shares necessary to be redeemed; T equal the total number of shares outstanding before the redemption; and N equal the number of shares owned by the redeeming shareholder before the redemption. Thus, if Brown owned 600 of 1,000 shares of voting common outstanding before the redemption, X = 231, the number of shares that must be redeemed to meet the 80% test.

The 80% rule is rigidly enforced. For that reason, in making your computations under the above formula, if you calculate X as a whole number plus a fraction of a whole number, the number redeemed should be the next whole number. For example, if X is computed as 100.3 or 100.8, the number of shares to be redeemed is 101.

3. The 80% test is applied a second time to all of the redeeming stockholder's common stock, whether voting or nonvoting. So, not only must the voting stock meet the 80% test, but also the *total* number of common shares—voting plus nonvoting.

EXAMPLE:

If Brown, in the above example, owns in addition to his 600 shares of voting common, 300 shares of nonvoting common (of 400 outstanding), he must redeem 140 of those shares in addition to the 231 shares of the voting common to meet the second 80% test:

$$T = 1{,}400 \qquad X = 371$$
$$N = 900$$

Subtracting from the 371 total, the 231 of voting common as computed above, leaves 140 of the nonvoting common to be redeemed.

It is permissible, in a redemption otherwise qualifying under the disproportionate rules, to include nonvoting preferred in any amount and receive capital gain on such preferred. In effect the nonvoting preferred "goes along for the ride." (But see the restrictions on redeeming preferred stock qualifying as "Section 306 Stock," at page 52.)

You may not attempt a disproportionate redemption where you are the sole shareholder or where a substantial number shares are owned by related persons.

In determining the percentage of stock ownership of the redeeming stockholder before and after the redemption, the constructive ownership rules are applicable. Under these rules ownership of stock is attributed from one related person to another, sometimes making it more difficult to qualify under the redemption rules.

If a redemption meets the 50% and 80% tests, but it is found to be one of a series of redemptions constituting part of a single plan, the tests will be applied against the total result, after all the redemptions have been completed.

If the redemption does not qualify under the disproportionate rules, the redemption may qualify for capital gain treatment by showing that the redemption was not "essentially equivalent to a dividend."

If your ownership is more than 62½% of the outstanding voting stock, you must be especially careful to meet the 50% rule. Meeting the 50% rule automatically covers the 80% test. But coming only within the second may leave you short of qualifying on the first. If your holdings are 62½% or less, satisfying the 80% rule qualifies you automatically under the 50% rule, since 80% of 62½% is 50%.

How the Constructive Ownership Rules Are Applied

You may own stock in a corporation either directly or indirectly. Directly owned stock is the stock which is registered in your name. Indirectly owned stock is stock registered in the name of another but which is attributed to you. A person might transfer 51% of control of a solely owned corporation to his close family members and then assert that he is no longer in control of the corporation. However the realities are clear. He and his family will with few exceptions act as a unit. Merely by changing paper ownership his tax treatment should not be altered.

1. *Family relationships.* You are considered as owning the stock owned by your spouse (except where you are legally separated under a decree of divorce or separate maintenance), your children (which includes a legally adopted child), your grandchildren and your parents.

Stock held *for* these family members by corporations, trusts or partnerships are considered as owned by that family member in proportion to the total amount of stock held by the corporation, trust or partnership. Thus, if your son is a 25% partner and his partnership owned 100 shares of stock of your corporation, your son is deemed to own 25 shares, and in turn you are deemed to own all of the 25 shares owned by your son, resulting in a double attribution of those 25 shares.

There is an important exception to the double attribution rule: Stock owned directly by reason of family ownership cannot again be attributed to a third family member. Thus if in the previous example, your son's wife owned 25 shares of stock, those 25 shares would be attributed to your son who would be deemed to own them, but they cannot be reattributed to you.

2. *Corporate ownership.* If you own 50% or more of the *value* (not the number) of the shares in a corporation, you are treated as owning any stock owned by that corporation in the proportion that the value of your stock in that corporation bears to the total value of all the outstanding stock of the corporation. For example, if A Co. owns 100 shares of B Co., and you own A Co. stock which is 75% of the total value of all the A Co. stock outstanding, you are considered as owning 75 shares of B Co. On the other hand, if you own 50% or more of the value of the shares in a corporation, the corporation is treated as owning *all* of the shares owned by you—either directly or indirectly—in any other corporation. For example, you own 50% of the value of A Co.'s outstanding stock; you also own 20 shares of B Co.; and your son owns 50 shares of B Co. A Co. is treated as owning: The 20 shares in B Co. which you own directly, and the 50 shares of B Co. which you are treated as owning through your son.

3. *Partnerships and estates.* Stock owned directly or indirectly by a partnership or estate is considered as owned *proportionately* by its partners or beneficiaries. Stock owned directly or indirectly by a partner or beneficiary of an estate is considered as owned by the partnership or estate.

4. *Trusts.* If you are a beneficiary of a trust, any stock owned by the trust is attributed to you according to your actuarial interest in the the trust. Likewise, all the stock owned by you is deemed to be owned by the trust, unless your beneficial interest in the trust is less than 5%.

In tracing your relationship to corporations, partnerships, estates and trusts, there is a limitation on double attribution similar to the limitation discussed in the family attribution rules: Stock which is considered as owned by the corporation, partnership, estate or trust is *not* considered as owned by it, if the purpose is again to attribute that stock to an individual. For example, you own 50% of A Co.; your sister (who does not fall within the list of prohibited relationships, so that you are not deemed to own her A Co. shares) owns the other 50% of A Co., and in addition she owns 100 shares of B Co. A Co. is treated as owning through your sister the B Co. stock; but that B Co. stock cannot again be attributed to you because of your 50% ownership of A Co.

5. *Option.* If you own an option to buy stock you are treated as owning that stock. An option to acquire an option, and each of a series of such options, is treated as an option to buy stock.

Where you are deemed to own stock because of a family relationship *and* because you hold an option to acquire the stock, that stock is considered as owned by you by reason of the option and not by reason of the family relationship. In other words, the option rule takes priority over the family relationship rule. The effect of this rule is illustrated in the following example: You hold an option to acquire 100 shares of A Co. Your son owns directly 100 shares of A Co. If you were deemed to own the 100 shares of A Co. stock solely by reason of your son's ownership of that stock, then that stock could not be reattributed to, for example, your daughter. But because you are deemed to own the 100 shares by reason of your option to acquire that stock, those shares *can* then be reattributed to your daughter. There is no rule against reattribution where the original attribution is by reason of an option.

The application of the constructive ownership rules to the disproportionate redemption test is illustrated in the following example:

EXAMPLE:

A Co. has 1,000 shares outstanding. You own 700; your wife owns 50; a trust of which you are the only beneficiary owns 100, and an unrelated person owns 50. In order to meet the 50% test, you must redeem at least 451 shares, since the 100 shares owned by the trust and the 50 owned by your wife are attributed to you. The 451 shares may come from the shares owned by any of the parties except the unrelated person. Likewise with the 80% rule. When using the formula on page 164, the figure for "N" includes your shares plus the share attributable to you.

Termination of a Stockholder's Interest

A redemption of your stock will receive capital gain treatment if it results in a complete termination of your entire interest in the corporation.

The constructive ownership rules (*see* above) apply to a limited extent in determining whether you have successfully terminated your interest in the corporation. The attribution rules concerning corporations, partnerships, estates and trusts continue to apply, *but they will not apply between family members* if the following conditions are met under the 10-year "look forward" rule and the 10-year "look backward" rule.

The 10-year "look forward" rule. The 10-year "look forward" rule restricts your future relationship with the corporation as follows: (1) You may not after the redemption have any interest in the corporation, such as, officer or director, except as creditor. That there is an obligation in the form of a debt does not necessarily show the individual holding it is a creditor. According to the Treasury, a creditor should have rights which are not greater or broader than necessary for the enforcement of his claim. An obligation will be viewed by the Treasury as a proprietary interest rather than a creditor interest in the following instances: The debt is subordinate to claims of general creditors, or payment of principal or interest is conditioned on corporate earnings, or payment is deferred for more than 10 years. (2) You may not acquire any interest in the corporation for a period ending ten years from the date of the redemption, except if the interest acquired is by bequest or inheritance. (3) You must file in duplicate with your tax return for the year of the redemption, an agreement to notify the District Director of any acquisition described in (2), within 30 days of such acquisition, and to retain your records and tax returns during the 10-year period which would enable the District Director to compute the amount of tax you would have owed if the redemption distribution had originally been taxed as a dividend.

The 10-year "look backward" rule. The Treasury will examine the 10-year period immediately preceding the date of the redemption to see if you have given stock to or received stock from any person listed

in the constructive ownership rules. "Person," as it is used in this con-
text, means an individual, corporation, partnership, trust or estate. If,
during the preceding 10-year period, you have received stock from
any person whose ownership of that stock—if that person owned it on
the date of the redemption distribution—would be attributed to you,
then you fail to satisfy the 10-year look backward rule and the family
attribution rules apply. Also, if, during that 10-year period, you have
given away stock to any of those persons and that stock is not also
redeemed at the same time that your stock is redeemed by the corporation, you fail to satisfy the requirements.

You may be saved however if you can show that the stock was not
given away or received by you in an attempt to avoid income taxes.
The Treasury states that the mere fact that the recipient of the stock
was in a lower tax bracket than the transferor of the stock is not in
itself proof that there was a tax avoidance motive behind the transfer.

The 10-year "look forward" and 10-year "look backward" rules are
illustrated by the following examples:

EXAMPLES:
   1. A owns 100 shares of X Co. stock. His wife, W, owns the remaining
20 shares. In 1966, A transfers 20 shares to W. Then in 1968 X Co. redeems all 40 shares of W. Unless W can show that A's transfer of the 20
shares had no tax avoidance motive, the family attribution rules will apply,
and W will be deemed to own A's 80 shares after the redemption so that her
termination will not have been complete.
   2. Assume the same facts as above, but all 80 of A's shares were redeemed by X Co. If A could not show absence of a tax avoidance motive,
then unless the 20 shares which he transferred to W were redeemed at the
same time, the family attribution rules would make him constructive owner
of W's 40 shares and A would not qualify under the termination rule.

If you do not satisfy the termination requirements because of the
application of the family attribution rules, that does not necessarily
mean that you lose capital gain treatment. You might qualify under
the "substantially disproportionate" redemption rule, or a court might
decide that the redemption distribution was not "essentially equivalent
to a dividend."

Tax planning considerations. If the look backward and look forward rules are met, one family member can have all of his stock re-

deemed, realize a capital gain, and the other family members can continue to own stock and control the corporation. Often, to take advantage of this rule, the wife should be issued stock when the corporation is formed. Later her interest can be redeemed at capital gain rates at a time when the corporate values have appreciated. This redemption can coincide with the husband's retirement. The family unit will be able to withdraw from the corporation a substantial amount of its earnings and profits at capital gain rates and the husband can continue as a stockholder and receive dividends in his post-retirement years.

Redemption "Not Essentially Equivalent to a Dividend"

This type of redemption is resorted to only when you cannot qualify under the "substantially disproportionate" rule, the termination rule or the redemption to pay death taxes rule. You should not rely on this approach to qualify the redemption for capital gain treatment. It may be necessary to go to court to win your position. The requirements here are vague. Facts the court will look for will be: (1) Has there been a substantial change in the proportionate ownership and control of the corporation as a result of the redemption? (2) Was there a corporate business purpose rather than a nonbusiness purpose of the redeeming stockholder for the redemption? (3) Has the corporation a history of dividend distributions? (4) Is there sufficient earnings and profits in the corporation to cover the distribution? (5) Did the redemption result in a pro rata distribution of earnings?

No single factor will decide a case. Needless to say, your chances improve as more of the above questions are answered in your favor.

In the following cases, the courts found that the redemptions were not "essentially equivalent to a dividend," and therefore the gain was taxable as capital gain:

1. Squier and his wife owned stock in A Co. in the percentages set out below. Schilling, an unrelated party, owned the remainder. Squier died and, according to a buy-sell agreement among the stockholders, the corporation redeemed 30% of the stock held by his estate, part of the proceeds from which was used to pay estate taxes, funeral and administrative expenses. After the redemption, the percentages held by the stockholders were as indicated below.

	Before Redemption	*After Redemption*
Squier (Estate)	51%	41%
Wife	13	16
Schilling	36	43

The portion of the redemption proceeds used to pay estate taxes and other death expenses were conceded capital gain, since the death tax provision covered it. The court found that the remainder, although it did not fit into the disproportionate redemption or complete termination rules, was not "essentially equivalent to a dividend" for the following reasons: (1) The redemption resulted in a significant reduction in control of the Squier family; (2) there was dissension between Schilling and the others prior to the redemption, which indicates that a "bail out" of earnings was not intended; (3) the corporation had a history of paying regular dividends, and (4) Schilling, after the redemption, held a substantial minority interest and received nothing from the redemption.

2. Hinrichsen owned 90% of the corporation's common stock and 77% of the 6% preferred; the remainder was owned by an employee. The corporation redeemed all the preferred and the Treasury claimed it was "essentially equivalent to a dividend." The court disagreed. It said: (1) There was a valid corporate purpose in the redemption: profits were declining and the corporation wanted to float a bank loan which would charge less than the 6% payable on the preferred. (2) If the corporation declared a dividend on the common stock, Hinrichsen would have gotten 90% of it; here he got only 77% of the total proceeds from the redemption distribution. Therefore there was no pro rata distribution of earnings. (3) Over the years, the corporation's record showed annual dividend payments averaging 47% of before-tax profits. (4) Of the $103 paid on each redeemed share, $100 represented paid-in capital and $3 represented the required redemption premium.

3. Lewis incorporated his solely-owned Ford auto dealership. As his sons came of age, he introduced them to active management of the business, in conformity with Ford policy to keep young people in management. When Lewis reached age 69 and retired, he had allowed his sons to acquire 51% of the stock and to control most of the manage-

ment of the business. He then surrendered all active interest in the business and his monthly salary, retaining only the titular positions of vice-president and director. The corporation, which had never in its history paid dividends, redeemed his stock over a five-year period. The Treasury argued that the amounts received by Lewis in redemption of his stock were dividends, pointing to the fact that the corporation had accumulated profits during the redemption period of between $42,000 and $86,000. A court held Lewis was entitled to capital gain on his redemption gain. A substantial and meaningful change in control occurred. Lewis's interest was terminated, having surrendered all his stock and all direct and indirect participation in business management. Furthermore, his age and Ford policy of keeping young people at the heads of the dealerships were evidence of business purpose.

Combining Redemptions With the Sale of a Business

Stock redemptions may be used when you are selling your business. Assume that your prospective purchaser is not willing or cannot afford to buy the entire corporation. You may do the following: Sell to him an amount of stock equal in value to the operating assets plus any surplus he is interested in acquiring. Immediately afterwards the corporation redeems the remainder of your stock. The courts and the Treasury agree that where this procedure is followed, the redemption of your remaining stock will be given capital gain treatment under the complete redemption rules. In this way, the buyer acquires only that part of the business in which he is interested, and you will realize capital gain on the full value of the corporation.

Your tax position will be strengthened if the stock sale precedes the redemption. Where it does not precede the redemption, it will be difficult to show that the redemption was a complete termination. If such an oversight is made, however, and the Treasury refuses to accept the redemption as in complete termination of your interest, it may still be possible to qualify the redemption for capital gain treatment under the "substantially disproportionate" tests (page 163) or the "not essentially equivalent to a dividend" test (page 170).

Redemption of Stock to Pay Death Taxes

When the owner of a substantial interest in a closely held corporation dies, it is often necessary to liquidate part or all of his stock holdings to raise the cash needed to pay estate and inheritance taxes, funeral expenses, and other estate expenses. If the redemption of that stock by the corporation does not fit into the requirements of the disproportionate-redemption or complete-redemption rules, the estate would receive a taxable dividend.

To overcome this potential dividend problem, the tax law permits redemptions that meet certain tests to avoid dividend treatment. Since the basis of the stock redeemed will usually be its fair market value at the date of the death of the stockholder, his estate or heirs redeeming the stock will usually have no gain on the redemption; the stock will likely be redeemed at the same value as its basis.

Although this type of redemption is referred to as a redemption to pay death taxes and administration and funeral expenses, the proceeds from the redemption need not be applied for those uses. The total of the death taxes, administration and funeral expenses is merely a measure of the maximum amount that can be received under these special redemption provisions.

Rules for redemptions to pay death taxes. The redemption of the stock (preferred as well as common stock) will be treated as a capital gain transaction rather than a dividend distribution if these tests are met:

1. The value of the stock has been included in the decedent's gross estate. This can include stock of which the decedent made a gift before his death but which is included in his estate because it was determined that the gift was made "in contemplation of death."

2. The value of the stock of a single corporation included in the estate has to be *more than* either (a) 35% of the value of the gross estate, or (b) 50% of the value of the taxable estate. If 75% or more in value of all the outstanding stock of two or more corporations is included in the gross estate, the value of those stocks can be added together in order to meet the 35% or 50% requirement.

3. The distribution in redemption must be made after death of the stockholder and within three years and 90 days after the due date of

the estate tax return. If a petition is filed in the Tax Court concerning the estate tax of the estate, the redemption deadline is extended to 60 days after the Tax Court decision becomes final. If the corporation has insufficient funds to make the redemptions within the required period, it can issue notes in payment within the required period and thus meet the requirements of the special redemption.

4. The total amount of the redemption cannot exceed the total of (a) estate, inheritance, legacy and succession taxes (including interest), and (b) funeral and administration expenses allowable as deductions to the estate.

Whose stock can be redeemed? Usually the estate's stock is redeemed. But any other stockholder's stock can qualify if that stock was included in the gross estate. Thus if stock is specifically left to a legatee, his stock can qualify for redemption. If a donee received stock from the decedent before the decedent died in a transaction which was later held to be a gift in contemplation of death (which makes that stock subject to Federal estate tax in the decedent's estate), the donee's stock is also eligible for redemption. Stock accepted by a legatee in satisfaction of a monetary bequest does not qualify for redemption.

As previously noted, the total of the death taxes and funeral expenses is a ceiling for the amount of the redemption distribution that can qualify under this special rule. A legatee may have some of his stock redeemed and get the advantages of this special redemption rule without paying death taxes or expenses. However, once the ceiling is reached additional redemptions will not qualify for the special redemption treatment. In most cases, this does not present a problem because all the beneficiaries of the estate and the executor agree that the estate is to redeem its stock first and thereby get the money needed to meet the necessary expenses. But if there are hostile legatees who have stock that qualifies for the special redemption, the estate should act promptly to get its stock redeemed or at least make certain that the corporation does not redeem any other stock first.

If the stock that is included in the gross estate is exchanged for new stock in a taxfree recapitalization or other exchange that requires the owner of the new stock to take as his basis the basis of the old stock, a later redemption of the new stock (within the required period after the due date of the estate tax return) also qualifies for this special redemption.

EXAMPLES:

1. X's gross estate is $1,500,000, his taxable estate is $750,000. Included in the gross estate are stocks of:

	Value Included in Gross Estate	Percentage of Ownership Represented by This Stock
Corporation A	$300,000	50
Corporation B	300,000	100
Corporation C	250,000	100

No one of the three stocks meets the 35% or the 50% requirement. But the stock of B and C can be totaled because more than 75% of each corporation's stock is included in the gross estate. The A stock cannot because less than 75% is in the gross estate. The total of B and C stock ($550,000) meets both the 35% test ($525,000) and the 50% test ($375,000). Either or both stocks can be redeemed, up to the allowed total of death taxes, funeral, and administrative expenses, under the special redemption rules.

2. The gross estate of Y is $1,000,000; the taxable estate, $700,000. The total of the death taxes and funeral and administration expenses is $275,000. Included in Y's gross estate is stock of three corporation, having the following values for estate tax purposes:

Corporation A	
Common stock	$100,000
Preferred stock	100,000
Corporation B	
Common stock	50,000
Preferred stock	350,000
Corporation C	
Common stock	200,000

The stock of A and C included in the gross estate is all the stock outstanding of each corporation. The combined value of stock in these two corporations (and they can be combined because more than 75% of each company's stock is in the estate) is more than $350,000 (35% of the gross estate or 50% of the taxable estate). Also, the stock of Corporation B included in the gross estate has a value of more than $350,000. Thus, a redemption of any of the stock listed above (in any combination) that does not exceed the $275,000 death tax and funeral and administrative expenses total meets the rules of the special redemption.

Redemption By Means of a Sale of Stock to Related Company

Selling stock you own in one corporation to another corporation you control rather than having it redeemed may not give you capital gain. Sale to a controlled corporation is treated as if the stock was redeemed by that corporation. A sale to a subsidiary is treated as if the subsidiary transferred the redemption price to the parent and it redeemed the stock. In these transactions, your sale is viewed as a redemption. Whether you have capital gain or ordinary income as a result depends on where you fit under the various redemption rules discussed above.

For the corporation receiving the stock from you, that stock is a contribution to its capital. The corporation's basis for that stock is the basis that stock had in your hands.

It does not always follow that you will have to include as ordinary income the proceeds from the sale of stock to a "sister" corporation. Check the redemption rules that do give capital gain. If they apply, you can use them.

A sister corporation is one controlled by the same person or persons who control the corporation, the stock of which is being sold to the sister corporation. In this instance, control means ownership of either 50% of the total voting power or 50% of the total value of all the shares of a corporation. If you control a corporation which, in turn, controls (by the 50% ownership tests) another corporation, you are treated as controlling the other corporation as well.

The constructive ownership rules at page 165 have to be used in computing the percentage of stock you own. You have constructive ownership of stock held by a corporation in which you own less than 50% of the stock. Regardless of how much you own, you are the constructive owner of that proportion of the corporation's holdings in other stock.

If you have a redemption under these rules, you compute whether you have a disproportionate redemption or a redemption of an entire stock holding based on your holdings in the corporation *which issued the stock* you are selling or exchanging, *not* in the sister corporation that is acquiring it.

If your receipt from the sister corporation in payment for your stock is taxed as a dividend, it is the earnings and profits of the sister corporation that measure the amount of dividend income you have.

Tax Consequences of a Partial Liquidation

On a partial liquidation of a business, a stockholder has capital gain or loss measured by the difference between the fair market value of what he receives and the basis for his stock surrendered in the partial liquidation.

A partial liquidation occurs when a separate and distinct business activity of the corporation is sold off or the assets of that activity are distributed to the stockholders.

The tests for a partial liquidation are: (1) The corporation adopts a plan of partial liquidation. (2) The distribution in partial liquidation is made within the year in which the plan is adopted or within the following tax year. (3) The distribution is attributable to the corporation's ceasing to conduct a trade or business in which it has been actively engaged during the five-year period immediately before the distribution. This distribution can take the form either of a distribution of the assets of the trade or business in which it has ceased to engage or a distribution of an amount not exceeding the net proceeds from the sale of the business assets of that discontinued trade or business. (4) Immediately after the distribution in partial liquidation, the company is actively engaged in a trade or business which has been in existence for the five-year period ending on the date of the distribution.

In either (3) or (4), you cannot include within the five-year period a business acquired during that period in a transaction where no gain was recognized in whole or in part. In other words, if during the five-year period, your corporation acquired another business in a taxfree reorganization, liquidating either the acquired business or your old business (and retaining the acquired business) does not meet the five-year test even though the acquired business (taking into account the time of its existence before your corporation acquired it) has been in existence for five years. On the other hand, assume your corporation paid cash for a business in a taxable transaction. Assume further that the purchased business, taking into account its existence before and after your corporation acquired it, has at least a five-year life. A liquidation of that business (or a liquidation of your old business and retention of the acquired business) qualifies under the five-year requirement.

A corporation can also include in the liquidating distribution that portion of its working capital reasonably attributable to the terminated business activity and no longer needed in the operation of the remaining business. Presumably, if the corporation distributes assets of the terminated business instead of selling first and distributing proceeds, it can also include the allocable working capital.

A partial liquidation requires a redemption of part of the corporation's outstanding stock. The law is specific in allowing that the redemption need not be pro rata among the stockholders. Thus, a distribution in partial liquidation can be made to some stockholders and not to others, or in greater proportion to some than to others. But the Treasury is clear that the amount of stock redeemed in a partial liquidation is not necessarily determined by how many shares were turned in. The stock redeemed must be the same proportion of the outstanding shares as the fair market value of the distribution bears to the fair market value of the corporation's net assets before the distribution. So, if the distribution in partial liquidation is equal to 25% of the fair market value of the net assets of the corporation before the distribution, there is deemed to be a redemption of 25% of the outstanding stock regardless of the number of shares that are actually turned in to the corporation.

EXAMPLE:

You own all 100 shares of the Brown Corporation, each share having a basis of $1,000. The corporation has owned three pieces of rental property for more than five years. The properties have the following fair market values: A—$50,000, B—$50,000 and C—$100,000. Pursuant to a plan of partial liquidation, you turn in 50 shares, receiving back property A in a liquidating distribution. Using the above formula, the Treasury will treat the transaction as if you turned in only 25 shares, so that you must report a gain of $25,000 ($50,000 fair market value of the property distributed less $25,000 basis of 25 shares of stock). The remaining $75,000 of basis is allocated pro rata among your remaining 50 shares.

CHAPTER XI

Planning Reorganizations of Your Corporate Business

THIS CHAPTER COVERS various transactions grouped together by the tax law as reorganizations. You will generally have to deal with the reorganization law when—

You are planning a merger or consolidation with another company,

You are going to recapitalize your company,

You are planning to buy another company, paying the purchase price in the form of your company's stock,

You are going to sell your company to another firm in exchange for its stock,

You are planning to merge your parent company into one of its subsidiaries or a subsidiary into the parent, or

You are going to split up your present company into two or more companies.

At first glance, these transactions seem too diverse to have anything in common. But in fact they have common features. In all, the original business form has changed. For example, a local store is now part of a large supermarket chain; two former competitors may be combined; a former lumber and pulp company is now two separate companies, a lumber company and a pulp and paper company. But despite the change of form, substantially all of the original capital remains in active business use.

The major tax question in all the transactions is: Are the transfers that took place, such as, the exchange of stock for stock or stock for assets, taxfree? Generally they are, provided some of the original investors remain part of the rearranged organization and there was a good business reason for the reorganization.

The tax that would have resulted, but for the special taxfree rules, is postponed to a time when the stockholder or other investor in the reorganized groups sells his interest.

The chance that the reorganization will fail to meet the taxfree rules is increased when the transfer begins to resemble a sale. For example, compare these two situations: (1) Jones, the sole proprietor of A Corporation, exchanges his stock in A for stock in B Corporation plus cash equal to 5% of the total value of A. (2) Smith, the sole stockholder of C Corporation, exchanges his stock in C for stock in D Corporation, plus cash equal to 95% of the total value of C. It is clear in (1) that Jones' interest in his business continues substantially after the reorganization. The 5% cash can therefore be separated out and the transaction made taxable to that extent. But in situation (2), Smith's interest in Corporation C is almost eliminated. 95% of the value of that corporation was bought from him. The mere fact that he continued a 5% interest in the form of stock does not detract from the fact that the transaction was really a sale. This is not the kind of transaction that comes within the taxfree reorganization rules.

A taxfree reorganization must conform to the rules explained below under a plan of reorganization. At times a court will infer a plan, even though there was none actually written.

Reorganizations Recognized by the Tax Law

The tax law recognizes six types of reorganizations, each designed to fit a different business purpose:

1. A merger or consolidation that conforms with the law of your State. For tax purposes, such a reorganization is called an (A) reorganization. A merger results where one corporation absorbs another. It makes no difference whether the corporation being absorbed is the smaller or the larger. In a consolidation, two or more corporations combine into a new corporate entity.

You may be interested in arranging an (A) reorganization if you receive an offer from a large, publicly-held corporation to acquire your business. On the other hand, you may wish to join with a competitor or a supplier to form an entirely new corporation combining your production, management and marketing facilities. This too could be worked out in the form of an (A) reorganization.

2. An acquisition by one corporation of the controlling interest of another corporation in what is called a (B) reorganization. The only consideration that may be paid by the acquiring corporation is its voting stock. If part payment is in cash or other property, the transaction is subject to tax. The acquisition of a subsidiary is a typical example of a (B) reorganization.

3. An acquisition by one corporation of "substantially all" of the assets of another corporation in exchange for voting stock is what is called a (C) reorganization. Here, the exchange is between the two corporations. In a (B) reorganization, the transaction is between the acquiring corporation and the stockholders of the acquiring company. The end result of both transactions is often the same. However, when a (B) reorganization is used (stock for stock), the acquiring corporation becomes the owner not only of the acquired company's assets but also of any hidden liabilities (for example, tax liabilities for past years not uncovered until a Treasury audit in subsequent years). This fact should be considered when choosing between a (B) and a (C) reorganization.

4. A division of a corporation into two or more corporations in what is called a (D) reorganization. It is used to split off part of a business into a new controlled corporation. The transfer of assets is made by your corporation which receives back the stock of the new corporation. For this type of reorganization to be allowed by the Treasury, the plan of reorganization must provide that the stock of the controlled corporation must be promptly distributed to your corporation's stockholders.

5. A recapitalization is called an (E) reorganization. It differs from the other reorganizations in that only one corporation is involved, the original corporation. It is used when the existing capital structure is insufficient to meet present business purposes. You may seek to recapitalize, for example, when your creditors agree to exchange their bonds for a participating equity in your corporation, or nonvoting preferred stockholders with dividend arrearages demand a voting interest in the corporation.

6. Class (F) reorganization. This is the least frequently used reor-

ganization and is available only when the purpose of the reorganization is to change the identity, form or State or organization of your corporation. If any other purpose is also sought in the transaction, this category is not available. Thus, for example, you would use the (F) reorganization when you wish to reincorporate in a different State because of more favorable tax rates.

Now that the basic differences among the six classes of reorganizations have been described, each will be discussed in more detail.

Class (A) Reorganizations

A merger or consolidation to qualify as a taxfree reorganization must meet the conditions set up by the law of the State in which the transaction occurs. But this is by no means the sole requirement. There are three other tests that must be met before a merger or consolidation qualifying under State law is allowed taxfree reorganization treatment. They are: (1) The continuity of interest test, (2) the business purpose test, and (3) the continuity of business enterprise test. The three tests apply to all classes or reorganizations but are most important in the Class (A) type, since the others have the three requirements built into them, as will be explained in the following paragraphs.

The Continuity of Interest Test

In a sale, the selling party is completely divorced from his former interest in the property sold. He takes his cash and disappears. But in a true reorganization, the "selling" stockholder receives back an ownership interest in the acquiring corporation. His interest in the assets of his old corporation is continued into the acquiring corporation. He has an equity interest in his former corporate assets. This remains true even though the former stockholder was a local hardware store owner and received a minority interest of shares in a large mail order house as a result of the merger of the two companies. It makes no difference that prior to the merger he owned 100% of the assets of his hardware store, and afterwards, his two shares amounted to a small minority ownership interest. The continuity of interest test is satisfied.

Thus, for a merger to be accepted as a reorganization for tax law purposes, the stockholders of the acquired corporation must continue to have an equity interest in the absorbing corporation. It is not neces-

sary that all former stockholders receive stock from the acquiring corporation, but if too many receive securities, such as notes and bonds or
other boot, the continuity of interest requirement will not be satisfied.

But what constitutes an equity interest? Clearly, voting common
stock qualifies. An ownership interest is evidenced by a right to vote
on corporate policy and a right of participation in profit distributions.
Both voting and nonvoting preferred stock also meet the continuity of
interest requirement.

Generally, the receipt of notes and bonds by the seller of assets does
not give him a proprietary interest in the debtor corporation.

If in consideration for the transfer of assets by the acquired corporation, the acquiring corporation assumed liabilities (such as creditor
obligations) of the acquired corporation, the continuity of interest test
is not passed.

If stock purchase warrants are the only consideration given by the
acquiring corporation, the continuity of interest test is probably not
met.

If the acquiring corporation is a controlled subsidiary, it meets the
continuity of interest test by paying for the acquired assets with common stock of its parent corporation.

Continuity of proprietary interest. Although a proprietary interest
is required, it is not necessary that the participation of the acquired
corporation's stockholder extend to the management of the acquiring
corporation. That is, voting stock is not necessary. However, how
much of the total consideration paid by the acquiring corporation
must consist of stock? For example, if Corporation B is acquiring the
assets of Corporation A and the price set by the parties is $1 million,
will the transaction be a taxfree reorganization if the price is paid in
the form of: (1) $900,000 common stock and $100,000 cash; (2)
$500,000 common stock and $500,000 cash; (3) $100,000 common
stock and $900,000 cash? Court decisions make it clear that (1)
would certainly satisfy the continuity of interest requirement; and it is
just as clear that (3) will not. Some place in the middle is the cutoff
line beyond which the consideration is too diluted with cash to constitute a continuing ownership interest. One court said 56% common
stock (or other proprietary consideration) meets the requirement. The
Treasury has this rule of thumb: If stockholders of Corporation A (the

acquired corporation) receive stock of Corporation B equal to at least 50% of the total value of the A stock, the continuity of interest requirement is satisfied and an advance ruling will be issued by the Treasury. This 50% is measured in the aggregate, not on a stock-holder-by-stockholder basis. Therefore, some stockholders can be bought out entirely for cash without spoiling the reorganization.

How to treat consideration other than stock. Any property other than stock or its equivalent meeting the proprietary interest test is either cash or "boot." "Boot" may consist of securities of the acquiring corporation, stock in other corporations, inventory of the acquiring corporation or investment property held by the acquiring corporation.

Cash and "boot" are not received taxfree, even though the transaction qualifies as a reorganization. Whether they are taxed as a dividend or as capital gain depends on how the transaction is set up. If there are accumulated earnings and profits in the acquired corporation, then the Treasury will probably maintain that any distribution of cash or "boot" in a reorganization is a dividend to the extent of the stockholder's prorata share of accumulated earnings and profits of his corporation.

In any event, there is no tax, capital gain or dividend, if there is no gain on the exchange. This is illustrated by the following examples.

EXAMPLES:

1. Corporation A, owned by Jones, had a value of $100,000 when Corporation B proposed a statutory merger in which Corporation B would absorb Corporation A. Jones agreed to the merger. Jones's stock in A has a basis of $50,000. The consideration paid by Corporation B consists of B nonvoting preferred stock, fair market value $75,000 and cash of $25,000. Jones's gain is $50,000 ($100,000 less $50,000, basis of stock surrendered). Of this $50,000, $25,000 (the cash) is taxed.

2. Same facts, except Jones's stock basis is $100,000. Since there is no gain on the exchange, Jones pays no tax on the cash.

3. Same facts, but Jones's stock basis is $125,000. The $25,000 loss is not allowed, since losses are never recognized on reorganizations whether or not cash or "boot" is received. But the loss is reflected in the basis of the new stock of Corporation B received by Jones.

The Business Purpose Test

It is not difficult to tailor a transaction to meet the requirements of the reorganization rules. To prevent the use of the reorganization rules to avoid tax, the courts have developed the business purpose rule. If the purpose of the "reorganization" was to avoid taxes and nothing more, then the court will disregard the fact that the exchange meets the terms of the law and tax the transaction.

EXAMPLES:

1. A Corporation, with $100,000 of earnings and profits, owned stock in Corporation B, worth $50,000. Gregory, the sole stockholder of Corporation A, wanted the B stock in order to sell it on the market. He knew that if his corporation distributed it to him outright, the full $50,000 value of those shares would be taxed to him as a dividend. To avoid this tax, he had A Corporation set up Corporation C. In exchange for the C stock, A Corporation gave it the B stock as its sole asset. As part of this reorganization, A Corporation distributed the C stock to Gregory. Since the receipt of the C stock was part of a reorganization, Gregory paid no tax on its receipt. The next day, Gregory liquidated C Corporation, receiving the B stock as a liquidation distribution. On the liquidation, he paid capital gain tax on the difference between the value of the B stock and his basis in the C stock. Since the basis of the B stock in his hands was its fair market value, he had no further taxable gain when he sold the stock. Thus, Gregory appeared to avoid a dividend tax on the receipt of the B stock, using a reorganization involving the temporary Corporation C. However, the Treasury challenged the transaction which became the subject of the famous *Gregory* case before the U. S. Supreme Court. The Court said that the only reason for the elaborate plan of reorganization was to avoid a dividend tax on the direct distribution of the B stock by Corporation A. There was no business purpose other than tax avoidance in setting up the intermediate corporation. Therefore, the Treasury had the right to treat the reorganization as if it had never occurred and tax Gregory with a dividend.

2. Smith was sole stockholder of W Corporation which owned a 25% interest in a tract of land. Cole owned a 25% interest in two adjoining tracts. Both parties wanted to transfer all of the land to U Corporation (a publicly-traded corporation) in exchange for U's voting convertible preferred stock. Before the actual deal went through, but after it had already been set up, Cole and W Corporation transferred their interests in the land to a newly-formed corporation, M. In exchange, they received all the M stock in a taxfree incorporation. Shortly afterwards, they transferred all of their M stock to U in exchange for the voting convertible preferred stock of U. Then, U liquidated M to get the land. Smith and Cole argued that their exchange of M stock for U voting stock qualified as a (B) reorganization. Technically, they met the requirements of a (B) reorganization. Nevertheless, the Tax Court refused to recognize it as a taxfree reorganization, and Cole and Smith were forced to pick up a taxable gain of over $200,000. The Tax Court held that although the transaction falls literally within the requirements of a (B) reorganization, the formation of M corporation served no business purpose. So, the substance of the transaction was simply

an exchange by Cole and Smith of land for U stock. And that, of course, is a taxable transaction.

Examples of valid business purposes are: Eliminating dissenting stockholders, diversifying production, increasing efficiency by acquiring a supplier as subsidiary, eliminating a loss division.

Does the business purpose have to belong to the corporation or to its stockholder? The Treasury prefers that the business purpose belong to the corporation. But in a closely-held corporation, a valid business purpose on the part of its shareholder is sufficient. An example of a stockholder business purpose is the acquisition of a new corporation to increase the value of his stock in the acquiring corporation for future bargaining with prospective purchasers of the acquiring corporation.

The Continuity of Business Enterprise Test

All this test requires is that there be a continuity of *some* business activity by the acquiring corporation. It is not necessary that the same kind of business be continued after the reorganization. Thus, for example, if a steel mill merges into a bicycle manufacturing corporation, the test is met even if the acquiring corporation thereafter makes only baby carriages. It is not met if the acquiring corporation ceases all operations and begins to liquidate. In that case, the "reorganization" will be taxed as a sale.

Advantage of the Class (A) Reorganization

An advantage in using the (A) reorganization is that there is no restriction on the kind of consideration to be used. For example, only stock may be used in a (B) or (C) reorganization. In an (A) reorganization, boot may pass without destroying the major taxfree nature of the exchanges. However, this very fact has led some businessmen to use too much cash and securities instead of sufficient amounts of stock thereby violating the continuity of interest test and failing to qualify as a taxfree reorganization.

The acquiring corporation may transfer the assets of the acquired corporation to its subsidiary as part of the reorganization.

The Class (B) Reorganization

A (B) reorganization is the acquisition by one corporation of control of another corporation *solely* for voting stock of the acquiring corporation (or a corporation in control of the acquiring corporation).

This type of exchange is practical where the company being acquired has few stockholders since the exchange of stock is made directly between the stockholders of the corporation being acquired and the acquiring company.

Solely for voting stock. This requirement is strictly enforced by the Treasury and courts. If Corporation A is acquiring control of Corporation B by acquiring the stock from its stockholders, the only form of consideration that Corporation A may use in exchange for the B stock is its own or its controlling parent's voting stock. A *combination* of voting stock of the acquiring corporation and its parent is not allowed. The use of cash or any other nonvoting stock property will invalidate the reorganization and cause it, in most cases, to be treated as a sale. There may be a minor exception where cash is used to pay for fractional shares. Thus, if the exchange is to be on a three-to-one basis (three shares of B stock for one of A stock), the taxfree nature of the reorganization may be upheld if A corporation pays cash for an odd share of B stock; but it may have to go to court to win this right. Although one appeals court has allowed the payment for fractional shares, the Treasury so far has not changed its position that *any* cash will invalidate a (B) reorganization.

The acquiring corporation may not pay debts or claims against the acquired corporation or its stockholders, but the Treasury has said that the acquiring corporation may pay any stock transfer taxes on the acquired stock without running afoul of the "solely" rule. The Treasury generally does not allow the acquiring corporation to pay attorneys' fees, etc., of the acquired corporation's stockholders.

What is voting stock? Voting common and voting preferred both qualify as voting stock. If the right to vote is conditional, for example, only if there are dividend arrearages, it is not voting stock. The right to vote must be absolute. The voting stock may be Treasury stock. Stock warrants are not voting stock.

Although nothing but voting stock may be received in a (B) reorganization, contingent rights to additional stock may be given. Often, this approach is used when it is difficult to determine what price should be paid by the acquiring corporation in the form of voting stock for the acquired corporation. So, a contingent price is arrived at, based on future profits. Then, if and as the future profits are realized, additional voting stock is paid to the stockholders who had turned in their stock in the acquired corporation.

EXAMPLE:

The Treasury ruled that the requirements of a (B) reorganization were met in this case: Corporation X, which already owned 50% of the stock of Corporation S, acquired the other 50% for a good business purpose from Corporation Y for 40,000 shares of X voting stock and a nonassignable right to receive up to an additional 20,000 shares of X voting stock, depending on the future earnings of S. The only property that Y could receive was additional voting stock of X. In these circumstances, the requirement of a (B) reorganization that the exchange be solely for voting stock, said the Treasury, was met. If, in addition, the rights Y received were assignable, if Y could get the dividends on those additional 20,000 shares before it acquired the stock, or if Y could get anything else, then the requirements of a (B) reorganization would *not* have been met.

The use of a contingent stock payment arrangement amounts to a deferred payment for the stock of the acquired corporation. If the payments take more than a year, part of the gain on the transaction will be treated as interest received under the "imputed interest" provisions of the tax law. However, though imputed interest can arise when stock is distributed in the later years, nevertheless the transaction may still qualify as a (B) reorganization.

What is control? In order to be in control, the acquiring corporation must acquire at least 80% of all voting stock *and* at least 80% of all other classes of stock. Thus, if Corporation X, whose stock is being acquired by Corporation Y, has outstanding 100 shares of voting common, 50 shares of voting preferred and 100 shares of nonvoting preferred, Corporation Y must, to qualify under the (B) rules, acquire a total of 120 of the voting common and preferred, and 80 of the nonvoting preferred.

Control may be acquired in one transaction or in a series of transactions over a relatively short period of time such as 12 months. But what if the acquiring corporation had made a recent cash purchase of stock of the company being acquired. Does that spoil the (B) reorganization? A prior cash purchase is disregarded by the Treasury if it is not part of the plan of reorganization. There is no definite Treasury rule fixing how long before the reorganization the cash purchase must have been made to be unrelated. But Treasury regulations imply that a 16-month interval would be acceptable.

The acquired corporation can redeem the stock of dissenting stockholders prior to the reorganization without that redeemed stock being included in the 80% control test. If the acquiring corporation cannot or refuses to give more of its stock for the preferred stock, or if the preferred stockholders dissent from the reorganization plan, the acquired corporation can give call notice, which eliminates the entire class from the transaction. The redeemed stockholders will generally get capital gain treatment on gain from the redemption.

Possibility of recognizing a loss. The rule that gains or losses are not recognized in a reorganization may be at times undesirable. If a loss is incurred in the exchange, you may wish to avoid the (B) reorganization rules and recognize the loss. One possibility is to include a significant amount of cash in the purchase price. This would violate the first rule of the (B) reorganization and probably invalidate it.

Note: If your corporation already has control of another corporation (at least 80% stock ownership), any further acquisition of the controlled corporation's stock solely in exchange for your corporation's stock qualifies as a (B) reorganization.

There are basis problems in (B) reorganizations. For example, the value of the net assets of Corporation X is $100,000. X's basis for the assets is $70,000. The X stockholders' bases for their stock in X is only $20,000. They accept an offer from Corporation Y which wants to acquire X Corporation as a subsidiary. An exchange is made of all the X shares for 1,000 shares of Y voting stock, fair market value $100,-000, in a transaction qualifying as a (B) reorganization. Under the reorganization basis rules, Y's basis for its newly acquired X stock is the same as it was in the hands of the X stockholders, namely, $20,000. Y is not satisfied with this result; it gave its own stock worth $100,000 for stock having such a low basis. Y can solve its problem by liquidating its new subsidiary, thereby getting a $70,000 basis for the X assets. Alternatively, it could use a (C) reorganization to acquire just the X assets (as opposed to the X stock), and wind up with a $70,000 basis for the X assets.

The Class (C) Reorganization—"Practical Merger"

A (C) reorganization is commonly referred to as a "practical merger" because of its similarity to an (A) reorganization. In both cases, the acquiring corporation emerges as owner of the acquired corporation's assets. However, where there are dissenting stockholders, the (C) form is more practical since, under most State statutes, a two-third majority is needed to enable a corporation to sell its assets. In addition, the stockholders of the acquiring corporation do not, under most States' law, have to vote on the acquisition.

A (B) reorganization "becomes" a (C) reorganization if the acquiring corporation liquidates its new subsidiary after acquiring 80% control. If liquidation is part of the plan of acquisition, the reorganization is considered by the Treasury and courts as a (C) reorganization. In such a case, the reorganization may fail if the prior acquisition of stock by the acquiring corporation had occurred over a long period of time instead of at once.

If eventual liquidation of the newly acquired subsidiary is planned, the Class (C) offers a more flexible method; the acquiring corporation is not limited to exchanging voting stock as in a Class (B) reorganization. A (C) reorganization may be preferable to a (B) reorganization for another reason. As only 80% of the stock of the acquired corporation must be acquired, a dissident minority of the acquired corporation can be eliminated by using the (C) reorganization and acquiring only the assets. Moreover, the danger of acquiring hidden liabilities is eliminated in a (C) reorganization.

There are two main requirements for a Class (C) reorganization: (1) Substantially all of the properties of one corporation (the acquired corporation) must be acquired in the reorganization and (2) the consideration given by the acquiring corporation must be *solely* its voting stock (with important exceptions discussed below).

What is "substantially all assets"? In an asset acquisition, the acquiring corporation would like to select the assets that would benefit it and reject those which are of no use in its business and which are tied to mortgages and other liabilities. This business motive is not easily carried out, because in a reorganization there must be a continuity of interest. In a (C) reorganization this is expressed in the rule that "substantially all of the properties" of the acquired corporation must be transferred to the acquirer. This is to ensure that the interests of the acquired corporation's stockholders are substantially continued in the acquiring corporation.

Suppose the acquired corporation wishes to retain 25% of its gross assets to pay debts and other liabilities not assumed by the acquirer. Is the remaining 75% substantially all of the assets? This would be considered by the Treasury substantially all and would not invalidate the reorganization, if the 25% were retained to pay off claims, but not if the 25% constitutes operating assets which are retained to continue the old business. In the latter case, the transfer of 75% looks too much like a sale.

Need for advance ruling. There is another problem connected with the "substantially all" requirement. The implementation of a reorganization is almost wholly dependent on securing an advance ruling from the Treasury. Without one, even though you feel practically certain that your plan will qualify as a taxfree reorganization, the cost of going to court and the amount of taxes usually involved makes the possibility of failure a formidable impediment.

The Treasury has a standard for what constitutes "substantially all of the properties" of the acquired corporation. An advance ruling approving the reorganization will be issued if the assets transferred by the acquired corporation represent at least 90% of the fair market value of the net assets, and at least 70% of the fair market value of the gross assets owned by the acquired corporation immediately before the transfer.

The acquiring corporation must give solely its voting preferred or common as consideration for the assets acquired. However, there are two exceptions to this rule: (1) The acquiring corporation may assume liabilities of the acquired corporation; (2) The acquiring corporation may pay cash or notes if the total cash, notes and any assumed liabilities do not exceed 20% of the total consideration.

Assuming liabilities. If the acquired corporation were forced to pay all of its liabilities, it often would have to retain some operating assets needed by the acquiring corporation. This fact would seriously hamper the reorganization. Recognizing this, the law allows the acquiring corporation in a (C) reorganization to assume any liabilities attached to the acquired assets. This concession does not violate the "solely for voting stock" requirement. However, where the amount of assumed liabilities approaches the 50% mark, the Treasury might consider the voting stock too diluted to properly satisfy the continuity of interest rule and attempt to treat the transaction as a sale. Note that an assumption of liabilities may in some cases be considered as "boot" if there was no business purpose for the assumption or it was merely a device to avoid taxes.

Liabilities arising out of the reorganization are treated differently from liabilities existing prior to the reorganization. So where the acquiring corporation assumed liabilities of the acquired corporation such as attorneys' fees that accrued out of the reorganization, the Treasury treats their value as the payment of cash by the acquiring corporation, which may disqualify the reorganization entirely, if the "cash" payment does not fall within the following exception.

20% exception. The "solely for voting stock" requirement can be bypassed to the extent of 20% of the total fair market value of all the properties of the acquired corporation. Put another way, if 80% of the total fair market value of *all* the properties is acquired for voting stock, then the remaining 20% may consist of cash or other property, such as notes, inventory of the acquiring corporation, etc. It is possible, under this exception, to buy out dissenting stockholders of the acquired corporation, or to provide cash for the acquired corporation for any other use it may have.

WARNING. If you use the 20% exception, any assumed liabilities of the acquired corporation are, *for this purpose alone,* regarded as cash.

EXAMPLE:

X Corporation, having properties with a total fair market value of $500,000, is being acquired by Z Corporation in a (C) reorganization. Z Corporation pays $50,000 cash, $350,000 fair market value of its voting stock, and assumes $100,000 of B's liabilities. The reorganization fails. Note that if no cash was paid but the assumed liabilities amounted to $150,000, the reorganization would qualify. The reason is that the 20% exception would not then come into play.

The 20% exception has still another drawback. It is usually difficult at the time of the reorganization to determine exactly the total fair market value of the assets, or else the Treasury on audit may deflate fair market value. For this reason, it is good policy to stay far short of the 20% mark as insurance against a subsequent downward adjustment.

If the above problems cannot be solved, you may be forced to abandon a (C) reorganization for an (A) reorganization.

Voting stock of the acquiring corporation's controlling parent may be used to make the acquisition. A combination of parent and subsidiary stock is not acceptable.

"Creeping control," as discussed in the section dealing with (B) reorganizations, is a gradual acquisition of the acquired corporation's stock and is an acceptable method of accumulating the requisite 80% control. However, the same form of "creeping control" may not be acceptable in a (C) reorganization, especially if you intend to liquidate the acquired corporation immediately following the reorganization.

(If your corporation owns at least 80% of the voting stock and 80% of all other classes of stock of the other corporation, you may bypass the reorganization route entirely and use the special parent-subsidiary liquidation described at page 59).

The Class (D) Reorganization

A (D) reorganization can be used when: (1) You want to split two lines of your present business into separate corporations, (2) you and your associates want to go your separate ways, each taking with him a part of the business, or (3) you want to move part or all of your business to a new locale. All these business rearrangements can be carried out without tax consequences by using a (D) reorganization.

(D) reorganizations fall into two general patterns:

1. One corporation, P, creates another corporation, S, transferring all or substantially all its assets to S in exchange for stock, securities and other property of S. P then liquidates, according to the original plan of the reorganization. The two features of this form of (D) reorganization are the requirements that all or substantially all of the assets be transferred to S, and that the plan of reorganization requires that what is received by P from S be distributed to the stockholders and

security holders of P. If there is no distribution, the transaction is treated as a taxfree incorporation. This form will be used when you need to relocate your corporation or to combine a relocation and a recapitalization. A recapitalization can be carried out by having the newly created S issue stocks and securities and after the exchange P distribute them to its stock and security holders in a new arrangement.

2. Corporation P has two active businesses and wants to separate them, perhaps for reasons of economic efficiency or perhaps to give Smith and Jones, the 50% stockholders in P, sole ownership of one business each. They draw up a plan of reorganization providing for a spin-off, split-off, or split-up. These divisions are discussed in detail beginning at page 206. Generally, they have the effect of splitting a single corporation into two or more smaller ones.

When "boot" such as cash is distributed in a (D) reorganization and the stockholder has realized gain, the distribution may be taxed. Whether the gain is taxable as capital gain or as a dividend depends on the circumstances surrounding the distribution. For example, if the gain reflects accrued dividends on preferred, then there is a taxable dividend to the extent of the stockholders' ratable share of earnings and profits. But no more than the recognized gain is taxable as a dividend. A dividend may also be present if there is a history of no dividend payments for many years.

In a (D) reorganization, if the assumed liabilities to which the property is subject exceed their basis, gain is recognized by the transferor corporation.

The Class (E) Reorganization

The following transactions are examples of Class (E) reorganizations, or recapitalizations:

1. A corporation with $100,000 par value of bonds outstanding, instead of paying them off in cash, discharges them by issuing preferred stock to the bondholders.

2. Stockholders surrender to a corporation for cancellation 25% of its preferred stock in exchange for no par value common stock.

3. A corporation issues preferred stock, previously authorized but unissued, for outstanding common stock.

4. An exchange is made of a corporation's outstanding preferred stock having certain priorities with reference to the amount and time of payment of dividends and the distribution of the corporate assets upon liquidation, for a new issue of the corporation's common stock having no such right.

5. An exchange is made of a corporation's outstanding preferred stock with dividend arrearages for a similar amount of that corporation's preferred stock plus an amount of stock (preferred or common) equal to the amount of arrearages. However if the purpose of transaction is solely to wipe out the dividend arrearages, then the stock that was issued in place of the arrearages is included in gross income.

What is a recapitalization? The first distinction between a recapitalization and the other forms of reorganization is that in a recapitalization only one corporation is involved. The corporate shell remains intact, the business operations, assets, management and name remain intact; all that is affected is the ownership structure. Any of the following exchanges would qualify as a recapitalization exchange: (1) Preferred stock for common stock; (2) Common stock for preferred stock; (3) Common stock for common stock; (4) Preferred stock for preferred stock; (5) Preferred stock for bonds; (6) Common stock for bonds; (7) Common or preferred stock for debentures, long-term notes or other securities; (8) Bonds for bonds.

Bonds for stock. This form of recapitalization has created some difficulties for businessmen, especially where the corporation involved is a family corporation or solely-owned, and has a large earnings and profits account.

The continuity of interest requirement in a recapitalization is not stringent as with other reorganizations. Some of the stockholders may receive cash or bonds in exchange for their stock without adversely affecting the reorganization.

The Class (F) Reorganization

This type of reorganization has a very limited use and overlaps with the Class (D) reorganization. Where the only purpose of the reorganization is to change the identity, form or place of organization of the corporation, the (F) reorganization is available. There are no restrictions as to how the reorganization is carried out.

Liquidation and Reincorporation May Be Treated As a Reorganization

You may want to avoid the taxfree reorganization rules. Assume Corporation A has cash in excess of what it needs. An outright distribution to stockholders would result in a dividend. Instead the stockholders liquidate the corporation, pay a capital gain tax on the excess of what they receive (cash and other assets) over the basis of their stock, and then reincorporate taxfree the noncash assets and continue the business. Here, the Treasury may argue that the proper way to look at what was done is to telescope the liquidation and reincorporation into one step. It was as though Corporation A had set up a new corporation, transferred its operating assets to it in exchange for its stock, but retaining the cash and distributing as a liquidation distribution the cash plus the stock of the new corporation. In other words, it was a Class (D) reorganization. As a Class (D) reorganization, the distribution of cash amounted to "boot" and is treated as a *dividend*. The Treasury is saying that the stockholders cannot, by using a circuitous route, convert ordinary income into capital gain.

The Treasury's position has been upset where the stockholders of Corporation A own less than 80% of the new corporation because of new stockholders brought into the reincorporation. In that case, the courts say, the old stockholders do not have the "control" required by the Class (D) reorganization, and there is no reorganization. An alternative Treasury argument in this case is that the transaction resulted merely in a change in corporate identity, that it is therefore an (F) reorganization, which has no such percentage of ownership requirement. The courts have rejected this Treasury argument.

The courts will, however, recognize a (D) reorganization even where there is no stock distribution to stockholders of Corporation A where such a distribution is meaningless.

EXAMPLE:

Brown owns all the stock of Corporations A and B. He causes A to sell most of its assets to B for cash. Then he liquidates A claiming capital gain on the cash. Brown argues there is no Class (D) reorganization because he received no distribution of the B stock. But in that case the court said no distribution was necessary; Brown already owned all the outstanding B stock. The result was a (D) reorganization and a dividend to Brown.

Suppose Corporation A above sells only some of its assets to B. Another requirement of the (D) reorganization is that "substantially all" of the assets be transferred to the other corporation. If the assets retained by A Corporation are not needed to carry on its business (for example, cash, unrelated investments) but all the assets required to carry on the business are transferred, then, say the courts, the "substantially all" requirement is met. The result would be the same even where the value of the retained assets exceeds the value of the assets transferred.

Parties to the Reorganization

Not only must there be a reorganization, but the taxfree exchanges must involve "parties to the reorganization." If stock or other property is received by a person not a "party to the reorganization" the transaction may be partially taxable. The Treasury considers the following to be "parties to a reorganization:"

Both corporations in a transaction qualifying as a reorganization where one corporation acquires stock or properties of another corporation.

A corporation which transfers all or part of the assets acquired to a controlled corporation remains a party to the reorganization.

A corporation controlling an acquiring corporation when the controlling corporation's stock is used by the acquiring corporation to get the properties.

Both Corporations A and B where A is merged into B.

All three corporations where A and B are consolidated into Corporation C.

Both corporations where a corporation transfers substantially all of its assets to another corporation in exchange for voting stock.

All three corporations where Corporation A transfers substantially all of its assets to Corporation B in exchange for C voting stock, C being in control of B.

Both corporations where Corporation A transfers all or part of its assets to Corporation B in exchange for stock and securities of B but only if (1) immediately after the transfer, A or one or more of its stockholders is in control of B and (2) the B stock and securities are distributed or transferred to the A stockholders.

Corporations A and B but not Corporation C where A acquires B stock from C in exchange solely for A voting stock if the B stock does not make up substantially all the assets of C, C is not in control of A immediately after the acquisition, and A is in control of B immediately after acquisition.

Figuring Gain or Loss on Reorganization

In a reorganization, property of one corporation is transferred to another in exchange for stock and securities. Or the stock of one corporation is acquired by another and the acquiring corporation can then continue to run the acquired corporation as a subsidiary or liquidate it. In each of these transactions, the stockholders of the acquired company usually turn in their stock in that company for stock or securities of the acquiring company. Sometimes, that can be a direct exchange, where the *stockholders* of Corporation A, for example, turn in their A stock to Corporation B in exchange for Corporation B stock. More often, however, the transaction will be between Corporation A and Corporation B, with Corporation A turning over its properties to Corporation B in exchange for Corporation B's stock and then, in the liquidation of Corporation A, the Corporation A stockholders will turn in their A stock for B stock. A taxfree reorganization may be permissible even if A does not liquidate. It merely holds on to the B stock and perhaps becomes an investment company. Thus, whenever there is a reorganization, the tax consequences at both the corporate level and at the stockholder level must be reviewed.

Exchanges on the stockholder level. In a reorganization, no gain or loss is recognized for tax purposes when, pursuant to the plan of reorganization (1) the stockholder turns in stock or securities of one of the corporations that is a party to the reorganization and (2) he gets back *solely* stock or securities of that same corporation or any other corporation that is a party to the reorganization.

Where the stockholder gets other property (cash, for example) in addition to stock or securities, that other property is called "boot." The value of the boot is taxable to him to the extent it does not exceed his gain. It is important to keep in mind that to the extent the distributing company has earnings and profits, the taxable boot received may be treated as distribution of a dividend and taxed as ordinary income. If the taxable boot exceeds earnings and profits, the excess is then taxable as a capital gain.

In a (B) reorganization, however, the stockholder must get *solely* voting stock and nothing else. Otherwise, the entire transaction becomes taxable.

Exchange on the corporate level. If boot is received by a corporation, it will be taxable to the corporation to the extent the boot does not exceed the gain. However, if the boot is distributed to the stockholders in carrying out the provisions of the plan of reorganization, the corporation is not taxable on the boot.

Where a stockholder receives securities other than stock (bonds, for example), the exchange is taxfree only if he gives up securities having at least a face value equal to the face value of the securities he receives. Otherwise, the difference between the higher face value of the securities he receives and the lower face value (or zero, where he gives up none) of the securities he gives up is treated as "boot."

The tax treatment of the corporate parties to a reorganization is illustrated by the following examples:

EXAMPLES:

1. Corporation A, pursuant to a reorganization plan, transfers its voting stock, worth $400,000, and cash of $50,000 to Corporation B, in exchange for all of the assets of Corporation B, worth $400,000. Corporation A also assumes liabilities on the B property of $50,000. Corporation A has a loss of $50,000 determined as follows:

Property received		$400,000
Less: Stock	$400,000	
Cash	50,000	450,000
Loss		($ 50,000)

The loss is not deductible by Corporation A, but is reflected in the basis of the acquired assets in A's hands.

Corporation B has a gain of $100,000 determined as follows:

Voting stock	$400,000
Cash	50,000
Assumed liabilities	50,000
Total amount received	$500,000
Less: Assets transferred	400,000
Gain	$100,000

Corporation B will pay tax on the $50,000 cash *unless* pursuant to the plan of reorganization, it distributes the cash to its stockholders who may have to pay tax on the cash distribution.

2. Assume the same facts as in (1), except that Corporation B's plan of reorganization calls for its liquidation with a distribution of all the A stock and cash to Smith, B Corporation's sole stockholder. Assume also that Smith's basis for his B stock is $350,000. Smith's gain on the liquidation of B is calculated as follows:

Amount received in liquidation—	
A voting stock	$400,000
Cash	50,000
	$450,000
Less: Smith's basis for B stock	350,000
Gain	$100,000

If *only* voting stock of A had been distributed to Smith in liquidation of B, there would be no tax to Smith regardless of how much gain he had realized. But where the distribution includes "boot" as well as A stock, Smith is taxed on the "boot" to the extent of his gain. Since here Smith's gain ($100,000 as calculated above) exceeded the amount of "boot" received ($50,000 cash), all of the boot is taxed. If, for example, his gain had been only $25,000, then only $25,000 of the "boot" would be taxed. If the basis for his B stock exceeded what he received in the liquidation, so there is a loss, he cannot deduct the loss.

3. C Corp., under a plan of recapitalization issues $500,000 of voting common and preferred stock in exchange for the surrender and cancellation of common stock having a basis to C stockholders of $300,000. None of the $200,000 gain is taxed to the stockholders, since stock was exchanged for stock.

If bonds are received as well as stock, the bonds may be treated as "boot."

If you turn in stock and receive only securities (notes or bonds), the entire amount received will be taxed as a dividend to the extent of earnings and profits, unless the exchange qualifies as a redemption in which case you pay a capital gain on your gain from the exchange.

Figuring Basis for a Transferor Corporation

The "transferor corporation" in an (A) reorganization is the corporation absorbed in the merger or consolidation. In a (B) reorganization, it is the corporation being acquired as a subsidiary. In a (C) reorganization, it is the corporation, all or substantially all of whose assets are being acquired. In a (D) reorganization, it is the parent corporation which is exchanging its assets for stock of the subsidiary. In an (F) reorganization, where there are two corporations involved in the change, it is the originally existing corporation which will ultimately be dissolved.

Stock or securities received by a transferor in exchange for its property receives a substituted basis. This means that the basis for the received stock or securities is the basis of the transferred property given up by the transferor corporation. This basis is increased by gain taxed to the transferor. It is decreased by fair market value of "boot" received, the amount of money received, and any loss on the exchange that was recognized by the transferor.

The computation of basis by the transferor corporation is not important when it is liquidated as part of the reorganization plan. However, in a (C) reorganization where a liquidation is not required, the computation may be necessary.

Figuring Basis for a Transferee Corporation

A transferee corporation in an (A) reorganization is the surviving corporation in a merger or consolidation. In a (B) reorganization, it is the parent corporation acquiring the subsidiary solely for its voting stock. In a (C) reorganization, it is the corporation acquiring the assets of the transferor, solely for its voting stock. In a (D) reorganization, it is the controlled subsidiary corporation to which the assets are being transferred. In an (F) reorganization, where there are two corporations involved in the change, it is the successor corporation.

The transferee corporation generally takes a "carryover" basis equal to the basis of the property in the hands of the transferor. This basis may be increased by any gain taxable to the transferor on the transfer. Since a transferor recognizes gain only if it did not distribute boot received to its stockholders, if the boot is distributed under a plan of reorganization, the transferee corporation cannot step up the basis. There is no step-up in basis for gain taxable to the stockholders of the transferor.

Figuring Basis for Stockholders of Transferor Corporations

The basis of stock or security received by stockholders is the basis of stock or securities given up on the liquidation. This basis is increased by gain taxed to the stock or security holder, and the amount that was treated as a dividend. The basis is decreased by fair market value of any other property and money received and any loss on the liquidation distribution that was recognized to the stock or security holder.

Basis is allocated to fair market value when several classes of stock or securities are received in the exchange.

EXAMPLES:

1. Jones was the sole stockholder of Corporation B. Corporation A acquired all the assets of Corporation B in a Class (C) reorganization. In exchange, Corporation B received the following: 100 shares of A stock, valued at $400,000, $80,000 cash, and A Corporation inventory valued at $10,000. Under the plan of reorganization, B was liquidated, distributing all of the stock, cash and inventory to Jones in exchange for his B stock, having a basis of $350,000. Jones' *realized* gain is $140,000. But only the cash and inventory ($90,000) are taxable. His basis for the A stock is calculated as follows:

Basis of B stock surrendered		$350,000
Decreased by boot—		
Inventory	$10,000	
Cash	80,000	90,000
		$260,000
Increased by—		
Taxed gain (up to amount of boot)		90,000
Basis for A stock		$350,000

The basis for the inventory is its fair market value, or $10,000.

2. Assume the same facts, except that Jones' basis for the B stock is $450,000. His realized gain is now $40,000. His basis for the A stock is calculated as follows:

Basis of B stock surrendered		$450,000
Decreased by—		
Inventory	$10,000	
Cash	80,000	90,000
		$360,000
Increased by—		
Taxed gain		40,000
Basis for A stock		$400,000

In this example, the $50,000 of gain that went untaxed shows up in Jones' new basis. If Jones now sells his newly acquired A stock (presumably for

$490,000, the fair market value of the assets of the former Corporation B), he would be taxed on that $50,000. If he never sells the stock, but holds on to it until his death, and the value of the transferred assets remains constant (or appreciates), the basis for the A stock $490,000 fair market value at date of death, and the gain has escaped tax forever.

Carryover of Tax Attributes in a Corporate Reorganization

When one corporation acquires another, what happens to the acquired corporation's loss carryovers, accounting methods, depreciation accounts, etc.? Do they disappear, or does the acquiring corporation continue them in its own corporate shell? The tax law specifically provides which types of acquisitions will enable the acquiring corporation to "inherit" these attributes; and also which attributes may be inherited. The following types of acquisitions qualify the acquiring corporation as an heir to the tax attributes (which in turn are listed below):

1. Liquidation by a parent of its subsidiary (except where the stock of the subsidiary was acquired within two years of the liquidation);

2. An (A) reorganization;

3. A (C) reorganization;

4. A (D) reorganization, but only if: (a) the acquiring corporation acquires "substantially all" the transferor's assets, and (b) the stock, securities, and other properties received by the transferor—in addition to other properties formerly owned by the transferor—are distributed according to the plan of reorganization;

5. An (F) reorganization.

The (B) reorganization is not included since only the stock is acquired and the controlled corporation remains alive. If it is later liquidated, it is treated as a (C) reorganization. The (E) reorganization is not included because only one corporation is involved in a recapitalization.

Which attributes are carried over? Following is a list of the tax attributes allowed to be carried over into the acquiring corporation, when the acquisition qualifies within one of the five categories described above.

Net operating loss carryovers
Earnings and profits
Capital loss carryovers
Method of accounting

Inventories

Method of computing depreciation allowance

Amortization of bond discount or premium

Treatment of certain expenses deferred by the election of distributor or transferor corporation

Contributions to pension plans, employees' annuity plans, and stock bonus and profit-sharing plans

Recovery of bad debts, prior taxes, or delinquency amounts

Involuntary conversions

Dividend carryover to personal holding company

Indebtedness of certain personal holding companies

Certain obligations of distributor or transferor corporation

Deficiency dividend of personal holding company

Percentage depletion on extraction of ores or minerals from the waste or residue of prior mining

Charitable contributions in excess of prior years' limitations

Carryover of unused pension trust deductions in certain cases

Pre-1954 adjustments resulting from change in method of accounting

Certain items with respect to successor life insurance companies

The investment credit

The availability of net operating loss carryovers are subject to the limitations described at page 67.

Dividing an Existing Business

There are advantages in creating two or more companies out of an existing organization. Taxes may be reduced when income is spread among two or more corporations or partners. You benefit this way if you can:

1. Decrease taxes by dividing the income among several corporations. Where corporate earnings are high, a tax saving results if at least one of the new corporations earned less than $25,000. At this point the corporate tax rate jumps from 22% to 48%. But also check the multiple corporation rules at page 118.

2. Extract cash or other assets from the corporation. Is all the property in one corporation? Then the liquidation may be costly. If the

property had been spread among several corporations, then only one might have to be liquidated. You could liquidate one corporation, the one with the most cash and least goodwill.

3. Sell part of the corporate assets. Sale by the corporation of part of its properties and distribution of proceeds results in double taxes unless you can qualify for a special type of partial liquidation (see pages 177, 240). Having the property divided among several corporations can avoid this. You might just sell the stock in one corporation or you could liquidate the corporation and then sell the property, or, you might have the corporation sell and liquidate within 12 months. Whichever way is used you are taxed once and at capital gains rates. It is very important to avoid a split-up of corporations just before you are ready to sell part of the assets. The transaction might be regarded by the Treasury as being a sham.

4. The losses of one company may be offset against profits of another by filing a consolidated return after the division. But you might get an equal advantage, without consolidating, through the carryback of operating losses. You get this if you are willing to wait for future years to absorb present losses.

5. You may split up a corporation and have a partnership or proprietorship take over part of the business. This has been approved in some cases, although done to reduce taxes. The Treasury may attempt to attribute the income of the partnership or proprietorship to the corporation. However, if you can show a legitimate division of the business into separate operations, the courts say the division will be recognized.

Creation of Subsidiaries and Related Corporations

An existing corporation can create a subsidiary taxfree by transferring property to it in return for all of its stock. This is the same type of taxfree exchange as is used where a sole proprietor or partnership incorporates.

Another way of creating a new entity is for the stockholders of an existing corporation to set up a new corporation independently, using funds that are *not* in the existing corporation. This is possible, and sometimes preferable, where you do not need any of the original corporation's property in the new corporation. In creating a subsidiary of an existing corporation by transferring property to it from the original corporation, or by indirectly transferring property through the stockholders, your new corporation might lose its $25,000 exemption from surtax and $100,000 allowable accumulation of surplus (see page 156), if you cannot disprove that a major purpose in setting up the new corporation was to gain the $25,000 exemption and the $100,000 surplus credit. But you may have to pay an additional 6% tax on each corporation's first $25,000 of income under the multiple corporation rules.

Spin-Offs, Split-Offs, and Split-Ups

Dividing a corporate business can be done in these three ways:

1. *Spin-off*. Your corporation transfers property to another corporation and distributes the new corporation's stock to your stockholders.

2. *Split-off*. This is the same as a spin-off except that the stockholders turn in part of their stock in your corporation in exchange for the new stock.

3. *Split-up*. You transfer your property to two or more new corporations. The stock in the new corporations is transferred to your stockholders in exchange for the stock in your corporation, and your original corporation probably goes out of business.

These divisions can be taxfree to your stockholders if you follow these rules:

1. At the time you distribute the stock of the other corporation, you must have at least 80% of that company's stock. Also, you must distribute all your holdings in that company, including securities other than stock. You may distribute at least 80% of the stock in the other company and retain the rest of the stock and any amount of other securities. But then you have to show that you did not retain any of that extra stock or securities to avoid income taxes.

2. Your transaction was not principally intended as a method of distributing your profits or the other corporation's profits. An agreement before the distribution for the stockholders to sell the stock distributed to them will be considered by the Treasury as evidence that the transaction was a profit-distributing device. If there is no agreement, but after the transaction stockholders did sell stock distributed to them, the sale will not be considered as proving that the purpose of

the distribution was to distribute corporate profits to them at capital gain rates. But the Treasury says that, although it does not prove the case, such sale is evidence that a profit-distributing motive was present when the transaction took place.

3. Your corporation and the other corporation must be engaged in the active conduct of a trade or business immediately after the distribution. If your corporation had only stock immediately before the distribution, then only the company whose stock is distributed has to meet the active trade or business requirement. This trade or business must have been carried on for a five-year period before the distribution. The business activity need not have been carried on by the distributing or controlled corporation for the entire five-year period. A predecessor carrying on that business counts in figuring the five-year period. But the predecessor's business had to be acquired in a wholly taxfree transaction.

In addition to the three requirements listed above, the Treasury insists that you must show good business purpose for the transaction in order for it to be taxfree. The same requirements of business purpose in reorganizations are to be applied here. In general, the Treasury insists there be a continuity of interest in the divided business by those who had an interest in the business before division.

Active Business Requirement in Spin-Offs, Split-Offs, and Split-Ups

The Treasury had insisted that to effect a taxfree spin-off, split-off, or split-up, the existing corporation had to have two or more distinguishable businesses. Then, it could spin-off or split-off one business into another corporation, or it could put each of the businesses in a new corporation and undergo a split-up. Of course, each of the identifiable businesses had to meet the five-year rule. This Treasury position has been rejected by the courts. The courts said that if a corporation had a *single* business that met the five-year rule, it could spin-off (or split-off or split-up) part of that business to a new corporation. After the spin-off, if the old corporation and the new corporation carried on that business (that is, each carried on the complete business), the taxfree spin-off (or split-off or split-up) rules were met.

The Treasury has announced that it will follow these cases and has abandoned its earlier two-business requirement.

Treatment of Stockholder or Security Holder in Spin-Off, Split-Off, or Split-Up

In a permissible spin-off, a stockholder can receive taxfree the stock of the spun-off company. He need not give up stock in the controlling company, although if he does, it would not change the taxfree nature of the transaction. The corporations may go through some form of reorganization as well. That, however, is not necessary to get the taxfree division of the business.

A security holder (bondholder or holder of any other security but stock) may receive stock in the spun-off corporation without giving up any securities and the transaction would be taxfree. But if he receives securities, he has to give up securities of at least an equal face value to avoid tax. Otherwise, the excess of the face value of the securities he received over the securities he gives up is treated as "boot" and taxable. Similarly, if no securities are given up but securities are received (by either a stockholder or a security holder), the full face amount of the securities is treated as "boot."

"Boot" is property other than that allowed to be distributed taxfree in these types of business divisions. "Boot" includes cash and stock or securities of corporations not included in the spin-off, split-off, or split-up. It also includes the average of the principal value of securities (other than stock) distributed in excess of the principal value of securities (other than stock) turned in by the security holder.

Receiving "boot" does not necessarily make the whole transaction taxable. Only the "boot" is taxed. And if the total gain in a split-off (where the stockholder surrenders part of his original stock) is less than the "boot," then only the gain is taxed. Gain is the difference between the higher value of all he receives in the distribution (stock, securities, and "boot") over the basis of what the stockholder gives up. This gain is taxed as a capital gain, unless it is a distribution that has the effect of a dividend. But the taxed amount cannot be more than the "boot." If he gives up nothing in return for the distribution, as in a spin-off, "boot" received is treated as a corporate distribution and, if paid out of earnings and profits, is an ordinary dividend. If not a dividend, the distribution of "boot" reduces the basis of his stock. If the "boot" is more than his basis, the difference is taxed as capital gain.

Non Prorata Distributions in Spin-Offs, Split-Offs, and Split-Ups

In taxfree divisions of a business, the distribution of the stock or securities to the stockholders or security holders need not be in proportion to their holdings.

EXAMPLE:

A and B own all the stock of Corporation X, a corporation actively engaged in two businesses. A and B want to split up, each taking one business. One way to do that taxfree is to transfer one of the businesses to a new corporation in exchange for all of its stock. X then distributes all of the new corporation's stock to A in exchange for all of A's X stock. After the transaction, A owns all the stock of the new corporation and B owns all the outstanding stock of X.

Variations of non prorata distributions can be used to get other desired results. In the above example, the parties may have wanted both to remain stockholders in the new corporation (but in different proportions to their present stockholding in X) and B to become the sole owner of X. This could be accomplished with a non prorata distribution:

EXAMPLE:

70% of the new corporation stock is given to A in exchange for all of his X stock. 30% of the new corporation stock is given to B and he is not required to give up any of his X stock.

Non prorata distributions also apply where there is an existing subsidiary and the corporate divisions described above (or variations of them) are desired.

The Treasury says that the non prorata taxfree arrangements do not apply where the transaction amounts to an exchange between stockholders of stock or securities in two corporations. Thus, the taxfree rules would not apply in this case:

EXAMPLE:

C and D each own 50% of the stock in Corporation M and 50% of the stock in Corporation N. C and D then transfer all their stock to Corporation P, a new corporation they form, each getting 50% of the P stock. P then distributes all the M stock to C and all the N stock to D.

CHAPTER XII

Selling or Liquidating a Business

YOUR METHOD of doing business as a proprietor, partner, or corporation directly affects the type of assets you sell and the tax consequences of the sale. The following introductory pointers illustrate this statement.

If you are selling as a proprietor, the law considers that you are selling separate assets of the business. Some assets give capital gain or loss, others ordinary income or loss. This individual breakdown is required regardless of the fact that the business is being sold for a lump sum.

If you are selling as a partner, you can sell your individual partnership interest or if the entire partnership is selling out, the partnership can sell individual assets, the proceeds of which may be distributed to you, or individual assets may be distributed to you for your eventual disposal.

If you are selling a corporate business, you can sell your stock or the corporation can sell its individual assets. In the sale of a corporate business, double taxation must be avoided. If you can sell stock, there is no problem of double taxation. But often a stock sale cannot be negotiated; the buyer insists on buying only assets, so the corporation has to make the sale. If the corporation is dissolved, it will liquidate, distributing all of its assets to you as a stockholder. Normally, a sale at a gain by the corporation produces a tax to the corporation; and a subsequent liquidation of the corporation will usually produce another taxable gain. This may be avoided however if certain rules are followed by the use of the special 12-month liquidation (see page 227).

Sale of a Sole Proprietorship

The sale of a sole proprietorship is treated as the sale of separate assets rather than of a going concern as one unit. There are three classes of assets: (1) Inventories, (2) the physical plant, (whether owned outright or leased) and the equipment required in the business (office furniture, factory machines, delivery trucks), and (3) intangible assets such as goodwill, patents, and secret processes.

Profits realized on inventory are treated as ordinary income. Land and physical business equipment can produce capital gain or ordinary loss (these are called Section 1231 assets; see below). However, part of the gain can also be ordinary income to the extent there is depreciation recapture involved (see page 245). Gains from sales of intangibles are usually capital gains.

The following property, frequently described as "Section 1231 assets," are considered property used in a trade or business:

Depreciable property such as buildings, machinery, and other equipment held for more than six months.

Land (including growing crops and water rights underlying farm land) held for more than six months.

Timber, coal or domestic iron ore subject to special capital gain treatment.

An unharvested crop on farm lands, if the crop and land are sold, exchanged or involuntarily converted at the same time and to the same person and the land has been held for more than six months. (Such property is not included here if you retain an option to reacquire the land.)

Dairy, breeding, or draft animals (but not poultry) held for at least 12 months.

Sales and involuntary conversions of the above types of property are subject to a special rule that allows profits to be taxed as capital gain (except for profits on equipment and real estate allocated to depreciation); losses to be deducted as ordinary losses. The exact tax result depends on the net profit and loss realized for sales of such property made during the tax year. The net result of all such sales determines the tax treatment of each individual sale. To find that result, you add together all losses and gains (except gains allocated to depreciation according to the rules on pages 245 to 253) from:

Sales of such assets held for more than six months (12 months for dairy, breeding and draft animals).

The involuntary conversion of such assets held for more than six months (12 months for dairy, breeding and draft animals). But in this calculation, do not include casualty and theft losses incurred on uninsured business or investment property held for more than six months. The uninsured losses are fully deductible and are not included with the sales of the above types of property.

The involuntary conversion of any capital assets (including personal assets held for more than six months.)

A net loss is fully deductible by reporting all of the above sales as ordinary asset transactions. A net gain is taxed as a long-term capital gain by reporting all of the above sales as capital asset transactions.

EXAMPLES:

1. You realize these gains and losses:

	Gain	Loss
Gain on sale of rental property held six years (no part attributed to rapid depreciation)	$5,000	
Loss on sale of business equipment held four years		3,000
	$5,000	($3,000)
Net gain subject to long-term capital gain treatment	$2,000	

As your gain exceeded losses, each gain and loss (including the personal casualty loss) is treated as from a sale of a capital asset held more than six months.

2. Assume the same facts as above but that your gain on the sale of rental property was $2,500. Since the gain does not exceed the losses and a net loss of $500 was realized, all of the transactions are treated as dispositions of noncapital assets. The gain on the rental property is not reported as

a long-term capital gain. It, along with the sale of equipment, is reported on Schedule D in the part entitled "Property other than capital assets."

Under the above aggregation rule, gain realized on the installment sale of business or income-producing property held for more than six months may be long-term gain one year and ordinary gain another year. Actual treatment in each year depends on the net result of all sales including payments received in that year.

Allocation of Sales Price

You allocate the selling price among all the assets sold in the same proportion that the fair market value of each asset bears to the total fair market value of all the assets. After allocating the selling price, you compute gain or loss. You make separate computations of the gain or loss for each asset sold, and then report it according to the classification of each asset.

Because the seller's tax objectives conflict with the buyer's in making allocations of the sale price, the allocations made in the contract will usually be recognized for tax purposes, on the assumption that the allocations were subject to bargaining.

High value allocation. Goodwill and land are items to which the seller would like to allocate considerable value because gain on these assets is capital gain. The buyer wants a low value because these items are not depreciable.

The sale of a going business usually involves the transfer of goodwill. The buyer usually demands as an incident to the transfer of the goodwill that the seller give a covenant not to compete. This is an enforceable agreement that for a stated period and within a stated geographical area the seller will not operate in competition with his buyer. Under the tax law, the part of the purchase price allocated to goodwill is capital gain, whereas the part allocated to the noncompete covenant is ordinary income. The seller therefore is interested in allocating more to the goodwill than to the covenant. His argument is that the covenant not to compete is a means of protecting the goodwill and thus part of the goodwill. But the buyer's interest is directly opposed: The cost of the covenant is amortizable over the covenant's life, whereas the cost of the goodwill is a capital investment and not recoverable until the business is later sold by the buyer. How the purchase price is allocated between these two items usually depends on the strength of the parties' bargaining positions.

Intermediate value allocation. On the sale of depreciable assets, the seller may realize a mixed gain, part capital gain and part ordinary income. The amount of ordinary income depends on whether there is depreciation recapture. And that, in turn, depends on (1) whether the property is real estate or depreciable business equipment; (2) how much depreciation was deducted on that property and when, and (3) the total gain on the sale.

Depreciation on business equipment deducted after 1961 is subject to recapture. Depreciation of real estate deducted after 1963 is subject in part to recapture, where a rapid depreciation method had been used.

Where the recaptured depreciation (taxed as ordinary income) on a particular asset or group of assets is not large, the seller may want to allocate as much as possible of the purchase price to them; gain in excess of the recaptured amount is capital gain. The buyer may be willing to agree to the allocation since higher cost gives him a higher depreciation base. Where there is substantial depreciation recapture, the seller will want to allocate as little as possible to the particular depreciable asset.

On the other hand, a conflict between buyer and seller may arise when both equipment and real estate are being sold. All depreciation taken after 1961 on personalty is subject to depreciation recapture. But, in most cases, only part of rapid depreciation taken after 1963 is subject to recapture in the case of real estate. If no rapid depreciation has been claimed on the realty, there is no recapture. Where real estate and personalty is being sold, the seller may then want to allocate more to the real estate and less to the equipment. The buyer's interest may be in conflict. If the investment credit is available, he will want a greater allocation to the equipment.

Low value allocations. A seller wants to minimize the amount allocated to inventory to reduce ordinary income.

Normally, the sale of accounts receivable will not give rise to any gain because the seller's basis is equal to the amounts receivable. However, where the seller has a bad debt reserve on the books, he should seek to allocate to the accounts receivable their net value, that is, after reducing them by the bad debt reserve. Otherwise, where the accounts are sold for their full face amount, while the seller does not realize any gain on their sale, the bad debt reserve, now no longer needed since the accounts receivable were sold, becomes taxable as ordinary income.

When a cash basis business (usually a service organization) is sold, the amount received for accounts receivable is ordinary income, since at the time the accounts arose, no income was reported to give them a basis.

Sale of a Partnership

All or part of a partnership business may be sold by all or some of the partners.

If the partnership sells all of its assets and then distributes the proceeds to the partners, it reports the sale on the partnership information return as a sale of the assets. Gain or loss is computed on each of the items or class of items. (For an allocation guide, see the previous pages.) Each partner, on his individual return, reports his proportionate share of the partnership profit or loss on the sale.

Instead of selling a partnership interest, a partner may receive distributions from the partnership. He can usually recover his entire partnership basis before he has any taxable gain.

Another form of distribution from a partnership occurs when the partner retires or dies and the partnership buys out his interest. The distribution may be part capital gain and part ordinary income. Details of these rules are discussed below.

Sale of a Partnership Interest

Instead of selling the partnership assets, the partners may sell their partnership interests. One or more partners may each sell his interest. Where 50% or more of the partnership interests change hands, the partnership terminates.

The sale of a partnership interest can give rise to both capital gain or loss and ordinary income or loss. The taxable year of the partnership for the selling partner ends when he sells his entire partnership interest. For example, you are a 25% partner in a partnership that uses the calendar year as its taxable year. You, too, are a calendar year tax-payer. On June 30, you sell your entire partnership interest. As far as you are concerned, the current partnership taxable year ended on June 30. You report your distributive share of income or loss (and all the other distributive items, such as your share of partnership charitable contributions, capital gains, etc., as of June 30). Any income or losses incurred thereafter by the partnership have no tax effect on you. The part of the sales price for your partnership interest attributable to your share of unrealized receivables or appreciated inventory (these terms are defined at page 218, results in ordinary income or ordinary loss. Any excess results in capital gain or capital loss. In figuring the ordinary income, you must allocate part of your partnership basis to the receivables and inventory. The allocation is based on your proportionate share of the partnership basis for these properties. If you are relieved of any partnership liabilities, you include the amount as part of the sum realized for the partnership interest.

Timing the Sale of Your Partnership Interest

Poor timing of the sale of your partnership interest can be costly. If you are not on the same taxable year as your partnership, in the year of sale you may bunch more than a year of partnership income. In the year you sell out, you report your share of earnings up to the time of sale, in addition to the earnings from the regular partnership year ending within your individual taxable year.

EXAMPLE:

You are a member of a fiscal year partnership whose tax year ends July 31. You sell your interest on December 31, 1968. On your 1968 tax return, you have to report not only your share of partnership income for the year ending on July 31, 1968 but also your share for the period beginning August 1, 1968 and ending December 31, 1968, the day you sold out.

A sale of only a part interest does not close your partnership tax year.

The buyer of the partnership interest includes his share of the partnership income for the balance of the partnership year, using the same method of proration that was used by the selling partner to determine his share of partnership income up to the date of sale.

EXAMPLE:

A partner selling his partnership interest on June 30, 1968 for $21,000, has an adjusted basis for his interest of $5,000. His prorata share of partnership income to June 30 is $15,000, which is includible in his income. The $15,000 distributive share increases his partnership basis to $20,000. Therefore, his taxable gain on the sale of his partnership interest is $1,000 ($21,000 − 20,000). The purchaser of the partnership interest includes in his income as his distributive share his prorata part of partnership income for the remainder of the partnership taxable year.

How to Treat Partnership Distributions

Partnership distributions are usually not taxed; they are generally treated as payouts of income that are (or have been) reported by each partner as his distributive share of partnership income. But some distributions can result in capital gain and ordinary income or deductible losses. In addition to these tax consequences, you must consider the rules determining the basis for distributed property. Electing and applying the proper basis rules can affect not only the partner receiving distributions but also the partnership after the distribution.

When partnership distributions are taxed. You usually have no gain or loss on receipt of a partnership distribution. This is true whether you get a current or partially liquidating payment or a payment in complete liquidation. However, there are two exceptions to this rule: (1) In a current distribution or one in partial liquidation a loss is never recognized, but gain is recognized when the distributed cash exceeds the basis of your partnership interest. For example, you have a basis for your partnership interest of $10,000. You receive a distribution of $11,000 in cash. This gives you a gain of $1,000 which is taxed at capital gain rates. But no gain is recognized if you received $3,000 in property and $8,000 in cash. (2) In a complete liquidation, no gain is recognized except where the cash received exceeds your basis in the partnership. Loss is recognized if the distribution consists solely of money and unrealized receivables or inventory, and these items are less than your partnership basis. But the loss is not recognized if property other than inventory or unrealized receivables is distributed. This rule is valuable when you want to postpone recognition of a loss. You have the partnership distribute noninventory or receivable property to you and you control the time of the loss by timing the sale of the property.

What Are Unrealized Receivables and Substantially Appreciated Inventory?

The existence of unrealized receivables, appreciated inventory, and depreciable property in a partnership has tax consequences on sales and distributions. Unrealized receivables are rights to income, such as uncollected fees that have not been included in income because of the partnership's method of reporting income, for example, on the cash basis method, where receivables are not reported until actually received. The term unrealized receivables also includes the ordinary income potential in certain depreciable property owned by the partnership, to the extent of the gain that would have been recaptured if the partnership had sold the depreciable property at its fair market value at the time of the following transactions: (1) A distribution by a partnership to its partner; (2) A payment made in liquidation of an interest of a retiring partner or deceased partner; (3) A sale or exchange of an interest in a partnership by a partner. (A fuller discussion of how recapture applies to partnership distributions *see,* page 253.)

Substantially appreciated inventory is inventory whose fair market value exceeds: (1) 120% of its basis to the partnership and (2) 10% of the fair market value of all partnership property.

Inventory items for purpose of this rule are not limited to stock-in-trade or merchandise. The term includes all partnership assets except capital assets (such as security investments) and Section 1231 assets (such as depreciable property). Note that capital assets and Section 1231 assets under certain circumstances if held by the selling or distributee partner can be treated as inventory items.

Sale. When you sell your partnership interest, any part of the price attributable to partnership property qualifying as unrealized receivables or substantially appreciated inventory is ordinary income.

EXAMPLES:

1. Assume Smith sold his one-half interest in a partnership. The partnership is on the accrual basis and had the following assets and no liabilities:

Assets	Adjusted Basis	Fair Market Value
Cash	$ 10,000	$ 10,000
Accounts receivable	5,000	2,500
Trade notes receivable	2,000	2,100
Merchandise on hand	4,000	9,500
Machinery and equipment	80,000	100,000
Total assets	$101,000	$124,100

The inventory items, such as the accounts receivable, and trade notes receivable, and merchandise had a total adjusted basis of $11,000 and a fair market value of $14,100. The total value of all assets, other than cash, was $114,000. Since the fair market value of the inventory items, $14,100 was more than 120% of the adjusted basis of such items, $11,000, and also more than 10% of all assets other than cash, $114,100, there has been a substantial appreciation of inventory items. Therefore Smith can realize ordinary income to the extent the amount received for his interest in the inventory items exceeds his basis.

2. Jones' basis for his 50% partnership interest is $10,000. The partnership has assets with a basis and market value of $20,000 and unrealized receivables (such as fees) of $12,000. Jones sells his entire interest to Smith for $17,000, realizing a gain of $7,000. Of this, $6,000 is attributable to the unrealized receivables and is ordinary income; $1,000 is capital gain.

3. Same facts as above, but the selling price is $15,000. The first $6,000, attributable to the partnership's unrealized fees, is still ordinary income. Since the remaining $9,000 is exceeded by Jones' partnership basis of $10,000, he realizes a $1,000 capital loss.

Distribution on retirement. If you receive a distribution in kind on your retirement from the partnership of your proportionate share of appreciated inventories and unrealized receivables, there is no tax as the distribution is not treated as a sale or exchange. When you receive a disproportionately small amount of substantially appreciated inventories and unrealized receivables, the transaction is taxed. Even though you have not received your proportionate share of the appreciated inventory and unrealized receivables, you are treated as though you did. You receive ordinary income for the difference between the basis allocated to your interest in the unrealized receivables or inventory and the value of the capital assets received in exchange. The partnership has capital gain for the difference between the basis allocated to the distributed property in excess of your proportionate share and the value of the interest in receivables or inventory relinquished by you.

When you receive a distribution of appreciated inventory which you contributed to the partnership, the distribution is not taxed.

Receipt of more than proportionate amount of appreciated inventory and unrealized receivables. The partnership can realize ordinary income when one of the partners in a complete liquidation picks up more than his share of unrealized receivables and inventory. In this situation, the partnership realizes ordinary income for the difference between the basis of receivables and inventory allocated to the disproportionate part of the distribution and the value of the partner's interest in the other assets of the partnership given up in the exchange for the unrealized receivables and inventory. The partner realizes capital gain to the extent that the value of the unrealized receivables and inventory received by him in excess of his share exceeds the basis allocated to his interest in the other property given up in the exchange.

How to Figure Your Basis for Distributed Property

Figuring the correct basis of distributed property is necessary to determine the amount of your future depreciation deductions (if allowed to you) and the amount of your gain or loss on a subsequent sale of the property.

The way you figure basis depends on whether you received a current or partially liquidating distribution or a complete liquidating distribution.

Current distribution. The basis of the distributed property is the basis it had in the hands of the partnership immediately before the distribution. But the basis of the distribution cannot be more than your interest in the partnership reduced by any cash received in the same distribution. If the remaining basis of your interest is zero, the basis of the distributed property in your hands becomes zero.

EXAMPLE:

Smith receives $10,000 in cash and property having a partnership basis of $5,000. His partnership interest is $8,000. Since his interest is eliminated by the cash distribution, his basis for the property received is zero. In addition, he has a $2,000 gain (the excess of the cash over his basis before the distribution). Note: You may have to allocate basis if the bases of distributed properties exceed the basis of your interest in the partnership (see below).

A completely liquidating distribution. Your basis of the distributed property is an amount equal to the basis of your partnership interest reduced by any money distributed in the same distribution. That is, the distributed properties are allocated over your partnership interest after it has been reduced by any cash received.

When an allocation is required in either a current or liquidating distribution your interest in the partnership is first applied to any unrealized receivables and inventory; but these items cannot take higher bases in your hands than they had in the partnership immediately before the distribution. If your basis is less than the total bases of the unrealized receivables and inventory, the allocation is made in proportion to the bases of such items in the hands of the partnership. Any portion of your basis that is not applied to the receivables and inventory is then allocated to the other distributed properties. This final allocation is made in proportion to the respective bases of the properties in the hands of the partnership. Where only unrealized receivables or inventory is distributed in a liquidating distribution, that part of your basis not allocated to such property gives you a capital loss.

EXAMPLE:

The basis of Crow's partnership interest is $10,000. The partnership distributes the following to him: Cash $4,000, inventory with a basis to the partnership of $5,000, property X with a partnership basis of $2,000, and property Y with a partnership basis of $4,000. The cash reduces Crow's basis from $10,000 to $6,000. The $5,000 inventory further cuts it to $1,000. The $1,000 remaining is less than the partnership's bases for properties X and Y. So it is allocated to these properties in the same proportion as their bases in the partnership bear to each other: Property X gets a basis of $333.33 and Y a basis of $666.67. Crow's basis for his partnership interest is completely used up. Any further distribution of property to him would have a zero basis in his hands.

How the Sale of Distributed Property is Taxed

When you sell partnership property that has been distributed to you, the character of your gain or loss is the same as would be realized by the partnership if it had made the sale. That is, where the sale of property would be treated as ordinary income if made by the partnership, your sale of that property is also treated as ordinary income. So where you receive a distribution of unrealized receivables, any gain or loss realized when you sell these is ordinary gain or loss. The same rule holds for the sale of inventory unless it is sold after you have held it for more than five years. In that case, you realize capital gain or loss.

EXAMPLES:

1. A partner receives, in dissolution, inventory which has a basis to him of $19,000. After a year, he sells the goods for $25,000. The $6,000 gain is taxed as ordinary income. If he held the inventory for more than five years, his gain would be capital gain, assuming the merchandise was a capital asset in his hands.

2. A partner in the dissolution of his law firm received his share of accounts receivable amounting to $25,000. Since he received only his share, he is not taxed on the distribution. As the partnership used the cash method, the receivables had a basis to the partner of zero. If the receivables are later collected, or if the partner sells them, the amount received is ordinary income. The five-year rule, illustrated in the example above does not apply to accounts receivable.

In computing the holding period for distributed property, except inventory, you can include the time the property was held by the partnership. For inventory items, the holding period starts from the time you received the distribution.

When the Partnership Adjusts its Basis After a Distribution

In some situations, distributed property may take a basis in the hands of a distributee-partner that differs from the basis previously used by the partnership. In such case, the basis of the remaining assets of the partnership may be increased, if it so elects. For example, property with a partnership basis of $5,000 is distributed to a partner who has to take it at a basis of $4,000. The assets remaining in the partnership can be increased to take up this $1,000 loss in basis.

To make the adjustment, an election is filed. Once made, the election applies to all property transfers until revoked. Examples of circumstances under which an election may be revoked include: A change in the nature of the partnership business, a substantial increase in the assets of the partnership, a change in the character of the partnership assets, or an increased frequency of retirements or shifts of partnership interests.

The partnership after making an election adds to the basis of its remaining assets: (1) Any gain recognized to distributee. This covers the case where the distributed cash exceeds the partner's interest. (2) The excess of the adjusted basis of the distributed property to the partnership immediately before the distribution, over the basis it has to the distributee. For example, property with a basis of $15,000 is distributed to a partner whose interest in the partnership is $10,000. Under the election, the partnership can increase the basis of the remaining assets by $5,000 for the partner's $5,000 loss of basis. This increase-in-basis-rule applies whether or not the distribution is in complete liquidation of a partner's interest.

An election may work to the detriment of the partnership. An electing partnership is required to decrease the basis (but only in the case of a complete liquidation of a partner's interest) of its remaining assets by: (1) Any loss recognized by a partner. For example, where only money, unrealized receivables and inventory were distributed and these are less than the distributee's partnership interest. (2) The excess of the basis of distributed property to a partner over the basis of the distributed property to the partnership immediately before the distribution.

EXAMPLE:

Jones' partnership interest is $10,000. He receives, in a complete liquidation, property X with a partnership basis of $1,000 and property Y with a partnership basis of $4,000. The basis of X to Jones is $2,000 and of Y, $8,000. To account for this $5,000 increase to Jones, the partnership would have to decrease the basis of its remaining assets by $5,000.

The method of allocating these increase or decrease adjustments is as follows: An adjustment is made only to the remaining property which is similar in character to the distributed property which has created the adjustment. And it must have an effect of reducing the difference between the fair market value and the adjusted basis of the remaining property. Therefore, if an increase adjustment is allocated, the adjustment is spread only to those assets whose market values are more than their adjusted bases in proportion to the differences between the value and basis of each. No adjustment is made where the property's basis is more than its market value because the adjustment would increase rather than reduce the difference between its market value and basis.

The basis of any property cannot be reduced below zero. So, if a decrease adjustment is greater than the basis, the basis of such property is reduced to zero and the balance of the adjustment is applied against property of a similar character acquired in the future.

How a Retired or Deceased Partner's Interest is Taxed

In the liquidation of a retiring partner's or deceased partner's interest, ordinary income is realized on the amount of the distribution attributed to the partner's distributive share of income or guaranteed salaries or interest. Capital gain treatment is extended only to the value attributed to his partnership interest. And for this purpose, the partnership interest does not include payments for unrealized receivables which, if present, will be reflected as ordinary income.

Goodwill may be included as part of the partnership interest if the partnership agreement provides for such payment. But it cannot exceed the reasonable value of the distributee's share of the partnership goodwill.

Generally, the valuation placed by the partners upon a partner's interest in partnership property in an arm's length agreement will be acceptable. If such valuation reflects only the partner's net interest in the property (total assets less liabilities), it must be adjusted so that both the value of the partner's interest in property and the basis for his interest take into account his share of partnership liabilities.

Payments made to a retiring partner for his interest in substantially appreciated inventory items are ordinary income.

The remaining partners' distributive shares are not reduced by payments in exchange for a retired partner's interest in partnership property. They are reduced by payments in exchange for a retired or deceased partner's interest when the payments are considered as a distributive share of partnership income or a guaranteed payment.

Sale of a Corporate Business Requiring a Liquidation

What is the best way to sell a corporate business? The answer will in part be dictated by the demands of the prospective buyer. Does he want to purchase the entire business or only some of the corporate assets? Is he refusing to buy your stock for fear of acquiring hidden liabilities of the corporation? If so, he will want you to sell the assets and this in turn requires you to decide whether you want the corporate business to continue after the sale, in which case you can have the corporation sell the assets to the purchaser. The corporation can liquidate, selling some assets to the purchaser and distributing the remainder of the assets and the proceeds from the sale to you as stockholder.

There are several forms of complete liquidation which can be tailored to fit the type of liquidation you have in mind and at the same time provide favorable tax results: One tax and at capital gain rates. To reach these tax objectives, you must know definitely the result you wish to obtain and plan the transaction from beginning to end.

This section analyzes the possible forms of complete liquidation and the steps required to achieve tax advantages. Partial liquidations, which essentially are bona fide business contractions, are discussed at pages 177 and 240.

The Basic Liquidation Rules

When a corporation is liquidated it distributes its assets pro rata to its stockholders in exchange for their stock. Under State law, some assets may be retained by the corporation in a complete liquidation in order to meet its present creditor obligations.

The exchange of assets for stock is a capital gain transaction. There are a few situations where capital gain is not available, and will be discussed further on. Your gain or loss is measured by the difference between the amount you receive from the corporation (cash plus fair market value of other property) and the basis for your stock.

The capital gain rules apply to liquidation even though the distribution consists of accumulated earnings and profits of prior years—

amounts, which if distributed while the corporation continued in business would be taxable as ordinary dividends. Thus, a complete liquidation can remove from the corporation at capital gain rates the earnings that have accumulated in the corporation over the years. Of course, the corporation files a tax return for its last year up to the date of liquidation. Any earnings from operations realized in that last year are subject to corporate income tax.

While a corporation may be liquidated for tax purposes, it may not necessarily be dissolved for State-law purposes. It may remain dormant and be revived later and become active again.

Stockholder's basis for property received. Your basis for the property received is its fair market value. If your stock basis, for example, is $10,000 and on liquidation you receive property worth $15,000, you have a $5,000 gain. Your basis of the property received is $15,000. On a later sale of that property, you will have gain or loss depending on whether you receive more or less than $15,000.

Liquidating dividends over several years. A corporation in the process of liquidation will not usually distribute everything to its stockholders in one year. Often, the liquidation may take several years so that you apply the distributions against the basis of your stock until the basis is eliminated. Distributions thereafter become fully taxable. Even if you surrender part of your stock with each distribution, you apply the liquidating dividend to the entire basis of all your stock.

Tax effect of liquidation on the corporation. Generally, when a corporation makes a distribution in liquidation it has no taxable gains or losses. There are these exceptions to this general rule:

(1) If the corporation distributes installment obligations (where it elected to report gain on a sale on the installment method) the corporation has gain equal to the difference between its basis for the installment obligations and the fair market value of those obligations at the time of the distribution. The fair market value of the obligations are reported by the stockholder as part of the total fair market value of the property received by him in the liquidating distribution.

(2) If depreciable property is distributed in liquidation, the "depreciation recapture" provisions apply and the corporation will realize ordinary income to the extent of depreciation recapture.

(3) If property on which the corporation took an investment credit

is distributed before the useful life on which the credit was computed has passed, the corporation will have to recompute its previous investment credit based on the period of time it actually held that property up to the time of the distribution in liquidation. The difference between the recomputed credit and the credit actually taken in the prior year is added to the corporation's tax in the year it makes the liquidating distribution.

A 12-Month Liquidation Can Avoid a Double Tax on the Sale of Corporate Assets

When the prospective purchaser of a corporation insists on buying assets only, rather than stock, there is a danger of double taxation, first to the seller-corporation and second to the stockholder when he receives the proceeds from the sale in the liquidation distribution. The danger exists even though the stockholder attempts in his own name to negotiate the sale with the buyer in anticipation of his receiving the assets in the liquidation. The Treasury will claim that the stockholder was the agent of the corporation and thus the corporation should be taxed on the sale.

Double taxation can be avoided by using the special 12-month liquidation. By following the steps explained below, the corporation pays no tax at all on the gain realized from the sale of its assets (other than nonbulk sales of inventory) during the liquidation period; the stockholders pay a capital gain tax on the gain realized from the proceeds distributed by the corporation in liquidation. The net result is one tax to the stockholders.

To come within the 12-month liquidation rules, the corporation must adopt a plan of complete liquidation before sale of its assets (although negotiations may begin prior to adoption of the plan) and distribute all assets within the 12-month period beginning on the date of the adoption of the plan of liquidation. "All assets" means all assets except those needed by the liquidating corporation to satisfy creditor claims. You may set aside reasonable amounts for contingent claims as well as fixed claims, but you may not retain assets for the satisfaction of stockholders' claims on their shares. Thus, if stockholders cannot be located within the 12-month period, the corporation should make their pro rata distribution to an independent trustee or a special escrow account for the benefit of those stockholders. You should also be wary of the situation where a stockholder has loaned money to his corporation receiving back a note. Although this is a "claim" in law, the Treasury may insist that it in reality is another class of stock that must be redeemed in liquidation during the 12-month period.

What Items are Taxed in a 12-month Liquidation

If the above rules are met, sales by the corporation during the 12-month period beginning with the adoption of the plan of liquidation are not taxable except for these:

(1) Sale of inventory in the ordinary course of business is not tax-free. But the sale of all the inventory to one buyer in a bulk transaction escapes tax.

(2) Sale or disposition of installment obligations can be taxable even if made within the 12-month period. If the corporation received installment obligations on the sale of inventory during the 12-month period on a *nonbulk sale* (a sale that would be taxable in any event if made within the 12-month period), and then disposed of those install-ment obligations within the same 12-month period, it would be taxable on the disposition of the installment obligations. The corporation de-ferred the tax at the time of sale by using the installment method but cannot avoid the tax altogether by later disposing of the installment obligation within the 12-month period. Also, should a corporation own installment obligations on transactions that took place before the adoption of the plan of liquidation, gain on disposition of those obliga-tions during the 12-month period would also be taxable to the corpora-tion.

Losses are not deductible. Neither gain nor loss is recognized to the corporation on sales of qualified property during the 12-month liqui-dation period. That means that not only are gains not taxable but losses are not deductible. So, where a corporation has some assets on which it will realize a loss on sale, it should sell these assets before it adopts a plan of liquidation. Then, those losses would be deductible by the corporation, either reducing the current corporate income, if any, or creating a carryback loss to recoup prior years' taxes. However, there is a danger in attempting to "straddle" losses (*see* below).

When is the Plan of Liquidation Adopted?

Since the 12-month period begins with the date of adoption of the plan of liquidation, it is important to know when the plan was adopted. The usual rule is that it is adopted on the date the stockholders adopt a corporate resolution of liquidation, but other evidence of adoption of a plan may be sufficient. An informal agreement among all the stockholders has been recognized as adoption of a plan. The safest course is to adopt a plan in a formal corporate resolution.

Sale of loss assets before adoption of plan. Often a corporation has assets which have depreciated in value below their bases and would produce a loss if sold individually. If sold within the 12-month period after adoption of the liquidation plan, the corporation does not get the benefit of this loss, but if sold outside the plan of liquidation, the corporation recognizes the loss which it can use to offset operating income during its final tax period or as a net operating loss carryback to prior years. Treasury regulations state that if substantially all assets are sold prior to the formal adoption of the plan of liquidation, the date of formal adoption will be allowed to stand. In other words, it gives its conditional sanction to the corporation that wants to recognize losses, the condition being that substantially all assets must be sold prior to the formal adoption of the plan. If less than substantially all assets are sold prior to the formal adoption of the plan, the Treasury holds that the plan is adopted on the date the first asset was sold or negotiated for sale. So, if one-half your assets are "loss" assets, and you attempt to sell them prior to the formal adoption to recognize losses, the Treasury is certain to contend that the plan was adopted when the first loss asset was sold. This may cause either of the following results: (1) No gain or loss is recognized on the sale of all the assets, or (2) if the period from the date of the first sale to the date on which the last asset is sold exceeds 12 months, all the gain and all the loss is recognized; in other words, the corporation forfeits the benefits of the special liquidation rules.

EXAMPLE:

You anticipate liquidating your corporation. However, before you formally adopt the 12-month plan, you sell your loss assets. The sale is consummated on September 1, 1967. On October 1, 1967 the corporation formally adopts its plan of liquidation and sells the remainder of its assets (less those retained to meet claims) by September 15, 1968. If the Treasury is successful in its contention that the 12-month plan was informally adopted on September 1, 1967, all of the assets will not have been sold within 12 months of that date. The corporation will be forced to recognize all of its gain as well as its losses, resulting in the unwanted double tax.

The Treasury, however, has not been too successful in the few cases involving splitting losses and gains. The courts generally allow the loss sale to stand independently if the stockholders can show that the sale of the loss assets occurred prior to the decision to liquidate. Similarly, where the stockholders formally adopt a plan of liquidation, a prior loss sale may be allowed to stand. Because of the paucity of cases on this issue and the Treasury's continued unwillingness to relax its position, you should not feel too confident about your chances for success, and you should anticipate having to incur the cost of a court battle to prove your point.

If you are going to attempt a sale of less than substantially all the assets prior to formal adoption of the plan, adopt the plan soon after the loss sale. In that way the remainder of the assets can be sold within the 12-month period beginning with the sale of the loss assets. You thus create an everything-to-gain-but-nothing-to-lose situation. The 12-month rule is observed; the worst that can happen is disallowance of the loss deduction.

When Does the "Sale of an Asset" Occur?

For the sale of an asset to come within the benefits of the 12-month liquidation rule, it must occur within the 12-month period. Exactly when the sale has occurred has caused litigation.

The Treasury regulations state: "The date on which a sale occurs depends primarily upon the intent of the parties to be gathered from the terms of the contract and the surrounding circumstances. In ascertaining whether a sale or exchange occurs on or after the date on which the plan of complete liquidation is adopted, the fact that negotiations for sale may have been commenced, either by the corporation or its shareholders, or both shall be disregarded. Ordinarily, a sale has not occurred when a contract to sell has been entered into but title and possession of the property have not been transferred and the obligation of the seller to sell or the buyer to buy is conditional." Thus, the contract of sale may be drawn up by the parties before adoption of the plan, so long as title to the property does not pass from seller to buyer before that date.

A trouble spot in this area is condemnations. Under the law of the most States, a condemnation is treated as a sale, and it may occur before you can plan the corporate liquidation. If the condemnation occurs before the plan is adopted, gain from the receipt of the condemnation proceeds will be taxed to the corporation. On the other hand, you do not wish to adopt the plan too soon, since that might seriously shorten the time in which the corporation must sell the remainder of the assets and distribute the proceeds. The best approach is to adopt a conditional plan and file the required notice of liquidation with the District Director of Internal Revenue, but specifying that the adoption of the plan is conditional on the vesting order of the condemnation authorities. Then, when the condemnation does occur, you will file a second notice of liquidation, specifying that the plan became effective on the date of the vesting order.

The Treasury regulations permit the plan of liquidation to be adopted on the same day as the sale of the first corporate asset. The sale may take place prior to the adoption, so long as both occur on the same day. For example, if your corporation is selling its real estate first, you may adopt the plan on the closing date. Some tax practitioners however prefer to adopt the plan a few days prior to the closing in order to avoid possible questions by the Treasury.

Installment Sales of Assets are Restricted

Often, on the sale of business assets, the transaction will involve a considerable sum of money, and the buyer will not be in a position to pay all cash. He will, therefore, give obligations payable over a period of years. The seller, to avoid having to report the entire gain in the year of sale and pay the full tax before he actually receives full payment, is permitted to adopt the installment method. Since the corporation has to make distribution in liquidation of all of its assets within the 12-month period, two problems are created by installment obligations: (1) Will the corporation have to pick up income at the time it distributes the installment obligations to the stockholders as liquidating distributions? Normally, a corporation *does* have to pick up income when it distributes installment obligations in a liquidation. But under special provisions in the tax law, the corporation is not taxed on the disposition of installment obligations on liquidation if they arose from non-inventory sales made within the 12-month period or from a bulk sale. (2) Will the stockholders, when they receive the installment obligations as part of their liquidating distributions, have to include the value of those obligations in the total amount received in figuring their gain or loss on the liquidation? The answer is yes. There is no provision in the tax law that keeps the value of the installment obligations out of the total value of the distributions received by the stockholders in liquidation under the 12-month liquidation rule. So, he has to pick up the full value of those obligations at the time he receives them (the value of the obligation, however, may be less than their face amount) and pay a tax. When he later collects on the obligations, he will have no tax to pay if he included the full face amount as their value at time of liquidation. If he included less than the face amount of the obligations as value at the time of liquidation, the excess will be taxable when he collects the face amount of the obligations. The excess will be taxable as ordinary income, even though he realized capital gain on the liquidation.

Paying a tax on the obligations before they come due is probably the major stumbling block to the use of the 12-month liquidation as a means of selling a corporate business.

One possible way to solve the problem posed by an installment sale may be to utilize a Subchapter S election. If the corporation is already subject to the election, it may stay in existence to pass the gain to the stockholders. However, the election may be endangered by the 20% income test applied to the receipt of interest on the installment obligation.

Where the corporation has not been subject to the election, its ability to make an election for purposes of passing through the capital gain may be limited by the restriction discussed at page 91 concerning one-shot elections.

Can the Corporation Minimize Its Taxable Income in Its Final Year?

Some of the corporation's assets may consist of uncollected receivables and fees. If it is a cash basis taxpayer, it has not yet included their value in income. What are the tax consequences if these assets are sold or distributed as part of the 12-month liquidation? Can the corporation avoid including the proceeds from the sale or the value of the items distributed in its taxable income for its final year? The Treasury's answer is no. It contends this is not the type of asset that may escape taxation under the 12-month liquidation rule. This argument is usually upheld by the courts.

If you decide to use the special one-month liquidation (under which the stockholders may postpone the recognition of gain on liquidation of their corporation), you may *not* at the same time use the 12-month liquidation. Likewise, where the special subsidiary liquidation is elected, the 12-month rules apply only to a limited extent.

Records to be Kept and Information to be Filed

The corporation must, within 30 days after its adoption of the plan of liquidation, file a return on Form 966 with the office of the District Director. Attach to the Form 966 a certified copy of the resolution or plan of liquidation. If at any time you amend the plan, a new Form 966 must be filed to which the new plan as amended must be attached. You must also include the following information: (1) A statement showing the number of shares of each class of stock outstanding at the time of the adoption of the plan of liquidation, together with a description of the voting power of each class; (2) A list of all the shareholders owning stock at the time of the adoption of the plan of liquidation, together with the number of shares of each class of stock owned by each shareholder, the certificate numbers thereof, and the total number of votes to which entitled on the adoption of the plan of liquidation; and (3) A list of all corporate shareholders as of January 1, 1954, together with the number of shares of each class of stock owned by each shareholder, the certificate numbers, the total number of votes to which entitled on the adoption of the plan of liquidation, and a statement of all changes in ownership of stock by corporate shareholders between January 1, 1954 and the date of the adoption of the plan of liquidation.

In addition, you should attach the following information to your liquidating corporation's tax return: (1) A copy of the minutes of the stockholders' meeting at which the plan of liquidation was formally adopted, including a copy of the plan of liquidation; (2) a statement of the assets sold after the adoption of the plan of liquidation including the dates of the sales; (3) date of the final liquidating distribution, and (4) a statement of the assets, if any, retained to pay liabilities and the nature of the liabilities.

How to Use a One-Month Liquidation

Under the one-month liquidation election, all the corporate assets must be distributed within one month from the date of adoption of the plan of complete liquidation. It is useful where the corporation has little or no accumulated and current earnings and a sizeable appreciation in the corporate assets. Most of the gain from the capital appreciation will go untaxed at the time of the liquidation.

There are these advantages with this type of liquidation. (1) The installment method of reporting gain from the sale of the assets may be elected by the stockholders; (2) Noncorporate shareholders of the liquidating corporation will be taxed on gain from the liquidation only to a limited extent, and if there is no cash or certain securities (see below) received by the stockholders, all of the gain will be taxed at capital gain rates; (3) Corporate shareholders are taxed on all of their gain at capital gain rates.

There are these disadvantages: (1) If there is substantial cash or certain securities distributed by the liquidating corporation, noncorporate shareholders will have to report gain to the extent of accumulated and current earnings as ordinary income; (2) The basis of the assets in the hands of the shareholders is usually lower than it would be in a regular liquidation; there will be a lower depreciation basis or more taxable profit if the recipient shareholder decides to sell the asset; (3) The one-month limitation is rigidly enforced, and if you fail to meet the deadline you will lose the benefits. However loss of the one-month liquidation benefits will in most cases merely result in *all* of the gain being taxed at capital gain rates.

Using a One-Month Liquidation to Make an Installment Sale by the Stockholder

Assume you have a corporation with an apartment house that has appreciated considerably in value but no earnings and no cash. Your buyer refuses to purchase the corporate stock but wants the building only. You want to elect the installment method of reporting gain from the sale. You cannot use the 12-month liquidation when the installment method is elected. You would therefore turn to the one-month liquidation. Within the month period, the corporation distributes the building to you, and since there are no accumulated or current earnings in the corporation, you pay no tax on your gain. The basis of your stock becomes your basis for the building. You can sell the building and elect the installment method of reporting the gain on the sale.

How to Elect the One-Month Liquidation

The corporation first adopts a plan of liquidation. Then certain of the stockholders must make written election, within 30 days after adoption of the plan, to qualify the liquidation as a one-month liquidation. The election on Form 964 (revised) is filed with the District Director for the district in which the corporation's final income tax return will be filed. The election is deemed filed when it is put into the mail and postmarked. Thereafter, the liquidation distribution of all corporate assets must occur within one calendar month. It is not necessary that the month fall within the taxable year of the corporation in which the plan was adopted. It is essential that no distributions be made to stockholders prior to the adoption of the plan. The Treasury regulations do not require that the corporation be dissolved during the one-month period, but only that the "status of liquidation" exists during that period. A status of liquidation exists when the corporation ceases to be a going concern and its activities are merely for the purpose of winding up its affairs, paying its debts, and distributing any remaining balance to its stockholders. The corporation is permitted to retain the necessary cash to pay contingent liabilities and expenses after the end of the one-month period.

The rules of the one-month election apply only to the stockholders making the election. You cannot have a one-month liquidation unless

there are sufficient elections. For shareholders who are not corporations, the total elections must equal at least 80% of voting power of
the corporation held by noncorporate shareholders at the time of the
adoption of the plan of liquidation. In determining the total voting
power to see if holders of 80% of the stock made the election, you do
not count the stock held by corporations. For shareholders who are
corporations, you need 80% of the voting power, too. Here, you leave
out of the total voting power (1) stock held by shareholders who are
not corporations and (2) corporations owning 50% or more of the
total voting power of the corporation at the time the plan of liquidation was adopted.

How Gain on One-Month Liquidation is Taxed

Only that part of the gain attributed to the corporation's (1) accumulated earnings and profits and (2) cash and stock and securities
(acquired by the corporation after 1953) is taxed. To the extent that
the gain reflects earnings and profits, the gain is ordinary income. To
the extent the total cash and stock and securities exceed the earnings
and profits, that gain is taxable as capital gain. If a corporation is the
stockholder receiving the liquidating distribution, the portion of the
gain reflecting the greater of the earnings and profits or cash and stock
and securities is taxable as capital gain.

The following technical steps must be followed to compute taxable
gain in a one-month liquidation.

1. Compare the basis of stock held in the corporation with the total
fair market value of property and cash received that is allocated to that
stock. (If there is a loss, the loss does not come under these rules; the
regular liquidation rules apply.)

2. Determine the corporation's accumulated earnings and profits
and how much of those earnings and profits are allocable to the stock
held.

3. Total the cash and the fair market value of securities the corporation has and how much of that is allocable to the stock. The only
securities you count are those acquired by the corporation after 1953.

4. Compare the amount computed in (2) with the amount computed in (3) and determine which is larger.

5. Compare the amount of the gain determined in (1) with the

amount computed in (4). If the gain in (1) is greater than the amount computed in (4), the taxable gain is the amount computed in (4). If the gain in (1) is equal to or less than the amount computed in (4), the entire gain is taxable.

6. To determine how the taxable gain arrived at in (5) is to be taxed where the stockholder is not a corporation, first compare that taxable gain with the amount computed in (2). If the amount computed in (2) is equal to or is more than the taxable gain computed in (5), the entire gain is taxable as ordinary income. If the amount computed in (2) is less than the gain computed in (5), that portion of the gain equal to the amount computed in (2) is taxable as a dividend; the excess amount of gain computed in (5) is taxable as capital gain.

7. If the stockholder receiving the liquidation distribution is a corporation, the entire gain computed in (5) is taxable as capital gain.

Obviously, you will not use the one-month liquidation if the amounts in (2) or (3) are substantial, especially if the amount in (2) is large, as that amount is taxable as ordinary income to noncorporate stockholders.

EXAMPLE:

Assume that the Green Corporation has cash of $7,500, stock and securities acquired after 1953 of $9,000, and other property having a fair market value of $24,000. Earnings and profits amount to $6,000. It has three equal stockholders, one of which is a corporation. Each stockholder's basis for his stock is $5,000.

In a one-month liquidation, each stockholder receives $2,500 in cash. $3,000 in stocks and securities, and $8,000 in other property, for a total of $13,500. Since each stockholder's basis for his stock is $5,000 each has a gain of $8,500. Of the $8,500 gain, $5,500 (the total of the cash, stock and securities) is taxable. To the corporate stockholder the entire $5,500 gain is capital gain. To each individual stockholder, $2,000 is taxable as dividend income (his share of the $6,000 earnings and profits); the balance of the gain ($3,500) is taxable as capital gain.

Stockholder's basis for the property received in liquidation. You spread the basis of the stock over the properties received in the liquidation. Since gain is not taxable in a one-month liquidation (except to the extent of earnings, cash, and stock and securities), the basis of the nontaxed property in the hands of stockholders is the same as the basis for the stock. To account for cash received, taxable gain, corporate liabilities assumed (or property subject to liens), the following steps are taken to determine the basis of the properties received: (1) Start with the basis of the stock. (2) Subtract the cash received in the liquidation distribution. (3) To the amount remaining, add: (a) Liabilities assumed; (b) specific lien against property acquired in the distribution (other than stock); (c) any gain recognized on the liquidation.

EXAMPLE:

In a one-month liquidation, a corporation distributes to an individual stockholder in exchange for his 100 shares of stock: (1) $1,000 in cash; (2) stock acquired after 1953 with a fair market value of $4,000; (3) other property with a value of $22,000, subject to a $1,000 lien. The stockholder also assumes a corporate liability of $2,000. The basis for his 100 shares in the corporation was $12,000 and his share of the company's earnings and profits is $2,500.

The total value of everything received is $27,000, but there was $3,000 in assumed liabilities, giving him a net amount received of $24,000. Since his basis for his stock was $12,000, his gain is $12,000. $5,000 of that gain is taxable (the total of the cash and the stock). Of the $5,000 taxable gain, $2,500, his share of the earnings and profits, is taxable as ordinary income, and the remainder as capital gain.

The basis of the total property received in liquidation (other than the cash) is $19,000, computed as follows:

Adjusted basis for the stock	$12,000
Less: Cash received	1,000
Remainder	$11,000
Liability assumed	2,000
Specific lien against property	1,000
Gain recognized	5,000
Basis of all property acquired on liquidation	$19,000

$19,000 is allocated over the various properties received in proportion to their fair market values. But the specific lien is allocated directly to the property on which it is a lien. Therefore, $18,000 is first allocated (leaving out the $1,000 specific lien).

The market value of the stock was $4,000 and the net market value of the other property (after deducting the specific lien) was $21,000, for a total of $25,000. $4,000 / $25,000 of $18,000 is allocated to the stock as its basis, or $2,880. $21,000 / $25,000 of $18,000 is allocated to the other property, or $15,120 to which the $1,000 specific lien is added giving a basis for the other property of $16,120.

SELLING OR LIQUIDATING A BUSINESS

Records to be Kept and Information to be Filed with Return

Permanent records must be kept by every electing shareholder receiving distributions in complete liquidation. He must file with his income tax return for his taxable year in which the liquidation occurs a statement of all facts pertinent to the gain realized by him on his stock owned at the time the plan of liquidation was adopted, including: (1) A statement of his stock ownership in the liquidating corporation on the date of the distribution, showing the number of shares of each class owned and the basis of each share; (2) a list of all the property, including money, received on the distribution, showing the fair market value of each item of property other than money on the date distributed and stating what items, if any, consist of stock or securities acquired by the liquidating corporation after December 31, 1953; (3) a statement of his ratable share of the earnings and profits of the liquidating corporation accumulated after February 28, 1913, computed without diminution by reason of distributions made during the month of liquidation, and (4) a copy of his written election (Form 964 (revised)).

The corporation must, within 30 days after its adoption of the plan of liquidation, file a return on Form 966 with its District Director of Internal Revenue. Attach to the Form 966 a certified copy of the resolution or plan of liquidation. If at any time you amend the plan, a new Form 966 must be filed to which the new plan as amended must be attached. You must also include the following information: (1) A statement showing the number of shares of each class of stock outstanding at the time of the adoption of the plan of liquidation, together with a description of the voting power of each class; (2) a list of all the shareholders owning stock at the time of the adoption of the plan of liquidation, together with the number of shares of each class of stock owned by each shareholder, the certificate numbers thereof, and the total number of votes to which entitled on the adoption of the plan of liquidation, and (3) a list of all corporate shareholders as of January 1, 1954, together with the number of shares of each class of stock owned by each shareholder, the certificate numbers, the total number of votes to which entitled on the adoption of the plan of liquidation, and a statement of all changes in ownership of stock by corporate shareholders between January 1, 1954, and the date of the adoption of the plan of liquidation.

Using a Partial Liquidation When a Corporate Business is Being Sold

Assume you have two businesses within your corporation and want to sell one. In this case, the sale of stock is not possible. But you may still pay capital gain tax (without a second tax to the corporation) by using a partial liquidation.

If the corporation sold the assets and then distributed the proceeds plus the unneeded working capital, you would come within the partial liquidation rules. But you do not avoid the double tax. The corporation realizes taxable gain or loss on the sale of the assets. Then, on the distribution to you, while the partial liquidation rules save you from a dividend, you still pay a capital gain tax if the amounts received by you exceed the basis of the stock surrendered in redemption. Since this is not a complete liquidation, you cannot use the 12-month liquidation rule to avoid the tax on the corporation level.

Instead of following the above procedure, you could have the corporation distribute the assets of the business to be sold to you. If a complete business is being terminated on the corporate level, this distribution qualifies as a partial liquidation, and you realize a capital gain for the difference between the fair market value of the assets received and the basis for your stock that would be redeemed in the transaction. The new basis for the assets received by you is their fair market value. Then, when you later resell the assets received in the liquidation, you would have little or no gain (since presumably you would be selling at the same market value at which the assets were valued when distributed to you). There is one tax on the entire transaction, the capital gain tax you paid on receiving the assets in the partial liquidation.

If you negotiate the sale before the liquidation, the Treasury may try to prove that you have acted as agent of the corporation. If so, the corporation will be considered to have made the sale, and there is a double tax. Consequently, you must be careful in using a partial liquidation. The best approach is to liquidate at a time you are contemplating selling off part of the corporate business but before you have entered into negotiations for its sale. Keep detailed records showing when and with whom the negotiations took place to prove that the sale was made by you after the liquidation and not by you on behalf of the corporation before the liquidation (with the actual transfer to the buyer taking place after the liquidation). The requirements of a partial liquidation are discussed at page 177.

Sale of Subsidiary Company: Liquidation Rules

The corporate business being sold may be a subsidiary of your parent company. To avoid double tax, the parent company can liquidate its subsidiary in a taxfree liquidation. The parent picks up as its basis for the assets received in the liquidation the same basis that the subsidiary had in the assets distributed. If the parent corporation acquired the stock in the subsidiary corporation within two years of the adoption of the plan of liquidation, the basis of the assets received in the liquidation are stepped up to the parent corporation's purchase price for its stock. (See page 59.)

The rules applying to the liquidation of a subsidiary are similar in scope to the 12-month liquidation rules applicable to individual stockholders and their companies. Consequently, when there is a plan to sell the assets of a subsidiary, the subsidiary can sell its assets, realize the gain or loss, and then be liquidated taxfree into the parent corporation. Or the liquidation can occur first taxfree without an increase in the basis of the assets to the parent, followed by a sale by the parent which would incur the taxes.

Installment sales. The subsidiary can arrange an installment sale, elect the installment method of reporting, and after its liquidation, the parent corporation can continue to report the sale on the installment basis. The tax law specifically covers this point. It provides that on the distribution of installment obligations to the parent, the subsidiary does not realize income. An exception to this rule applies to distributions after November 13, 1966 where the plan of liquidation is within two years of date on which 80% control was purchased by the parent. In such a case, the subsidiary is taxed on the installment obligations.

Requirements for a taxfree liquidation. Liquidation of a subsidiary is taxfree if you meet the following rules: (Note that they are not elective; they apply whether or not you want that result). (1) There is a plan to liquidate the subsidiary; (2) on the date of liquidation and through the date of the receipt of the property distributed by the subsidiary, the parent corporation holds at least 80% of the combined voting power of all classes of stock in the subsidiary and at least 80% of all other classes of stock (except nonvoting stock preferred as to dividends), and (3) the subsidiary transfers all of its property either in one year or within a three-year period beginning at the close of the year of the first distribution. Where a series of distributions are made, the parent must continue to meet the 80% rules throughout the period and the Treasury may require a bond to be posted and a waiver of the statute of limitations to be signed. If a liquidation in a series is not completed within the prescribed time, none of the distributions qualify as taxfree.

When to avoid a taxfree liquidation. You may not want a taxfree liquidation of a subsidiary. For example, property held by a subsidiary may have appreciated in value. The parent corporation may want to acquire the subsidiary's assets and may not object to paying a capital gains tax in order to step up the basis of the acquired assets and take depreciation deductions on the higher value. In this case, the parent should dispose of enough stock to avoid the 80% test. Perhaps the liquidation may be stretched out beyond the permissible three-year period, and thereby fall outside the requirements of the taxfree liquidation provisions.

Minority stock interests that receive distributions in the liquidation of a subsidiary are subject to the ordinary liquidation rules. They have gain or loss for the difference between the fair market value of what they receive in liquidation distributions and the basis of their stock in the corporation being liquidated.

Records to be Kept and Information to be Filed

The liquidating subsidiary corporation must file a Form 966 along with its income tax return for the year of liquidation. The Form 966 must be filed within 30 days after adoption of the plan of liquidation. Other information also required is: (1) A statement showing the number of shares of each class of stock outstanding at the time of the adoption of the plan of liquidation, together with a description of the voting power of each class; (2) a list of all the shareholders owning stock at the time of the adoption of the plan of liquidation, together with the number of shares of each class of stock owned by each shareholder, the certificate numbers thereof, and the total number of votes to which entitled on the adoption of the plan of liquidation, and (3) a list of all corporate shareholders as of January 1, 1954, together with the number of shares of each class of stock owned by each shareholder, the certificate numbers, the total number of votes to which entitled on the adoption of the plan of liquidation, and a statement of all changes in ownership of stock by corporate shareholders between January 1, 1954, and the date of the adoption of the plan of liquidation.

Every corporation receiving a distribution from the liquidating subsidiary should keep permanent records showing the information listed below. The plan of liquidation must be by each of the corporations involved, have been approved by an official of each corporation and appear on the official records of each corporation. If the liquidation occurs in one taxable year, only one statement is filed, but if there is a series of liquidations, you must file a statement containing the following facts with your corporation's tax return for each year involved: (1) A certified copy of the plan for complete liquidation, and of the resolutions under which the plan was adopted and the liquidation was authorized, together with a statement under oath showing in detail all transactions under the plan; (2) a list of all the properties received on the distribution, showing the basis of such properties to the liquidating corporation at the date of distribution and their fair market value on the date distributed, (3) a statement of any indebtedness of the liquidating corporation to the recipient corporation on the date the plan of liquidation was adopted and on the date of the first liquidating distribution. If any indebtedness was acquired at less than face value, the cost to the recipient corporation must also be shown, and (4) a statement showing the ownership of all classes of stock of the liquidating corporation showing the number of shares and percentage owned and the voting power of each share on the date of adoption of the plan of liquidation, and at all times since to and including the date of the distribution in liquidation. The basis of the stock and the dates purchased must also be shown.

Retaining the Selling Corporation as a Personal Holding Company

After a sale of corporate assets, it may pay to continue the corporation in existence. The corporation holds and invests proceeds received on the sale of the assets in much the same way the individual stockholders would have invested the funds had they been distributed to them in liquidation. The company will be a personal holding company and will have to distribute all of its income to the stockholders to avoid the 70% penalty tax on personal holding companies. But the amount distributed to the stockholders, while taxable as ordinary income to the stockholders, may well be more than they would have earned before taxes had the corporation been liquidated in the first place and they had invested the funds personally.

This may be possible where the corporation will realize some capital gain on the sale of its assets, but the greatest portion of the gain will result on liquidation where there is a substantial difference between the basis of the stockholders' stock and the amounts to be distributed in liquidation. Also, by leaving the funds in the corporation, the corporation can receive dividends at a low tax rate.

EXAMPLE:

Your corporation has cash of $20,000 and other assets worth $200,000 but with a tax basis of $150,000. The basis of your stock in the corporation is $40,000. You own all of the corporation's stock. You have a buyer for the corporation's assets. Assume you have a choice of using a 12-month liquidation or retaining the corporation after sale of the assets.

Assume you use a 12-month liquidation. The corporation will sell its assets for $200,000, paying no tax. Adding the $200,000 proceeds to the $20,000 cash it had, it will distribute to you in complete liquidation of the corporation $220,000. Your gain on the liquidation ($220,000 minus your $40,000 cost of your stock) will be $180,000. After paying a 25% capital gains tax of $45,000, you will have left $175,000 ($220,000 less the $45,000 tax). If you invest $175,000 in stock yielding a 5% dividend, you will have an annual return before taxes of $8,750.

Assume you do not liquidate. The corporation sells the assets for $200,000. It has a $50,000 gain ($200,000 less its $150,000 cost). It pays a capital gains tax of $12,500. So, it has left after taxes $187,500. Add to that the $20,000 cash and the corporation has $207,500 to invest. Say it buys the same 5% yielding stock that you would have bought with your after-tax proceeds from liquidation. The corporation will then get $10,375 in dividends each year. As a corporation it is entitled to an 85% dividend deduction before it figures its taxes; in other words the corporation pays a tax on only 15% of the dividends it receives. So, only $1,556 of the $10,375 dividends received are taxable to the corporation. At a 22% rate, the tax is only $342. Subtracting that $342 from the $10,375 dividends received leaves the corporation with $10,033 to distribute to you as a dividend. So, instead of having a before-tax income each year of $8,750 from the after-tax proceeds of the liquidation, you get a before-tax annual income of $10,033. That's a 15% boost in annual income by keeping the corporation alive as a personal holding company after the sale of the corporate assets. In addition, if the corporation is in existence at the time of your death, capital gain potential on your stock is not subject to tax. On death, the basis of stock is increased to fair market value at the date of death.

Depreciation Recapture Problems in the Sale of a Business

Limitations are placed on the capital gain treatment of property subject to depreciation. Ordinary income is imposed on that part of gain attributed to certain depreciation deductions that previously reduced the basis of the property before its sale or other disposition.

In imposing ordinary income tax, the law discriminates between depreciable real property (such as a rental building) and business equipment (such as machines, autos and trucks).

The details of computing ordinary income under the recapture rules are discussed first; afterwards their effect on the sale of a business.

Figuring How Much is Ordinary Income on Sale of Business Equipment

On the profitable sale of depreciable business equipment, ordinary income is limited to the depreciation taken on the property since 1961. To determine this amount, the law requires you to figure the sale in this fashion. You find the "recomputed basis" of the property by adding the depreciation (including any extra first-year depreciation claimed) after December 31, 1961 to the adjusted basis of the property. The amount of the gain that is ordinary income is the lower of the following two items:

1. The recomputed basis less the adjusted basis, or

2. The amount realized less the adjusted basis. (Use the fair market value of the property if sale or exchange did not take place.)

In other words, the ordinary income is not more than the amount of the depreciation added to the adjusted basis to find recomputed basis. If the amount realized exceeds the recomputed basis, the balance of the profit can qualify as capital gain.

EXAMPLES:

1. The adjusted basis of equipment is $2,000. Depreciation taken after 1961 on the equipment is $1,300. The equipment is sold for $2,900. The profit of $900 is ordinary income, the difference between the amount realized and the adjusted basis. The recomputed basis is not considered as it exceeds the amount realized.

2. Assume that the amount realized on the sale is $3,700 and no other sales of depreciable property were made in the year. The profit on the sale is $1,700 ($3,700 less $2,000). Of this, $1,300 is ordinary income, $400 capital gain. The difference between the recomputed basis of $3,300 and the adjusted basis of $2,000 is $1,300. This is less than the $1,700 profit realized on the sale. Thus, ordinary income is limited to the lesser amount of $1,300. The remaining profit of $400 is subject to capital gain rates.

Generally, the depreciation deduction taken into account for each year is the amount allowed or allowable, whichever is greater. For purposes of ordinary income (but not for purposes of figuring gain or loss), the depreciation deductions taken into account for any year will be the amount "allowed" rather than the amount "allowable" if the allowed deduction is smaller and you can prove its amount. "Allowed" means depreciation actually taken as a deduction in past years. "Allowable" means depreciation that could have been taken had the business deducted all it was legally entitled to.

How to Figure Ordinary Income on Sale of Depreciable Realty

If you sell depreciable realty at a profit within a year after you acquired it, the part of your gain attributed to depreciation taken in 1964 or a later year is subject to ordinary income tax (to the extent of the gain). Ordinary income is realized regardless of the type of depreciation method used.

If you sell depreciable realty more than a year after you acquired it, ordinary income is imposed on only the part of the gain attributed to rapid depreciation (such as the 150% or double declining balance method or the sum of the years-digits method) in excess of the straight-line method. In figuring the excess, consider only depreciation claimed in 1964 and later years. If the sale takes place within 20 months after acquisition, 100% of this excess is taxed. After 20 months, the amount of the excess subject to taxation decreases by 1% per month beginning with the 21st month, until, after 10 years, profit on a sale may be fully taxable as capital gain. In figuring the holding period, only full months are counted. For example, if property was sold after a holding period of 20 months and 21 days, the holding period for tax-ing the ordinary income element is 20 months.

The above time limits require a careful timing of profitable sales of depreciable realty in order to reduce the ordinary income tax penalty. Postpone, if you can, the sale of depreciable realty during the first year of your ownership, regardless of the method of depreciation you use. If you use the straight-line method, postponing a sale to a date more than a year after you acquired the property will avoid the ordinary income tax completely. If you use a rapid depreciation method, a sale at a date during the first-year ownership period will generally subject all of the depreciation to ordinary income tax. The postponement of a sale to a date more than a year after acquisition will subject to ordinary income tax only the part of the gain attributed to the rapid depreciation taken in excess of an assumed straight-line rate. Leasing the property to the prospective buyer for a period before the sale might extend the holding period. But this type of transaction might be subject to a Treasury attack on the grounds that it is in reality a sale.

Ordinary income may be realized on the sale of leaseholds and leasehold improvements if your depreciation of the leasehold and other costs did not consider optional renewal periods.

Follow these steps to determine the amount of ordinary income realized on the sale of real property on which depreciation has been taken through a rapid method and which is sold after a period of more than a year.

(1) Figure the profit on the sale, exchange or involuntary conver-sion.

(2) Figure the difference between depreciation claimed under the rapid method and depreciation that would have been claimed under the straight-line method.

(3) Figure the holding period of the property. The holding period for property generally begins on the day after it was acquired. Thus, if

property is purchased on January 1, 1967, the holding period begins January 2, 1967. If the property is subsequently sold on January 1, 1969 the holding period is exactly 24 months. For property constructed or reconstructed by you, the holding period begins on the first day of the month in which the property is placed in service.

(4) Find the percentage of depreciation subject to recapture. This is 100% minus one percentage point for each full month after the date on which the property has been held for 20 full months.

Property Held up to	Percentage
20 months	100%
24 months (2 years)	96
36 months (3 years)	84
48 months (4 years)	72
60 months (5 years)	60
72 months (6 years)	48
84 months (7 years)	36
96 months (8 years)	24
108 months (9 years)	12
120 months (10 years)	0

(5) Multiply the percentage against the lower of Step 2 (the difference between depreciation claimed using the rapid method and depreciation that would be taken using the straight-line method) or Step 1 (the gain on the sale).

EXAMPLES:

1. You depreciate a new building with a cost basis of $100,000 on the declining balance method. You take depreciation using a 40-year life. After five years, when the adjusted basis of the building is $77,378 ($100,000 less depreciation of $22,622), you sell the building for $90,000. If straight-line depreciation had been taken, the total depreciation would have been $12,500 ($2,500 × 5). Here is how the ordinary income element is figured:

(1) Profit on the sale is $12,622 ($90,000-77,378)
(2) Additional depreciation is $10,122 ($22,622-12,500)
(3) Holding period: five years or 60 months
(4) The percentage based on holding period of five years is 60% (see table above)
(5) 60% is applied to lower additional depreciation of $10,122 (60% × 10,122 = $6,073.20)

Thus, $6,073.20 of the $12,622 profit is subject to ordinary income. The balance may be capital gain.

2. Assume the property was sold for $85,000. The profit on the sale is $7,622 ($85,000 − 77,378).

The additional depreciation is $10,122 (See above).

The percentage of 60% is applied to the lower profit of $7,622. Therefore, only $4,573.20 is ordinary income ($7,622 × 60%).

The useful life and salvage value for determining the depreciation on the straight-line method for step 2 above is the same as that used under the actual depreciation method.

EXAMPLES:

1. On January 1, 1968, you sell real property costing $10,000 on January 1, 1961. You computed depreciation under the declining balance method using a rate of 200% of the straight-line rate and a useful life of 30 years. If you had computed depreciation under the straight-line method, you would have used a salvage value of $1,000. The depreciation under both methods is as follows:

Year	Declining Balance	Straight-line
1961	$ 667	$ 300
1962	622	300
1963	581	300
1964	$ 542	$ 300
1965	506	300
1966	472	300
1967	400	300
Sum of depreciation deductions for periods after December 31, 1963	$1,960	$1,200

The additional depreciation for the property is $760, that is, the depreciation actually deducted for periods after December 31, 1963 ($1,960), minus the depreciation under the straight-line method ($1,200).

2. You sell depreciable real property on January 1, 1971, which cost $10,000 on January 1, 1964. For the period 1964 through 1968, you compute depreciation under the declining balance method using a rate of 200% of the straight-line rate and a useful life of 10 years. If you had used the straight-line method, you would have used a salvage value of $1,000. On January 1, 1969, you change to the straight-line method. You redetermine the remaining useful life of the property to be 8 years and its salvage value to be $77. The depreciation of the property under both methods is as follows:

Year	Actual Depreciation	Straight-line
1964	$2,000	$ 900(1)
1965	1,600	900
1966	1,280	900
1967	1,024	900
1968	819	900
1969	400(2)	678(3)
1970	400	678
Sum of depreciation deductions	$7,523	$5,856

(1) 1/10 of $9,000 ($10,000 minus $1,000)
(2) 1/8 of $3,200 ($3,277 minus $77)
(3) 1/8 of $5,423 ($5,500 minus $77)

The additional depreciation for the property is $1,667, that is, the depreciation actually deducted ($7,523) minus the depreciation that would have resulted from the straight-line method ($5,856).

Separate computations for improvements. To figure the amount of gain to be reported as ordinary income, you may have to make several computations if you placed units of a building into service at different times or made substantial improvements to the building. Each unit or improvement has a separate holding period. For example, an apartment house of 100 apartments is built. 30 apartments are put up for rental on January 1, 1967, 50 on July 11, 1967 and the remaining 20 on January 19, 1968. The apartment house consists of three separate elements. The holding period for each element begins on the first day of the month in which it was placed in service.

A separate improvement is each improvement added to the capital account of the property if the total of improvements added to the capital account during a 36-month period ending on the last day of any one tax year exceeds the greater of (1) 25% of the adjusted basis of the property at the beginning of the first day of the 36-month period, or the day the holding period of the property begins if later; (2) 10% of the unadjusted basis of the property at the beginning of the first day of the 36-month period, or the day the holding period begins if later; or (3) $5,000.

The addition to the capital account is the gross addition, unreduced by the cost of the replaced property.

EXAMPLE:

If a roof, with an adjusted basis of $20,000 is replaced by a new roof costing $50,000, the amount of the improvement is the gross addition to the account of $50,000, not the addition of $30,000. The $20,000 adjusted basis of the old roof is no longer reflected in the basis of the property.

The adjusted basis or the unadjusted basis includes the depreciated cost of all improvements whether or not they qualify as separate elements.

In applying the above 36-month period test, do not include improvements in any of the three years if for such year the improvements do not amount to the greater of (1) $2,000 or (2) 1% of the unadjusted basis of the property as of the first day of such tax year.

EXAMPLE:

The unadjusted basis of property is $300,000. During the year improvements A, B, and C, costing $1,000, $600, and $700 respectively are made. Since the total of the improvements, $2,300, is less than 1% of the unadjusted basis ($3,000), the improvements are not treated as improvements for purposes of the three-year test.

The method of computing ordinary income on separate units is complicated and we suggest that you follow Treasury regulations for the method of computation.

Installment Sale of Depreciable Property

If you elect to report on an installment basis a profitable sale of depreciable property, ordinary income must be reported before any of the capital gain is reported. You do not allocate the profit element of each installment payment between ordinary income and capital gain. You first report all of the ordinary income until the amount is exhausted.

EXAMPLE:

Smith sells a machine used in his business for $10,000, realizing a $3,000 profit, $2,000 of which is subject to ordinary income, $1,000 to capital gain. He will receive annual installments of $1,000 over a 10-year period. He elects the installment method. For the first six years, he reports as ordinary income the $300 profit attributed to each installment payment. In the seventh year, $200 of the installment payment is reported as ordinary income; the balance of $100, as capital gain. In the remaining three years, all of the profit of $300 of each installment is reported as capital gain.

Effect of Recapture Rules on Sale of Sole Proprietorship

The sale of a proprietorship is treated as a sale of individual assets. Since some of the assets are depreciable and others not, the seller's interest is to minimize the amount of ordinary income from recapture of depreciation he will realize on the sale by allocating as little as possible of the selling price to those assets. The buyer, on the other hand, is usually directly opposed in interest on this matter. He wants a higher value assigned to the depreciable assets so he can have greater depreciation deductions. The extent of compromise will depend largely on the relative bargaining positions of the two. Since the eventual allocation is the result of arm's length bargaining, the Treasury will most often accept the values as fixed in the contract.

If you cannot come to terms with your buyer, you can consider leasing the assets to him. You realize rental income which is also subject to ordinary rates, but you can compensate for this by charging a higher rental. In this manner, you are compensated for the use of your property, you can continue to depreciate the property, and if any of the property is real estate, you may extend your holding period. After 10 years, there is no ordinary income element in the sale of real property that was subject to rapid depreciation.

Alternatively to leasing, a taxfree exchange of like-kind property may be considered. Like-kind property is property of the same character or nature, but not necessarily the same grade or quality. Thus, real estate can be exchanged taxfree for other real estate. The depreciation recapture does not apply to like-kind exchanges if they are completely taxfree.

You may use an installment sale of the assets subject to depreciation recapture if there will be large amounts of ordinary income resulting from the sale. This prevents bunching of all the ordinary income into one year. Note the rule stated above that on an installment sale, all of the ordinary income from recapture is reported as the notes come due before any capital gain element is realized.

Before the sale, the business may be incorporated under the taxfree rules. The corporation is then sold. On the sale of stock, no depreciation recapture is involved. The buyer now has the business in corporate form, but the corporate assets may have a low basis. The buyer can cure this by liquidating the corporation and getting a stepped-up basis. As the depreciation recapture rules apply to the liquidation, the buyer may object. But this objection may be softened by the fact that the amount of taxable ordinary income increases the basis of the assets if real estate is involved, providing large depreciation deductions. In addition, the holding period for real estate is carried over to the corporation in determining when the 10-year period has run. After 10 years from the purchase of real property there is no depreciation recapture.

If possible, time the sale of the depreciation recapture assets to a year where your business has a net operating loss, a net operating loss carryover, or where there is an excess of losses over gains from the sales of depreciable property used in the business.

The last alternative is to transfer the depreciable assets by gift to family members in lower tax brackets. The ordinary income from recapture will not be so costly to them.

Effect of Recapture Rules on Sale of Partnership Assets

The depreciation recapture rules apply to the following partnership transactions: (1) Distributions to a partner of more or less than his pro rata share of depreciation property; (2) distributions to the successor of a retired or deceased partner, and (3) sale of a partnership interest.

Distribution to the partner. If the partner receives only his pro rata share of the depreciation recapture property, neither he nor the partnership realizes ordinary income. Instead, the potential ordinary income is carried over and the partner will realize it when he subsequently sells the property. The amount of potential recapture income is computed by determining how much recapture there would have been at the time of distribution to the partner had the partnership instead sold it to a third party. Since the amount of recaptured income depends on fair market value, special care must be given to establishing fair market value at the time of the distribution. If the distribution is agreed upon at arm's length bargaining, the value will usually be accepted by the Treasury. This may not be the case where the distribution is pursuant to a buy-sell agreement and the partners are members of the same family.

If the partner receives more or less than his pro rata share of depreciation recapture property, it is treated as a sale of a noncapital asset, resulting in ordinary income to the partner or partnership. If the partner receives less than his pro rata share, he realizes the ordinary income. If he receives more than his pro rata share, the partnership is taxed with ordinary income.

EXAMPLE:

Adam owns a ⅓ interest in a partnership. The assets of the partnership are cash, land and a machine. The machine, purchased by the partnership, has an adjusted basis of $9,000 and a fair market value of $15,000. Depreciation taken on the machine after 1961 is $9,000. The machine is distributed to Adam in complete liquidation of her partnership interest of $10,000. At the time of the distribution, there is a potential ordinary income of $6,000 because of the recapture rules. The partnership is taxed on $4,000 of ordinary income on account of depreciation (⅔ remaining interest x $6,000 potential income). The basis of the property to Adam as a result of distribution equals his basis for his partnership interest of $10,000. However, if he eventually disposes of the property, he must account for $2,000 ($6,000 potential ordinary income less $4,000 reported by the partnership).

If the partner receives back his originally-contributed property as part of the distribution, there is no depreciation recapture to the partnership. The potential recapture is carried over to the partner who realizes it, if he subsequently sells the property.

Distribution to successor. Whether the recapture rules apply to a distribution to the successor of a retired or deceased partner depends on the form of the distribution. If the payment is made without regard to the partner's interest, it is treated as a distributive share of partnership income or as a guaranteed payment, and the recapture rules do not apply. If the payment is in satisfaction of the partner's interest, the recapture rules do apply. The rules outlined above apply in figuring how much ordinary income is realized.

Sale of partnership interest. Generally speaking, the depreciation recapture rules in this area are similar to the rules concerning unrealized receivables on sale of a partnership interest. The purchase price received by the selling partner is first allocated among all of his pro rata share of the assets according to their fair market values. The value allocated to the depreciation recapture assets (such as equipment) is used to determine if, at the time of the sale by the partner, there would have been ordinary income to the partnership if it had sold the assets. This amount is what the selling partner includes in his own income.

Effect of Recapture Rules on Sale of a Corporation

Sale of stock. The recapture rules do not apply to a sale of stock of a corporation. There may have to be an adjustment of price, however, to take into account the ordinary income that will result to the buyer's acquired corporation, if he plans to liquidate it after the purchase.

Sale of assets. The recapture rules apply to a sale of individual assets. The assets are treated as sold individually even though there may be a bulk sale. The allocation rules outlined for the sole proprietor should be consulted.

Liquidations. The recapture rules apply to liquidations including the following: The special 12-month liquidation; the special one-month liquidation; the special parent-subsidiary liquidation.

If you plan to use the special one-month liquidation, the recapture rule may increase the amount of *dividend income* to the stockholders, as well as ordinary income to the corporation. The amount of dividend income to individual stockholders depends on the earnings and profits in the liquidating corporation at the time of liquidation. This liquidation is generally elected when there are high-appreciation assets in the corporation and little or no earnings and profits. With high-appreciation assets, the depreciation recapture potential is correspondingly large. Assume there is $50,000 of recaptured depreciation which the corporation has to recognize as ordinary income. This increases its earnings and profits and thus provides an additional $50,000 of potential dividend income to its stockholders on the liquidation.

If you plan to use the special 12-month liquidation, consider this planning suggestion. Under the 12-month liquidation rules, the liquidating corporation does not recognize gain or loss. This means if the corporation sells the assets and distributes the proceeds to its stockholders, any gain on the asset sale is not taxed to the corporation, but any loss on the asset sale is not a tax deduction for the corporation. If there is depreciation recapture, the ordinary income that is taxed to the corporation on the sale or distribution to stockholders of its depreciable assets is not offset by any losses. To minimize this result, you should consider having the corporation if possible sell its loss assets before adopting the plan of liquidation. However, as indicated on page 229, sales of loss property may be restricted.

When a special parent-subsidiary liquidation is planned, there is no recapture problem if the subsidiary is liquidated more than two years after the parent corporation acquired its stock. However, distributions to minority stockholders will result in recaptured ordinary income to the liquidating corporation. This tax consequence can be avoided by distributing nondepreciable assets (such as land or inventory) to the minority stockholders. If the liquidation of the subsidiary occurs within two years from the purchase of 80% of the subsidiary's stock (and the other rules on page 241 are met), the recapture rules apply. One method of lessening the impact from the recaptured ordinary income is to cause the subsidiary to sell or retire its loss assets prior to adoption of the plan of liquidation. This will allow the ordinary income to be partially or fully offset by those losses.

CHAPTER XIII

Collapsible Corporation Danger to Capital Gain

THE COLLAPSIBLE CORPORATION rules are designed to prevent the prearranged use of a corporation to convert ordinary income into capital gain. But they are sufficiently broad to adversely affect bona fide corporations such as an operating company that holds assets that have substantially appreciated in value.

Real estate corporations have borne the brunt of the collapsible corporation penalty. More specifically, for real estate dealers its provisions make it difficult to use corporations to insulate profits from ordinary income tax rates. For example, two dealers organize a corporation to develop a tract of land. The corporation improves the tract which increases in value. Before the lots are sold, the dealers sell their stock in the corporation to a third party and claim capital gain treatment on the sale of the stock. If a Treasury agent examines the transaction he will probably apply the collapsible corporation rules and claim the sale is taxable at ordinary income rates. The stockholders will then have to prove that the corporation was not collapsible. How they might succeed is explained later in this chapter.

The collapsible corporation rules penalize the stockholders, not the corporation, on their disposition of their stock. The penalty is the treatment of the gain on the stock as ordinary income on the theory that the stockholders are trying through the stock disposition to realize capital gain on appreciated corporate property which, if sold by the corporation, would be taxed at ordinary income rates.

As the collapsible corporation rules are among the most complex in the tax law, no discussion can simplify all of the problems of interpreting the law. However, we hope that this chapter can alert you to when the collapsible corporation rules may be applied and to possible defenses.

When you are planning the following types of transactions, you must check that the collapsible corporation penalty does not apply: (1) Complete liquidation of the corporation. (2) Partial liquidation of the corporation. (3) Sale of stock by stockholders to third persons. (4) Exchange of stock for other stock or property, as for example, in a taxfree reorganization. (5) A nonredemption distribution by the corporation in excess of its current and accumulated earnings and profits. (Normally, this would produce a capital gain, see page 141.)

When is a Corporation Collapsible?

A corporation is collapsible when: (1) Its principal activity is the manufacture, construction or production of property, or the corporation has inventory, or real or depreciable property used in its business (other than property for production of inventory), and has been holding it for less than three years. (2) The corporation, at the time of the sale of its stock or its liquidation, has not realized a substantial portion of the total taxable income to be realized from the activities in (1). (3) The shareholders intended to realize capital gain or recognized the possibility of doing so by selling the stock or liquidating the company.

When the Treasury wants to impose the collapsible corporation rules, it will claim that your motive in the sale or liquidation was to realize capital gain rather than let the corporation sell the corporate assets at ordinary income tax rates.

The Treasury may infer your motive from facts surrounding your corporation's activities, or through a special percentage test. To rebut the Treasury claim, you must show you were not motivated by a desire to convert ordinary income into capital gain or that your sale comes within one of the statutory exceptions. You might show that the sale was forced by your poor health, the sale occurred at least three years after the corporation finished construction of the property, or the corporation realized substantially all of its profits on its assets. These defenses are discussed later in greater detail.

The Intent Test

To prove that your corporation is collapsible, the Treasury can use one of two methods: (1) Applying a percentage test to certain assets (usually property sold to customers) that have been held for less than three years. (2) Presenting facts from which a court can infer that you formed or used the corporation principally for the manufacture or purchase of property, with the intention of realizing capital gains on the sale of your stock.

Percentage test. The Treasury can use a percentage test to raise a presumption that your corporation is collapsible. The percentages described below are applied to the following property held for less than three years: (1) stock-in-trade included in the inventory, (2) property held for sale to customers, (3) depreciable property used in the corporation's business (Section 1231 assets), except if it is used to produce property held for sale to customers, (4) unrealized receivables, or fees not previously included in the corporation's income. Under this test, the corporation is presumed to be collapsible when:

1. The fair market value of such property is 50% or more of the fair market value of the corporation's total assets (not counting its cash, obligations that are capital assets to the corporation, certain Government bonds, and stock in other corporations); and

2. The fair market value of the property is 120% or more of its basis.

EXAMPLE:

A corporation owned the following assets (at fair market value) at the time it liquidated and distributed all of its assets to its stockholders:

Cash	$175,000
Note receivable held for investment	130,000
Stock of other corporations	545,000
Rents receivable	15,000
Building built by the corporation and held as rental property (having a basis of $600,000 and subject to a mortgage of $500,000)	750,000

The only asset affected by the presumption is the building itself; it is depreciable property. To find if the 50% requirement is met, the value of the building—$750,000 must be compared to the value of the total assets.

But in figuring total assets, cash, capital assets, and stock in other corporations are eliminated. The only other asset besides the building that goes into the total is the rents receivable of $15,000. Obviously the $750,000 value of the building is more than 50% of the total assets of $765,000. Further, the builder's value of $750,000 is more than 120% of its $600,000 basis (120% of $600,000 is $720,000).

On the liquidation of the corporation, there is a presumption that the corporation is a collapsible corporation.

You can attempt to disprove the presumption raised by the percentage test by presenting evidence that the corporation was not used to convert ordinary income to capital gain.

Other evidence. That the percentage test does not apply to property held by a corporation does not mean that the corporation is not collapsible. The Treasury can rely on presentation of evidence from which it can be inferred that there was an intention to use the corporation for collapsible purposes. The intent to sell does not have to be shared by all of the stockholders. The stockholders who make policy decisions can by themselves taint the entire corporation as collapsible. A number of courts, however, have held that where the only one to sell his shares is a minority stockholder, he escapes collapsible treatment. In one case the sale was a result of disagreements between the minority and majority stockholders enabling the minority stockholder to pull out of the business. Another case allowed capital gain treatment where the minority stockholder could not put up additional funds needed for the business and sold his stock to investors who could.

Treasury regulations state that a corporation is collapsible when the stockholders' intention to realize capital gain is contemplated at any time during the construction of property. One court has questioned the validity of this regulation. It held that the intention may be shown to have existed at any time during the corporation's life, not just during the period of construction but subsequently withdrew its objection to the regulation. This indicates that the court felt the Treasury test goes far enough. The intention is "evil" only if it exists during the period of construction. If you can present clear and convincing evidence of circumstances occurring after construction was completed that gave rise to the intention, you will probably be safe. For instance, in one case in which the taxpayers won, they showed that they had no intention of converting their apartment house into a co-operatively-owned building until a year after construction was completed when they were presented with the idea by a broker.

But when does construction end? This question has been a source of litigation. One court said that construction means "all construction required to perform the contract completely." So, if a whole shopping center has been constructed but for a retaining wall and the finishing touches to a parking lot, an intention to sell formed at that time results in ordinary income treatment to the stockholders. However, a building is completed when fully occupied even though there remain uncompleted landscaping, driveways, steps and walks. The Treasury has said that changes to an existing building, such as alterations to an office for a new tenant or changes in decor, that do not alter the character of the building are not "construction" for purposes of the collapsible rules. If the intent to sell forms during that period there is no worry about Treasury challenge.

A corporation was held not collapsible when the stockholders sold out after observing serious defects in the building owned by the corporation. In other cases, sales motivated by the seller's poor health cleared the corporations of the collapsible charge.

Defenses and Exceptions to Collapsibility

To rebut the Treasury charge that you used the corporation to convert ordinary income into capital gain, you might be prepared to show that the corporation had realized a substantial part of the taxable income to be realized on property it constructed or bought. If this proof can be sustained, the corporation is not collapsible. But this approach is difficult as the law in this area is not clear. In addition, the courts and the Treasury offer conflicting approaches. Neither the law nor the Treasury explains how to figure how taxable income is computed and how much of the amount is considered to be substantial. A court suggests that taxable income is to be figured as (1) taxable income already realized on corporate property (considered as collapsible assets) plus (2) taxable income that would be realized if the remaining collapsible assets were sold on the date of the disposition of the stock.

Courts have held that a realization of 33% and 51% of taxable income is substantial. One court has held a 17% realization is not substantial.

The Treasury does not agree to the holding that a 33% realization of profit is sufficient to clear the corporation as collapsible. It insists that to meet the substantial test the stockholders must show that the part of total income to be realized after the disposition of stock is not substantial, not whether substantial profits were realized before the disposition of stock. For example, if a housing project has a potential gain of one million dollars and the holding corporation is liquidated after 25% of that figure is realized from sales, under the Treasury's test, the $250,000 realized income is "substantial" only if the amount not yet realized (here, $750,000) is *insubstantial*. However, the courts are generally more liberal, looking only to the amount already realized to see if the "substantial" test is met.

Technical defenses and exceptions. Even if the Treasury can prove that the corporation is collapsible, ordinary income tax does not apply to the stock disposition unless:

1. *70% test.* At least 70% of the recognized gain on the sale or distribution comes from constructed or purchased property. Thus, if 30% or more of such gain is attributed to noncollapsible assets, all gain of the stockholder is capital gain. To find if this 70% rule is met, compare what you got through the liquidation or sale of your stock with what you would have gotten if the property involved had not been constructed or bought.

2. *5% test.* You own more than 5% of the value of the corporation's outstanding stock at any time after the corporation started constructing or at the time it made such purchases. Ownership by relatives and others is counted as your own stock ownership. The relatives and others whose ownership counts as yours are the same as in the case of personal holding companies (see page 149). In addition, you also count the stock owned by brothers-in-law, sisters-in-law, sons-in-law, daughters-in-law. But treasury stock held by the corporation is not counted.

3. *Three-year test.* Not more than three years have elapsed since the construction or purchase of the property was completed. The Treasury requires actual completion and not substantial completion.

A court held that a "certificate of occupancy" is not proof of completion. In the case of a multi-unit construction project, the three-year period does not begin until the last unit is completed. Above all, do not confuse this rule with the stockholders' holding of corporate stock.

If stock is sold on the installment method within the three-year period, gain is treated as realized within that period, even if an installment payment is received after the three-year period.

EXAMPLES:

1. (*70% test*) Brown organized Price Corporation, contributing $100,-000 in cash for all of its stock. The company invested $40,000 in one project of residential houses. By the end of the year, the houses had been sold and the corporation showed a profit after taxes of $10,000. At the same time as it went into the first project, the company also invested $60,000 in land to be subdivided into lots and distributed in liquidation, before profits (to any great extent) were realized from their sale. By the end of the year, the corporation realized $6,000 in profits after taxes from the sale of these lots. A few days after the start of the following year, the corporation liquidated distributing:

Cash and notes amounting to	$56,000
Lots with a value of	94,000

Brown had a $50,000 gain on liquidation ($150,000 as value of the distribution less the $100,000 basis for his stock). Brown's gain on liquidation, if the corporation had not undertaken the second project, would have been $10,000 (the $110,000 in cash the corporation would have had after realizing the profit after taxes on the first project minus the $100,000 basis for his stock). The gain attributable to the second project (the one that could make the corporation collapsible) is, therefore, $40,000. Since $40,000 is more than 70% of the entire gain of $50,000, the entire gain is ordinary income. The 70% rule is met.

2. (*Combining the three-year test and the 70% test*) More than three years have elapsed since Smith Corp. built the Class A homes. Only two years have elapsed since construction was completed on the Class B homes. Smith sells all of his stock, realizing a gain of $500,000, half of which is attributed to the Class A homes, and half to the Class B; an additional gain of $200,000 is attributable to noncollapsible property. The three-year test applies to the Class A homes so the $250,000 gain attributable here is taxed at capital gain rates. The Treasury ruled, however, though the Class A gain is not collapsible income, it is still considered in computing the 70% test to Class B gain (which cannot escape by the three-year rule). So, of a total gain of $700,000, $500,000 is attributed to collapsible property, which is greater than 70%. Hence, all the gain from the Class B homes is ordinary income.

Planning to Avoid the Collapsible Penalty

Where it seems that the collapsible corporation rules may affect your operations, consider these suggestions:

1. Take less than the full advantage of the collapsible rules. For example, the corporation constructs two buildings of equal value at equal cost, selling one at its appreciated value and paying tax at ordinary rates on it. The corporation distributes the proceeds after tax, plus the other building at its appreciated value. Less than 70% of the total gain on distribution will result from the second building that was distributed in kind. The collapsible corporation rules do not come into effect and the distribution is taxed at capital gain rates. You have failed to secure the full capital gain advantage since tax at ordinary rates has to be paid on the sale of the first building.

2. See to it that no stockholder owns more than 5% of the stock at the organization of the corporation. For this purpose, you will need 20 unrelated people to organize the corporation. This arrangement is useful when considering investment in a corporation. If you take 5% or less of the stock, you can subsequently sell at capital gain, although the corporation is "collapsible" to the other stockholders.

3. Use a corporation that has prior earnings. For example, a corporation constructs a building and, upon its completion, the building together with all the other assets are distributed in liquidation. If 30% of the gain on the liquidation is from the prior earnings, and only 70% from the appreciation in the value of the building, the entire gain is capital gain. But if these percentages are 71 and 29, the full gain is ordinary income.

4. Deal with the corporate stock after the termination of the three-year period following the construction of property. However, that stock is sold on an installment basis and installments will be received more than three years after the construction or purchase of property does not avoid the collapsible corporation penalty, if the sale has taken place within the three-year period.

5. Consider the possibility of planning the sale of corporate assets in a year when the corporation is a Subchapter S corporation. Capital gain of the corporation is generally taxed to stockholders. But note that Treasury regulations threaten to upset capital gain treatment in a

Subchapter S corporation if a substantial stockholder is a dealer in the type of asset which was sold by the corporation. In such a case, the sale of the asset is taxed at ordinary income tax rates. The regulations do not define what constitutes a substantial stockholder. Although there has been no legal challenge to this regulation, many tax authorities question its validity.

Limited Escape Routes from Collapsibility Provided by Law

The collapsible corporation taint can be avoided in a sale or liquidation if the increase in value of certain collapsible assets does not exceed 15% of the corporation's net worth. However, failure to meet this test does not by itself necessarily classify a corporation as collapsible. Whether or not a corporation is collapsible depends on the application of the intent test. Before looking at the specific transactions to which the objective test is applied, let us see what the law defines as (1) ordinary assets on which unrealized appreciation is computed and (2) net worth:

1. Ordinary income assets are generally those assets of a corporation which, if sold at a gain, would result in the imposition of an ordinary income tax on the corporation. Furthermore, if any stockholder owns more than 20% of the corporation's stock (5%, in case of a one-month liquidation), the ordinary income assets of the corporation also include those assets of the corporation which, if sold at a gain by the stockholder, would result in the imposition of an ordinary income tax on him. Thus, a dealer who owns more than 20% of the corporation's stock can jeopardize the corporation's ability to meet this test. For example, the corporation owns rental houses. One stockholder, who owns more than 20% of the stock, deals in houses. The corporate houses are considered ordinary income assets for all stockholders. One way in which the law determines dealer status is to look at the previous holdings of a stockholder who now owns more than 20% of a given company's stock. Perhaps he owns or owned more than 20% of another corporation's stock during a preceding three-year period. Perhaps more than 70% of the other corporation's assets are or were similar, or related in service or use, to more than 70% of the assets of the present corporation. Then any sale or exchange of stock of the other corporation that took place during the preceding three-year period is

regarded as a sale or exchange of the assets of the other corporation by the stockholder. This rule prevents a person from avoiding dealer status by using a separate corporation to operate each real estate venture. A stockholder who owns 20% or less of a corporation's stock, but more than 5%, must take into account the unrealized appreciation in assets of that corporation, which would be ordinary income assets in his hands if he did own more than 20% of the corporation's stock. But his dealer status does not "taint" the other stockholders. However, he does not have to account for his interests in other companies.

Ordinary income assets include property used in a trade or business (such as rental property), if the total unrealized depreciation on the property exceeds the total unrealized appreciation. Also included is property used in a trade or business (such as rental property), which has unrealized appreciation, and which, in the hands of a stockholder who owns more than 20% of the company stock, would be taxed at ordinary income tax rates.

2. Net worth. This means the amount by which the fair market value of all the company's assets exceeds its liabilities. However, the net worth does not include any capital contributions made within a one-year period, unless the contribution was for bona fide business reasons. This rule prevents the increasing of capital solely to meet the 15% test.

How the 15% test operates. The 15% test is applicable to only the following four transactions:

1. A stockholder's sale of his stock.

You sell your stock in a corporation that holds appreciated property subject to the collapsible corporation penalties. However, the net unrealized appreciation on the property does not exceed 15% of the net worth of the corporation. You get capital gain on your sale; the ordinary income tax penalty of the collapsible corporation rule does not apply. However, not coming within this exception are sales to your corporation, or if you are a stockholder owning more than 20% of your corporation stock, sales to your wife, children, or parents, or to a corporation you control.

2. Complete liquidation occurring within one month.

3. Sales and exchanges of property by the corporation during a liquidation occurring within a 12-month period. The corporation must

also sell substantially all of its properties, and not distribute to its stockholders any property on which depreciation or depletion can be taken.

4. Distributions to stockholders in a complete liquidation. For the distributions to qualify, sales and exchanges of corporate property must take place during the 12-month period and the distribution must also meet the requirements of test 3 above.

Special Corporate Election Avoids Collapsible Corporation Penalty on Sale of Corporate Stock

You plan to sell stock of a corporation which the buyer of the stock expects to continue to operate. The corporation holds properties that are worth substantially more than their cost and has not substantially realized these profits. You fear that your stock sale may be subject to collapsible corporation rules. Furthermore, you believe that you cannot fit your case under any defense or exception in the law.

You can avoid collapsible corporation rule penalties if the buyer is willing to buy the stock under the condition that the corporation consents in a special election to pay tax on the "Subsection (f)" assets (see below for definition) if it disposes of them at a gain in a sale, exchange, or disposition.

The theory behind the special election is that if you sell stock in a corporation that continues to operate and later realizes gain on the property, tax at the corporate level is assured.

The election applies only to sales of stock, not partial or complete liquidations or capital distributions.

The stock sale must be made within a six-month period after the consent is filed. The consent is irrevocable after the sale of stock, even if the corporation is subsequently held not to be a collapsible corporation.

When an election is made, land or any interest in real estate, such as a leasehold interest, is not treated as a capital asset. Also not treated as a capital asset is any asset the construction of which was started before the date the stock is sold or any improvements resulting from construction started by the corporation within two years after the date of the stock sale for which a consent has been filed.

Benefit of the consent election is not available to a shareholder if, during a five-year period ending on date of the sale, he or any person related to him sold any stock of another consenting corporation within any six-month period after the consent was filed by such other corporation.

If a corporation owns 5% or more in value of outstanding stock of another corporation on the date of the stock sale after the owning corporation's consent was filed, the consent is not effective unless the other corporation has filed a consent by the date of such stock sale with respect to sales of its own stock. Sale by a shareholder of stock in owning corporation which has filed a consent, is treated as a sale of stock in such other corporation. Similar rules are applied to a corporate chain connected by 5% or more stock ownerships.

How the consent is given. The consent of the corporation (or a 5% stockholder corporation) is given by means of a statement, signed by any officer who is duly authorized to act on behalf of the consenting corporation, stating that the corporation consents to have the provisions of Section 341(f)(2) of the Internal Revenue Code of 1954 apply. The statement must contain the names, addresses, and taxpayer account numbers of any corporations, 5% or more in value of the stock of which is owned directly by the consenting corporation, and any other corporations connected to the consenting corporation through a chain of stock ownership as described above.

The statement must be filed with the District Director with whom the consenting corporation will file its income tax return for the tax year during which the statement is filed. A stockholder who sells stock in a consenting corporation within the six-month period beginning with the date on which the consent is filed should attach a copy of the consent to his income tax return for the tax year in which the sale is made.

Each corporation which consents must maintain records adequate to permit specific identification of its "subsection (f)" assets. "Subsection (f)" assets are the following assets which at the time stockholders sell their stock are owned or under option to purchase by the consenting corporation: Inventory, property held for sale to customers in the ordinary course of the corporation's business; land, unrealized receivables or fees; any of the types of property mentioned above which, at the time of the sale of stock was being manufactured, constructed or otherwise produced. Also, any improvements on land which was a "subsection (f)" asset, which resulted from construction commenced by the consenting corporation or its purchaser within two years after the date of the stock sale.

Installment Sales, Income Averaging, or Charitable Contribution as a Solution

Where the corporation is unequivocally a collapsible corporation, and the stockholders cannot avail themselves of any of the exceptions, you might consider the installment sale to spread the tax on the ordinary income. This way you may avoid bunching up ordinary income in one year. If you decide on the installment sale, remember to set up the sale to meet the special 30% requirement for the first year of the sale, and the possible dangers involved in making an improper election of that reporting method.

An alternative method of alleviating the bunching of income may be income averaging if available.

You may avoid a high tax by setting up trusts for some or all of the collapsible stock (each trust you set up is a separate taxpayer) and by making outright gifts to your children. This does not cleanse the collapsible taint, but it does put the gain into lower tax brackets.

As a final alternative, an individual in a tax bracket of over 50% may consider making a charitable contribution of the collapsible corporation stock. Where a person is in an over 50% tax bracket, the tax deduction for the value of the stock is worth more than the net if he had sold the stock at ordinary income tax rates.

CHAPTER XIV

Buy-Sell Agreements Between Business Associates

Sᴛᴏᴄᴋʜᴏʟᴅᴇʀs ᴏғ ᴀ ᴄʟᴏsᴇʟʏ-ʜᴇʟᴅ ᴄᴏʀᴘᴏʀᴀᴛɪᴏɴ should consider buy-sell agreements. An agreement will assure that stock of any stockholder will not pass outside the corporation's or stockholders' control. It will help to eliminate natural friction that may develop between surviving stockholders and the family of the deceased. Finally, from the point of view of an outgoing stockholder or his estate, a ready market is provided for the stock, preventing either a forced sale or a "locked-in" interest.

A buy-sell agreement should be worked out at the inception of the corporation or soon afterwards. It should have these objectives:

1. Name the purchaser of the stock. Generally this is either another stockholder or the corporation. In some cases, it may be selected key employees or a pension or profit-sharing trust set up by the corporation. In this chapter, the discussion will deal with a purchase by another stockholder or the corporation. Regardless of who is the purchaser, the next objective is ensuring that the buyer will have sufficient funds to perform the contract.

2. Funding the agreement. This is usually done by insurance. The problems of insurance funding are discussed on page 274.

3. Fixing the price of stock in the agreement.

4. Resolving the tax problems which may be involved if the insurance is financed by the corporation or if there is to be a redemption of stock by the corporation.

Naming the Buyer

Generally, a buy-sell arrangement is made between the stockholders and known as a "cross-purchase agreement," or between the stockholder and the corporation and known as a "redemption agreement."

The redemption agreement is generally easier to arrange than the cross-purchase agreement. It also may ease the funding of the agreement. If the corporation is not endangered by the surplus accumulation penalty, it can set aside funds for a possible redemption. If insurance funding is used, the corporation assumes the cost of premiums. Although it gets no deduction for this expense, it relieves the stockholders of paying for the insurance, a cost which may be particularly onerous when, for example, there is a difference in the ages of two principal stockholders and premium cost is disproportionate to stockholdings.

Fixing the Price

The buy-sell agreement should fix the price of the stock or provide a formula for determining the price. It may be several years from the time the agreement is drawn up until it comes into operation, for example, at the death of a stockholder. At that time, it is almost certain that the financial and economic position of the corporation will not be the same as it was at the inception of the agreement. For this reason, a formula should be used that is flexible and adaptable to predictable and unforeseeable changes. If a price is fixed in dollars, there should be provision for mandatory periodic reappraisal and readjustment.

Book value is generally not an accurate measure of value. As a compromise a formula may provide for a price fixed as book value plus the last two or more years' profits as the value of goodwill. A requirement for an annual revaluation of the business is usually not practical because businessmen often neglect to perform this annual task. Therefore, a floor, such as book value plus two years' earnings, should be written in.

In fixing a price in a busy-sell agreement, there may be a tendency to set down restrictions to depress the value of the stock interest for estate tax purposes. This tax purpose should not be the motivating force in setting value. By restricting the price, you also restrict what can be realized on the stock. Estate taxes should not be a major concern when fixing the price. A sound plan would be one that will produce a fair price for the stock with additional planning to provide for liquid funds that will pay for the increased estate taxes. Special rules provide for redemption of corporate stock sufficient to pay estate taxes and funeral and administration expenses. (See page 173.)

Income Tax Consequences of Purchase By Either Corporation or Stockholders

If a stockholder buys the stock of a deceased shareholder, there are no immediate tax consequences to the buyer.

The selling party, usually the estate of the deceased, generally does not realize gain or loss on a sale or redemption as the basis for the stock becomes at death its fair market value (which is in most cases the selling price stated in the agreement).

Tax problems may develop when a redemption is combined with a purchase of some of the stock by the remaining stockholders or by an incoming stockholder. This may occur when the corporation does not have sufficient cash or sufficient surplus under state law to support a redemption of all of the stock. In such a case, the Treasury may claim that the outgoing stockholder is subject to dividend income because his stock was not completely redeemed. Proper timing of the steps of a sale or redemption can prevent this complication. Set up the transaction so that the redemption will be the last step. In that way the requirement for a complete redemption will be satisfied (see page 168), resulting in capital gain.

EXAMPLE:

Jones holds 50% of the corporate stock, worth $500,000, and is withdrawing from the corporation. It is intended that the corporation redeem $200,000 of the stock, Smith, the remaining stockholder, purchase $100,-000 of the stock and Brown, an incoming stockholder, purchase the remaining $200,000. If the transaction proceeds in the above order, the redemption of Jones' stock is not a complete redemption because at the time of the redemption all of his stock was not redeemed. Thus he is in danger of having the $200,000 received from the corporation treated as a dividend unless he can prove to a court that the three steps were all part of a single transaction. The safest procedure is to have Smith and Brown make their purchases first, followed by a redemption of Jones' remaining shares. In that way, Jones' interest is completely terminated by the redemption, and, barring special circumstances, capital gain will be realized on the transaction. A simultaneous purchase and redemption will also qualify the total gain for capital gain treatment.

Potential Redemption Problems if a Corporation has an Insufficient Surplus

If the corporation is designated as purchaser of the stock, you should anticipate the possibility that the corporation may not have a sufficient surplus under state law to carry out the agreement. To cover this possibility, your agreement may provide for adjustments to create an adequate surplus to meet the state law requirements. For example, the agreement might provide for an increase in the surplus by writing up depreciated assets to fair market value or by reducing the par value of the capital stock. The agreement may also provide that if the adjustments of corporate assets cannot provide an adequate surplus, the surviving stockholders may purchase the shares.

Funding a buy-sell agreement with insurance can help alleviate an inadequate surplus problem.

Tax Problems of the Remaining Stockholder Under Buy-Sell Agreements

Where the corporation originally has an obligation to redeem and does redeem, the remaining stockholder will not be charged with a constructive dividend. Thus, for example, under a stock retirement plan, the corporation redeems all of the stock of Jones. Smith, the remaining stockholder, is not charged with a constructive dividend.

Under a cross-purchase agreement, where the remaining stockholder pays for the stock with his own capital, there are no tax problems. But, should he turn to the corporation to redeem some of the shares of the outgoing stockholder, he invites tax difficulties. The amount paid by the corporation for the stock may be taxed as a constructive dividend. For example, Smith contracted to buy Jones' stock. After he makes a down payment and the stock is put in escrow to guarantee payment, he has the corporation complete the purchase. Under present authority, Smith received a taxable constructive dividend as the corporation satisfied his legal obligation. Similarly, if he bought the stock and then turned the shares over to the corporation for payment, the payment by the corporation is taxable as a dividend. However, the dividend attack may be defeated in the following type of situation: A corporation has no surplus and under state law cannot make a redemption of the stock. A stockholder buys all of the stock from the outgoing stockholder with the understanding the corporation will buy the shares as soon as there is sufficient surplus. Under court authority, the redemption by the corporation should not be treated as a dividend to the remaining stockholder.

What if the buy-sell agreement requires that the corporation redeem the stock, but instead the remaining stockholder buys out the withdrawing stockholder? Tax authorities are of the opinion that there is no dividend problem in this situation. Where, instead of a binding obligation, the remaining stockholder assigns his option to purchase the shares of the outgoing stockholder, there is no constructive dividend. No indebtedness of the remaining stockholder is being satisfied by the corporation.

Use of Insurance to Fund Plan

To fund a cross-purchase plan, each principal stockholder takes out insurance on the life of the other stockholder. He gets no deduction for payment of premiums; nor does he pay tax on the proceeds at the death of the insured. Similarly, when life insurance is used to fund a stock redemption plan, the corporation cannot deduct the premium expense; at the death of a stockholder, the corporation receives the proceeds taxfree.

When the corporation pays the premiums under a stock redemption plan, be careful to avoid a Treasury charge that the premium payments constitute constructive dividends to stockholders. Avoid any plan whereby the stockholders purchase policies on each other's life, name beneficiaries, and then have the corporation pay the premiums. The Treasury will exact a dividend tax because the stockholders are both the owners and unqualified beneficiaries of the policies. The corporation must be the owner of the policies, not the stockholders. If, for example, a stockholder has the right to borrow against the policy or possesses any other ownership rights, the stockholder may be considered the true owner of the policy and the premium payments by the corporation may be taxed to him as constructive dividends. If the corporation is the owner, stockholders can, without fear of adverse tax consequences, name beneficiaries other than the corporation *if* the right of the beneficiary to receive the proceeds is conditioned on his transferring the stock to the corporation.

In some cases, under a stock redemption plan, there may be a fear that when the proceeds are paid by the insurance company to the corporation, they might be diverted for purposes other than a stock redemption. To avoid this, stockholders might name a trustee as beneficiary of the company-bought policies. On the death of the stockholder, the proceeds are paid to the trustee which buys the stock from the deceased's estate and turns it over to the corporation for retirement.

In a cross-purchase agreement, the estate of the deceased usually owns the insurance policy on the life of the surviving stockholder. The estate can surrender it for cash or sell it to the survivor.

Gambling Feature of Insurance Funding

There is a hidden element of additional risk when insurance is used to fund a buy-sell agreement. Each of the principal stockholders or partners whose life is covered by insurance gambles that he will not die first. The estate of the first to die stands to lose a substantial portion of what it is entitled to. The following example illustrates the problem.

EXAMPLE:

Smith and Jones, each 50% stockholders, decide to fund their cross-purchase agreement with life insurance, each taking out a policy on the other's life. At the time the agreement is made, the total value of the business is $100,000, so each policy is for $50,000 face value. (Assume values remain constant.) When Smith dies, Jones collects the $50,000 insurance proceeds and turns them over to Smith's widow in exchange for all of Smith's stock. On the surface, it appears as though the widow has received full value for her husband's interest. But what really has happened? Jones has in effect purchased Smith's $50,000 share of the business for the cost of insurance premiums. Smith's widow winds up with $50,000, and Jones with a business worth $100,000. Smith could have done much better, if he had taken out $50,000 of insurance on his own life. In that way, at his death, his widow would have the same $50,000, but also the original one-half interest in the business. But this latter method would, of course, nullify the whole purpose of a buy-sell agreement, namely, to effect a buy-out of the deceased's interest in the corporation.

A solution to the problem is to consider the insurance as part of the value of what is to be paid out and give the estate of the deceased a proportionate share of the total. This approach will require the survivor to share the insurance proceeds with the decedent's estate in addition to paying out the deceased's interest in the business. But this solution would also nullify the funding purpose of the insurance.

To ease this problem, it is possible to use a formula that will fix how much insurance should be taken out to share the insurance gain and provide funds to pay for the business interest. In the case of two equal stockholders, the amount of insurance to be taken out would generally be double the value of one stockholder's interest.

EXAMPLE:

> Jones and Smith are equal stockholders. Assume the value of the business is $100,000. Each takes out a policy on the other's life for $50,000. If Smith dies first, Jones uses the proceeds of the policy on Smith's life to buy out his interest. In short, for $50,000 provided by the insurance he has taken over a business worth $100,000, while Smith's family has only the insurance proceeds of $50,000. However, assume Jones and Smith did not want this result. They could reach a more equitable solution if they took out policies of $100,000 each. Then, on the death of the first stockholder, his estate would receive $100,000 for his interest and the surviving stockholder would become the owner of a business worth $100,000.

The above example provides a simple statement of facts and only a general approach. An actual business situation is more fluid and complex. Unfortunately, it is impossible to work out a general solution to all the problems that may arise. Some of the variables that might have to be considered are: The useful lives of the company's assets (which would affect book values because of replacements), the differences in ages among the stockholders, the element of goodwill that a stockholder contributes, whether the estate of the deceased is entitled under the agreement to the cash value of the policy on the life of the survivor.

Effect of the Accumulated Earnings Tax on Buy-Sell Agreements

In Chapter IX, the tax on improperly accumulated earnings is discussed. There it is stated that in order to prod corporations into paying out earnings as dividends, a penalty tax of 27½% and 38½% is imposed on retained earnings in excess of $100,000 retained for reasons other than the reasonable needs of the business such as expansion.

Where earnings are accumulated to buy out a minority stockholder, especially a dissident one, the courts hold that there is a valid corporate business purpose for the accumulation. However, in a particular case, it may be necessary in this situation to go to court, since the Treasury has on occasion challenged the accumulation.

Stock of majority stockholders. Where the earnings are accumulated to buy out a majority stockholder, the reasonable needs of the business condition is not met on the grounds that the purpose of the accumulation is to allow the majority stockholder to bail out earnings of the corporation at capital gain rates.

Where the redemption may involve 50-50 stockholders, the Treasury holds that an accumulation for such purpose is not a reasonable need of the business, despite the fact that disharmony between 50-50 stockholders is as crippling to a business as that between a majority and minority stockholder. However, one court held an accumulation for redemption of a 50-50 stockholder's interest was acceptable when "no tax avoidance scheme was involved." However, the corporation in that case was aided by the fact that the earnings had been accumulated for another valid business purpose and it was diverted for the redemption only when a "serious dispute" arose between the 50-50 shareholders.

Change in corporate purpose. Assume that the earnings have been accumulated for a reasonable need of the business as in the case discussed above. The need disappears but stockholders fall out, and the accumulated earnings are used to buy out the majority stockholder. Thus, earnings originally accumulated for a business need are used for what would not have been a reasonable need of the business if it had been accumulated for that purpose from the beginning. In the few cases involving this point, opinion is split over whether the accumulation was improper and therefore subject to the penalty tax.

Value for Estate Tax Purposes

Between the stockholders of a corporation, the value stated in a buy-sell agreement is controlling in the absence of unusual circumstances such as fraud and duress. For estate tax purposes, the value stated in the agreement will be accepted if three conditions are present.

(1) A binding contract existing at death, under which the estate is obligated to sell and the survivor is obligated to buy; *or* at death, the survivor has a call on the stock of the deceased.

(2) The buy-sell agreement effectively prevented the decedent from selling his interest to third parties. An agreement that merely provides that at the death of a stockholder the corporation is obligated to purchase all of his stock, is not sufficient to fix the estate tax valuation at the agreement price.

(3) The agreement resulted from a *bona fide* business arrangement and not a device to pass decedent's stock to family members as a partial gift.

EXAMPLES:

1. Stockholders of the Brown Corporation had a buy-sell agreement providing that at the death of one of them, the others had the right of first refusal. The corporation or stockholders were not obliged to purchase the stock. The stock was valued in the agreement at book value. A court upheld the Treasury's valuation at more than double book value. The court said that a right of first refusal does not meet the first condition, since there is no binding obligation on the estate to sell, nor a duty on the corporation to buy in this type of agreement. All a right of first refusal does is act as a depressant on the market value, since it discourages third parties from purchasing the stock. It does not, however, in itself serve to fix a definite value.

2. A company was owned by a father and his two sons. Under their buy-sell agreement, each gave the other the option to purchase the shares of the deceased. Value was set at book value which, at the time of the death of the father was $113,000 less than market value. The court held that the price set in the contract was to be used for estate tax purposes. The difference here from example (1) is that if the remaining stockholder exercised his option, the estate of the deceased could not refuse to sell.

3. A buy-sell agreement provided that the corporation had an option to buy the stock of the deceased at book value; however, during his life there were no restrictions on the deceased's right to sell. In this case the court found the option price was not binding on the Treasury.

Buy-Sell Provision in the Partnership Agreement

The partnership agreement should provide for the event of the death of a partner. Without adequate planning, unnecessary problems are created. For instance, under partnership law, the death of a partner causes automatic dissolution unless state law or the partnership agreement otherwise provides. Also, without a buy-sell provision in the partnership agreement, the remaining partner or partners must often exhaust surplus funds or go into debt to buy out the decedent's interest.

Buy-sell provisions may be funded through a special bank account, where so much is contributed periodically according to actuarial guidelines. But this is undesirable for a number of reasons: (1) The partnership may not want to tie up surplus funds in this manner. (2) Partners do not with regularity live to their actuarial life expectancy. (3) A liability to fund may have a negative effect on the credit standing of the business. Consequently, most partnerships prefer to fund buy-sell provisions with insurance. The insurance may be carried by the individual partners on each other's lives, in a cross-purchase arrangement, identical to the type of agreement described for stockholders. The partnership, on the other hand, may own the policies, pay the premiums, and act as the conduit through which the insurance proceeds pass to the estate of a deceased partner in exchange for his interest. In either case, the premiums are not a deductible expense.

Where there are more than two partners, the cross-purchase set-up becomes cumbersome if a large number of policies must be purchased (each partner purchasing a policy on the lives of all the others). Consequently, the redemption arrangement may be favored.

If a partner is uninsurable, a sinking fund may be set up, into which is deposited each year an amount equal to the premiums paid on the life insurance for the other partners. The agreement should provide that upon the death of the uninsurable partner, the amount in the sinking fund should be applied as a down-payment on the partner's interest; the remainder to be paid in installments, secured perhaps by a transfer and leaseback of partnership property to the deceased's widow. Contributions to the sinking fund should cease when the fund reaches the value of the uninsurable partner's interest.

There should also be provision in the agreement, if the cross-purchase arrangement is used, for the purchase by the remaining partners of the policies on their lives from the estate of the deceased, the price being the cash surrender value at the time of death.

Valuation of the business. Any method of valuation, if it is reasonable and supported by the facts, will be acceptable by the Treasury. The following method illustrates one approach to valuing a partnership: (1) Find the average annual net earnings for the past five years. From that deduct 8% of book value. (2) Take the balance of the average annual earnings, which is the amount ascribable to the earning power of goodwill, and capitalize the figure at 15%. (3) Add book value to the figure obtained in step 2 to get the fair market value of the business.

EXAMPLE:

Average annual earnings for past five years	$15,000
Book value	$60,000

1. Earnings	$ 15,000
Less: 8% of book value	4,800
	$ 10,200
2. $10,200 capitalized at 15%	$ 68,000
3. Capitalized amount	$ 68,000
Book value	60,000
Fair market value	$128,000

Provision should be made in the agreement for periodic readjustments of valuation. To hedge against the fair probability that the partners will be lax in exercising this duty, a provision should be included appointing a special board in the event a reappraisal had not been made during a stipulated period prior to the death of a partner. The board's sole function is to fix a final valuation on the business, based on the most recent figure set by the partnership and taking into account the fluctuation in earnings and values since that time.

CHAPTER XV

Techniques of Withdrawing Corporate Profits Through Fringe Benefits, Pension and Pay Plans

Taxes and inflation have seriously affected the executive and other highly paid employees. Salary increases mean less and less as the employee's salary grows higher because taxes are based on a graduated rate. An executive whose salary is raised from $50,000 to $60,000 retains about $4,800 with the Treasury taking the rest. This tax erosion of income can be reduced by proper use of pay and other plans between you and your corporation. These techniques are outlined and discussed in this chapter.

Medical Expense Reimbursement for Stockholder-Employees

This is an important fringe benefit that a company can provide stockholder-employees. It can adopt a plan of reimbursement for medical expenses of employees and their dependents. The amount of the reimbursement, while deductible by the corporation, is not taxable to the employee. Thus, under a comprehensive plan, medical expenses may be reimbursed at a substantial financial saving.

To obtain the tax benefits, the company must adopt a plan for medical expense reimbursement. This is done by corporate resolution. In setting up your plan, you may discriminate in favor of select employees. Treasury regulations merely require that a reimbursement plan cover one or more employees. There may be different plans for different employees or different classes of employees. You might provide for full reimbursement for employees of one class, partial reimbursement for others, and no reimbursement at all for some.

The advantages of a medical reimbursement plan become apparent when you note the effects of having no reimbursement. When you pay your medical expenses, you are entitled to a limited tax deduction. Only the cost of drugs and medicines that exceed 1% of your adjusted gross income goes into the total of your medical expenses. Then, only to the extent that your total medical expenses exceed 3% of your adjusted gross income are they deductible for tax purposes. So, if you have substantial income, it is possible that none or very little of your medical expense is deductible. Consequently, you are paying the major portion or all of your medical expenses out of after-tax income. Suppose, however, the corporation reimburses you for all your medical expenses, including those of your dependents. Then, you have neither taxable income for the reimbursement nor deductions for the expenses. On the corporate level (if you look upon yourself and your controlled corporation as one), all medical expenses are tax deductible, not merely those expenses that exceed prescribed percentages of adjusted gross income.

Salary Continuation Plans

The corporation can have a plan under which employees continue to receive part or all of their compensation while they are out sick. Up to a certain limit, the amounts received by an ill employee are not taxable, while the company gets a tax deduction for the payments. Here, too, as in the case of medical expense reimbursement, the plan for salary continuation may be discriminatory.

Amounts a stockholder-employee receives while he is unable to work due to illness enable him to draw taxfree up to $100 a week after a 30-day waiting period.

You must make sure that the sick pay plan is recorded in the company minutes or as a resolution.

Group Term Insurance

An employer can provide insurance coverage of up to $50,000 without any tax to the employee under a group term policy covering all or a considerable number of employees. The cost of coverage is at a much lower rate than individual employees could obtain for similar insurance. The premium paid by the employer is tax deductible.

If the coverage is for more than $50,000, the premium for the excess coverage is taxable to the employee. But even if the tax is incurred, the employee may still be getting insurance at a lower cost than possible through his own resources.

EXAMPLE:

An executive, age 41, is covered by a group policy to the extent of $200,-000. The company pays the entire premium. According to Government tables for figuring the premium, the executive will have $414 of taxable income for the premiums on $150,000 of insurance in excess of the $50,000 allowed taxfree. His net cost will be the tax he pays on that $414 —which, if he is in a 40% tax bracket would cost him about $165. If he were to buy his own coverage for $150,000 (five-year term, renewable to age 65, convertible), the cost would be about $1,200 a year. And that $1,200 would have to come out of after-tax dollars.

Exceptions to $50,000 ceiling. Even if the coverage is more than $50,000 on a particular employee, he is not taxable on the premium costs of the excess if: (1) The employer is the beneficiary, (2) a charity is the beneficiary, or (3) the employee has terminated his employment because he has reached retirement age or has become disabled.

What is group insurance? To qualify as group term insurance, these requirements must be met: (1) The insurance must provide general death benefits under a master policy or a group of individual policies that make up a plan of group insurance. (2) Amounts of coverage cannot exceed the maximum allowed by state law under a master policy providing group term protection only. (3) Paid-up values may be included in the policy if (a) the policy specifies the portion of the premium allocable to the group term portion, and (b) the employer pays no part of the premium which is not allocable to the group term portion. (4) The plan of group insurance must be arranged by an employer for his employees. The plan can be in a separate written document or in a master policy and it must make life insurance available to a group of lives which include either all the employees of the employer or a class or classes which preclude individual selection. A plan will not qualify if eligibility for insurance protection under the plan at the time the employee first becomes eligible under the plan is conditioned on evidence of insurability. However, the Treasury will accept a plan as qualifying within the "evidence of insurability" requirement if ten or more employees have group term coverage at any time during a calendar year. (5) A plan will not qualify if it is available only to stockholder-employees. Presumably, if all employees are stockholders at the time the plan is put into effect but other employees, if they are employed, would become eligible for coverage, the plan would qualify. (6) The number of employees covered must at least equal the number required for a master policy under state law. (In many states, the minimum number required for a group plan policy is 10.) However, if the company does not have sufficient employees to meet that minimum, all employees must be covered. This can presumably be accomplished by using individual policies in so-called "baby-group" or "group wholesale." It may be done by having the employer join an association that provides group coverage to employees of their members.

You cannot discriminate in coverage amounts. The Treasury takes the position, for example, that if the stockholder-employee is covered for $100,000 and all the other employees are covered for $1,000 each, there is no true group term policy. Many State Commissioners of Insurance take the same position. So, to get the benefits of taxfree life insurance, you will have to supply substantial coverage to a number of employees.

Formulas for the amount of coverage must preclude employee-by-employee treatment. Factors that may be used in the formula include salary, years of service, position, or a combination of these factors. Also, alternative schedules of amounts of coverage based on the amount an employee elects to contribute may be used, but each schedule must satisfy the requirement that the formula precludes individual selection of amounts. Here, too, evidence of insurability cannot be a factor affecting the amount of coverage.

Qualified Pension and Profit-Sharing Plans

A qualified plan, pension, profit-sharing or stock bonus, is a method of deferring compensation. The term "qualified" means that it meets the fairly liberal Treasury requirements concerning nondiscrimination in eligibility and benefits.

Tax benefits flow both to the company and the employee in a plan meeting the qualification standards of the Treasury. (1) The employer deducts the amount contributed each year to the plan. (2) The employees participating in the plan are not currently taxed on their share of the employer contribution to the plan. (3) Assuming a trust is used as an intermediary between employer and employee, the income earned on the funds previously contributed into the trust are not currently taxable to the employee-beneficiary or to the trust. Thus, dividends, interests, rentals and the like earned by trust investments may accumulate and be reinvested with much greater turnover and profit than where there is a tax paid on current earnings. (4) Upon retirement or termination of employment, an employee pays capital gains tax on a lump-sum distribution received during one taxable year; if he receives the payout over a period of time, each payment is treated as an annuity payment. (5) If the distribution includes stock in the employer corporation, the employee is not taxed on appreciation of the stock while it was in the trust. The capital gain tax on the increase in value is deferred until the stock is eventually sold by the employee. (6) If the employee dies and the benefits accrued to him in the plan are paid out to his beneficiaries, the same tax rules apply as if the payments were made to the employee. And in addition, if a lump-sum payment is made, the first $5,000 of the payout can be taxfree to the beneficiaries. (7) As long as the beneficiary is someone *other than the employee's estate,* the value of his interest in the plan at the time of his death is not subject to estate taxes. (8) The plan can provide for voluntary contributions to the plan by an employee up to 10% of his compensation. This permits a taxfree buildup of his personal funds and an ultimate withdrawal of the profit at capital gain rates. A contributory plan can be set up so that the employee can direct the trustee of the plan how to invest his voluntary contributions to the plan. In effect, he can carry out his personal investment program within the shelter of the plan.

EXAMPLES:

1. Jones, an executive, earns a $50,000 salary. Assume the company is ready to pay him a 15% bonus, or $7,500. Of this $7,500 bonus, he will retain about one-half, or $3,750 after taxes. If he gets the same bonus each year for 25 years, and invests it at 5%, his after-tax income is about 2½%. At the end of 25 years, he will have built up a fund of close to $130,000.

Now assume that instead of an annual $7,500 bonus, Jones is a participant in his company's qualified profit-sharing plan and that the employer contributes 15% of his compensation to that plan. The $7,500 that would otherwise have been received as a bonus is now contributed directly to the plan. The contribution does not create taxable income to Jones.

Assuming again a 5% return, this time undiminished by taxes, over a 25-year period the annual $7,500 contributions built up to a total of nearly $376,000. If he gets that in a lump sum and pays a 25% capital gains tax, that will leave him with a net of $282,000, more than twice the $130,000 he would have built up by investing his $7,500 annual bonus on his own. Moreover, the employer gets the same annual tax deduction for the $7,500 contribution to the plan that he would have gotten had he paid the employee an annual bonus of $7,500.

2. In the previous example, if Jones accumulated $3,750 a year on his own at a 5% return, at the end of 25 years he would have a fund of $130,000. Suppose he puts the $3,750 each year into his company's profit-sharing plan which, we will assume, permits voluntary contributions. Assuming again a 5% return, the annual contributions of $3,750 will build up to a total of almost $188,000. If the total is distributed in a lump sum at retirement, Jones pays a capital gains tax on the income of $94,000 earned by his savings contributions. This is $23,500; which leaves him with about $164,500, or $34,500 more than he would have built up outside the plan with the same annual contributions.

Discrimination is barred. For the plan to be qualified, the company cannot discriminate in favor of officers, stockholders, or highly-paid employees. That means often that a substantial number, although not necessarily all, of the employees must be covered in the plan.

Where union employees have their own plan under their union contract, the plan put in for the other employees must often be such that the union employees have "comparable benefits." Often, by integrating the plan with Social Security, a satisfactory solution may be arrived at. Under this arrangement, the Social Security benefits are, in effect, considered part of the plan. So, it is possible for employer coverage to apply only to that part of salary in excess of the amount subject to Social Security coverage.

Pension v. Profit-Sharing Plans

The advantages of the qualified plan are available in both pension and profit-sharing plans. But there are some differences in approach and appeal.

A pension plan is geared to providing actuarially determined retirement benefits. For example, benefits may be based on a percentage of the average compensation of the executive during the last five years of employment prior to retirement. Once the benefits are determined, then the employer's contribution is actuarially computed. The actuary determines how much the employer must contribute to the plan each year to provide the necessary funds to pay the anticipated benefit when it comes due.

A profit-sharing plan does not have fixed benefits. Contributions are made out of corporate profits and allocated according to an allocation formula to each of the employees participating in the plan. At retirement or other payout date, the employee receives the amounts allocated to him plus the income and capital appreciation attributable to his allocated amount.

One form of pension plan, similar to a profit-sharing plan, is the money-purchase plan. Instead of determining the amount of the pension ahead of time, the distribution to the employee consists of whatever the amount of accumulated contributions for the employee will purchase (after adding appreciation and income to the contribution).

Many companies and their executives prefer profit-sharing plans because: (1) The company need not make contributions if there are no profits. (2) The percentage of profits to be contributed can be left open, so the board of directors can decide each year how much to contribute. On the other hand, there is a practical limit on how much can be contributed. Contributions in excess of 15% of compensation paid during one year are not deductible by the corporation. (3) There is no predetermined ceiling on how much will be paid out to the employees when they retire. Where an executive is comparatively young, he feels that over a fairly long period prior to his retirement the funds in the profit-sharing plan will build up to a greater amount than he can hope to get as a pension. (4) Where an employee leaves the company, under the plan, a good part of the amount contributed for him may not yet be vested. That is, he has no rights to that amount yet. This unvested or forfeited amount can be redesignated for the benefit of the employees remaining in the plan. Where there is a fairly high turnover of some classes of employees, the forfeitures can be a considerable factor in building up the funds for the employees, including stockholder-employees, who remain. In a pension plan, forfeitures do not benefit the remaining employees; they are used to reduce the employer's future contributions to the plan.

Pension plans find favor where the key employees are older and have less time to build up a substantial retirement fund. There is no effective ceiling on the employer's contributions to a pension fund similar to the 15% of compensation ceiling for profit-sharing contributions (although there are statutory limits). Where highly-paid key employees, entitled to substantial pensions under the plan, are not too far from retirement age, substantial contributions must be made for them to reach the actuarially-determined amounts by the time they retire.

While an advance ruling or determination letter from the Treasury that your plan qualifies for the special tax treatment is not required, it is advisable. In making a request for a determination letter, you should submit to your District Director the documentary evidence of the plan, together with certain data relative to the current operation of the plan.

Form 2950 must be filed after you have shown that your plan qualifies for each year the plan is in effect, with information to show that your plan continues to qualify.

Rules for Qualification of a Plan and Trust

The main rules for qualifying a plan and the tax-exempt trust to administer the plan are: (1) A trust which forms part of a pension, profit-sharing or stock-bonus plan must be created or organized in the United States. (2) The plan must be written and communicated to your employees. (3) The plan must be established by you, the employer, for the exclusive benefit of your employees. (4) It must be impossible under the trust instrument for any part of the fund or its income to be used or diverted for purposes other than the exclusive benefit of your employees or their beneficiaries prior to the satisfaction of all liabilities to the employees and their beneficiaries. In the case of an annuity plan the nondiversionary requirement is satisfied if there is a definite written agreement (as a provision in the contract form, or otherwise) between you, the employer, and the insurer, that refunds of premiums, if any, shall be applied toward the purchase of retirement

annuities within the tax year in which received, or in your next succeeding year. (5) The plan must benefit either 70% of all employees
(excluding certain short service, seasonal or part-time employees), or
80% of all eligible employees (excluding certain short service, seasonal, or part-time employees) if at least 70% of all employees are
eligible. Instead of meeting the percentage requirements, you may set
up a classification of employees which, if it does not discriminate in
favor of officers, shareholders, supervisors, or highly compensated employees, may satisfy the coverage requirements. Where some of your
employees are covered under a union-negotiated plan and you then set
up a plan to cover employees other than the union employees, your
classification may be acceptable. But the Treasury will insist that the
benefits the union employees get under their plan be comparable to the
benefits offered to the other employees under your plan. (6) There
must be no discrimination in favor of officers, shareholders, supervisors or highly compensated employees with respect to contributions or
benefits under the plan. (7) Upon termination of the plan or discontinuance of contributions under the plan, the rights of all employees to
benefits under the plan up to the date of termination or discontinuance
must be nonforfeitable. This requirement does not apply, however, to
the rights of employees discussed in item (6) above, where the requirement would result in the plan being discriminatory.

Under a pension plan, the benefits to be received by a given employee must be definitely determinable. He knows, for example, that at
age 65, he will receive a certain dollar amount. Forfeited benefits of
employees cannot be used to increase the benefits of others in the plan,
since that would defeat the "definitely determinable" requirement.
Forfeitures can only be used to decrease the cost in a later year. If you
have a profit-sharing plan, since there is no requirement for a definitely-
determinable benefit, forfeiture can be applied to increase the benefits
of other participants in the plan. You should consider this factor when
deciding between a pension and a profit-sharing plan. If your business
is the type where there is a high rate of employee-turnover, a profit-
sharing plan would enable you to apply the forfeited funds to the permanent employees which, of course, would include you.

You may not, under a *pension* plan, provide for the payment of lay-
off benefits, benefits for sickness, accident, hospitalization or medical

expenses. There is one exception: You may, to a limited extent, provide for medical and hospitalization expenses of retired employees. You may provide incidental life insurance under a pension plan. You may also provide incidental life, accident and health insurance under a profit-sharing plan.

The Treasury is very strict in its requirements that the plan must not be a device to siphon off profits from your business. The plan must prove to be nondiscriminatory in coverage and eligibility. That is, the plan must cover certain percentages of your employees (see above) or else you must submit a plan of coverage that satisfies the Treasury. In addition, the eligibility requirements must not discriminate. If your business requires only part-time employees, aside from yourself and other owners, you must not disqualify part-time employees from participating in the plan. If you did, the Treasury would view the plan as discriminating in favor of yourself and the other owners. The plan will also be disqualified if it looks good on paper, but in operation is discriminatory. Thus, in the above example, if your plan states that all full-time employees are eligible to participate, and all your employees are actually part-time, it will usually not be approved.

You may make provisions for granting loans to participating employees to the extent of their vested interests.

Qualified Stock Options

Two types of stock options can be made available to executives: a qualified stock option and a non-qualified option. There is a third type, a stock purchase plan, that has to be made available to all employees.

The qualified option is the better known plan. The executive has no taxable income when the option is granted nor when he exercises the option, even though the stock is worth more than the option price when he exercises it. When the executive finally disposes of the stock, presumably at a price substantially higher than what he paid for it, he is taxed at long-term capital gains rates. The company gets no deduction even though it issues the stock to the executive at a price lower than the market price at the time of issue.

In 1964, the tax law was amended to tighten up the stock option rules and, as a result, the qualified stock option is not as attractive as it used to be.

Here are the requirements that must be met to have a qualified stock option: (1) The option may be granted to an individual for any reason connected with his employment by a corporation or its parent or subsidiary corporation. (2) The option must be for purchase of stock of the employer corporation or its parent or subsidiary. (3) There must be a plan creating the stock option and it must state the total number of shares which may be used under the plan. (4) The plan must spell out the employees or class of employees eligible under the plan to receive options. But it can be discriminatory. (5) The plan must be approved by the stockholders of the corporation within 12 months before or after the date of adoption. (6) The actual option must be granted to an employee within 10 years from the date the plan is adopted or the date the plan is approved by the stockholders, whichever date is earlier. (7) The option must not be exercisable after five years from the date it is granted. (8) The option must not be transferable by the optionee during his life. During the employee's lifetime, it is exercisable only by him. If he dies without exercising it, his estate or those who inherit the option can exercise it. (9) If an executive has more than one option granted at different times, he cannot exercise the later one first, if that is at a lower price than the earlier one. (10) The optionee, immediately after being granted a qualified stock option, must not own stock equal to more than 5% of the total combined voting power or value of all classes of stock. If the equity capital of the corporation is less than $2,000,000, then the optionee may own an additional amount of stock, depending on the total capital. But the most he can own is 10%. (11) The option price must be not less than 100% of the fair market value of the stock on the date it is granted. (12) Stock acquired under the option must not be disposed of within three years from the day after the date the optionee acquires the stock. (13) From the date of grant of the option to the date three months prior to the date of exercise, the individual must have been an employee of either the corporation granting the option or its parent or subsidiary.

Thus, while the qualified stock option has some attractions, it presents a number of problems. For one, the option price has to be 100% of the value of the stock at the time the option is granted. Before the law was amended, option price could be as low as 85% of the value.

Also, the option has to be exercised within five years after it is granted. This may not be a sufficient time to see if the stock is really going to go up. Under the old law, an executive could be given 10 years to decide whether to exercise his option.

Most important and restrictive is the requirement that the stock be held for three years after exercise. Under the old law, only a six month holding period was required, although the stock could not be disposed of within two years of the time the option was granted. Under the old law, some of the stock could be acquired by exercising the option, held for six months and a day to give long-term gain, and then sold at a gain and the proceeds used to exercise additional options. The new three-year holding period discourages this type of financing of stock options.

Nonqualified Options

Stock options can be issued that do not meet the requirements of qualified stock options and can give advantages to both the company and the executive. The option can be issued at less than market value. Although the employee may have some immediate compensation income, he can come out ahead economically over the qualified option.

Furthermore, the company gets a tax deduction for the amount of compensation income that the executive has to report. This permits the company to issue the option at a substantial discount since the discount reduces its tax. Finally, the employee can cash in on the increased value of the stock after holding the stock as little as six months and a day (to get long-term capital gain).

The tax consequences of a nonqualified option are as follows: (1) If the option, when granted, has a readily ascertainable value, its value is immediately taxable to the employee. Except where options are traded in an active market, it will be the rare case where the option will have ascertainable value under the Treasury rules. (2) When the option is exercised, assuming the stock received has no restrictions on it, the executive has compensation income for the difference between the option price he pays and the market value at the time he exercises the option. For example, a company gives its executive an option to buy 100 shares of stock at $25 a share. When the option is exercised, the market value of the stock is $35 a share. The executive buys stock worth $3,500 by paying $2,500. The $1,000 difference is ordinary income to him. But now his basis for the stock is $3,500, the $2,500 he paid plus the $1,000 he reported as ordinary income. At the same time, the employer is entitled to a $1,000 deduction. (3) When the stock is subsequently sold, the executive will have long-term capital gain (assuming he holds the stock for more than six months) for the difference between his basis and what he gets for it. Continuing the example above, if he sold the stock a year later at $50 a share, he would receive $5,000. Since his basis is $3,500, he has $1,500 of long-term capital gain.

EXAMPLE:

Assume an executive earns $100,000 a year, has other income that equals his deductions, and files a joint return. The company gives him $100,000 of options to acquire stock having a market value at the time of the grant of the option equal to one year's salary. The stock is finally sold when it has increased in value to $140,000.

If a qualified option is given, the executive, when he exercises it, pays $100,000. He pays no tax at that time. He eventually sells the stock for $140,000, realizing a $40,000 long-term capital gain and paying a $10,000 capital gains tax. He nets an after-tax profit of $30,000. The employer, of course, gets no deduction.

Assume a nonqualified option is given and the option price is 85% of market value or $85,000. The employee pays $85,000 for the stock when he exercises the option and eventually sells it for $140,000. At the time he exercises the option, he has ordinary income of $15,000 (the difference between the $85,000 he pays for the stock and its fair market value of $100,000). In his tax bracket, he will have to pay a tax of $9,300. His basis for his stock then becomes $100,000 (the $85,000 he paid for it plus the $15,000 of taxable income he had to report). When he sells the stock, he will realize a $40,000 capital gain and have to pay a $10,000 capital gains tax. So, his total tax is $19,300 (the $9,300 paid on exercising the option and the $10,000 of capital gains tax on selling the stock). Subtracting the $19,300 from the before-tax profit of $55,000 ($140,000 − 85,000), leaves him with $35,700 after taxes, $5,700 more than he would have left if he had received a qualified stock option. And the employer is entitled to a $15,000 tax deduction at the time the employee exercises the stock option.

Index